THE LIVES OF FREDERICK DOUGLASS

The Lives of

Frederick Douglass

ROBERT S.
LEVINE

HARVARD UNIVERSITY PRESS

Cambridge, Massachusetts

London, England

2016

First printing

Library of Congress Cataloging-in-Publication Data

Levine, Robert S. (Robert Steven), 1953– author.

The lives of Frederick Douglass / Robert S. Levine.

pages cm

Includes bibliographical references and index.

ISBN 978-0-674-05581-0 (alk. paper)

1. Douglass, Frederick, 1818–1895.   2. African American abolitionists—
Biography.   3. Abolitionists—United States—Biography.
4. Slaves—United States—Biography.   5. Antislavery movements—
United States—History—19th century.   I. Title.

E449.D75L48 2015

973.8092—dc23

[B]

2015016183

In memory of George Dekker

❧ CONTENTS ❦

THE LIVES OF FREDERICK DOUGLASS

~ INTRODUCTION ~

Lives after the *Narrative*

NEAR THE END of his third autobiography, *Life and Times of Frederick Douglass* (1881), Douglass reflects on his extraordinary life, which he presents as a succession of lives: "It will be seen in these pages that I have lived several lives as one: first, the life of slavery; secondly, the life of a fugitive from slavery; thirdly, the life of comparative freedom; fourthly, the life of conflict and battle; and, fifthly, the life of victory, if not complete, at least assured."[1] In this schematic overview, the successive lives ultimately make up the one life of the 1881 *Life and Times*. But there was another life to come, and in the revised and expanded 1892 edition of *Life and Times* Douglass describes the failure of Reconstruction, his marriage to a white woman, a visit to Egypt, his diplomatic work in Haiti, and his appointment as Haiti's representative at the upcoming World's Columbian Exposition in Chicago. In this final version of *Life and Times*, Douglass continues to narrate his several and sometimes contradictory lives as one, at least within the covers of an autobiography that he hoped would find a wide readership. But there is nothing static about the man of this 1892 autobiography, and once the book was published, Douglass went on to lecture and write about his life history in ways that sometimes worked against the grain of *Life and Times*.[2] Revision, rather than completion, was among Douglass's highest values as an autobiographer.

Over the course of his long life (1818–1895), Douglass published three autobiographies: the 1845 *Narrative of the Life of Frederick Douglass, An American Slave* (his best known and most widely read autobiography), the 1855 *My Bondage and My Freedom*, and the 1881/1892 *Life and Times of Frederick Douglass*. While *Life and Times* covers the broad sweep of Douglass's life, the *Narrative* focuses on Douglass's life as a slave and fugitive, and *Bondage and Freedom* focuses on his life as a slave, fugitive, and reformer living in comparative freedom. *Bondage and Freedom* addresses "the life of conflict and battle" as well, with conflict and battle becoming even more central to *Life and Times,* which includes several chapters on the Civil War. Each autobiography can be read in isolation from the other, as an artfully constructed finished work, and that is typically how the *Narrative* is read. Douglass would probably be shocked that many now read his first autobiography apart from the institutional networks that helped to produce it, and without any great concern for how he would quickly revise it. At the very least, he would wonder why the majority of readers are interested in just this one life when he published a number of lives after the *Narrative*.

But what if we were to take seriously Douglass's notion of having lived several (or much more than several) lives as one? How would we read, or reread, the major autobiographies? Could they be regarded as one large autobiographical project? Such an approach would require reading across and through the several autobiographies with a heightened attention to the ways in which Douglass revises his representations of key moments of his life, such as his rebellion against the slave breaker Edward Covey. Critics have done extensive comparative work of this sort, and in *The Lives of Frederick Douglass* I do some of my own in examining Douglass's shifting, often conflicting accounts of his grandmother, the Aulds, and his fellow black slaves.[3] Reading the autobiographies in this way raises questions about how to recover what actually happened in Douglass's life. Moreover, when we enlarge the frame to include Douglass's many autobiographical lectures, essays, and letters from 1841 to 1895, even more inconsistencies become apparent. For example, Douglass portrays his relationship with Abraham Lincoln in positive terms in *Life and Times,* but he is more critical of Lincoln in his numerous autobiographical lectures, essays, and letters over the nearly thirty-year period between the time when he first met the president and the moment when he published the revised edition of his third autobiography. Douglass may celebrate Lincoln in *Life and Times* as a collaborator of sorts who brought about the end of slavery, but in other autobiographically inflected writings he expresses his frustrations with "the white man's President" who was "fettered by interpretations of the Constitution."[4] What is the "truth" about the relationship between Douglass and Lincoln? The story of their relationship emerges not simply from a close reading of *Life and Times* but through a consideration of Douglass's multiple and often shifting accounts, which, when brought together in the manner of a collage, offer a fuller and more complex picture. Another example: Douglass wrote and spoke about his slave master Thomas Auld over an approximately forty-year period. At times he seems fond of the man; at other times he conveys his disdain. Auld in some tellings is relatively kind and in others is absolutely vile. Where in Douglass's extensive comments and descriptions of Auld is the true Auld, and if Douglass lived a life in relation to Auld, how should we read that life? These are among the autobiographical and biographical questions that I take up in this study. I propose that the best way to understand Douglass's relationship with Auld, as with Lincoln, is by attending to his numerous reappraisals and revisions.

The Lives of Frederick Douglass is a book about Douglass as an autobiographer, but with a difference. Rather than focus on the three major autobiographies as discrete texts, subject to close readings and comparison, I consider them as part of a larger autobiographical project that encompasses a wide range of Douglass's writings. I approach the published autobiographical volumes as Douglass regarded them: as finished products that he hoped to sell in large quantities, but ultimately as unfinished lives that from the moment they were completed were subject to revision. This is a study of the autobiographical Douglass in which there are no stable or fixed texts. Instead, there are the three autobiographies, including several versions of those autobiographies (such as the 1845 and 1846 Dublin editions of the *Narrative*), numerous autobiographical lectures, essays, letters, and even a novella, all of which address aspects of Douglass's life from complementary and sometimes contradictory perspectives. While there are sections in this book that develop close readings in somewhat traditional fashion—i.e., that view a published autobiography as a skillfully made verbal construction that profits from close reading—my larger interest is in investigating Douglass's autobiographical project itself, not only for what we can learn about Douglass as a writer, but also for what we can learn about Douglass's career as a social reformer.

In short, this is a book about autobiography that is also a literary biography. In *The Lives of Frederick Douglass*, I examine a wide range of Douglass's autobiographical writings from the 1840s to the 1890s, focusing on his efforts over time, and often in very different historical and rhetorical contexts, to describe his relationships with a number of nineteenth-century figures, not only Lincoln and Thomas Auld, but also John Brown, William Lloyd Garrison, Gerrit Smith, and others. I explore Douglass's evolving and sometimes contradictory positions on race, violence, nation, and black diasporic community. By emphasizing the complex seriality and performative nature of Douglass's autobiographical writings, I present a new and less familiar Douglass who is surprisingly canny and elusive, capable of depicting himself as both a black Benjamin Franklin and a Toussaint L'Ouverture, while ever aware of what his autobiographical writings and lectures might accomplish (as political and cultural interventions) at specific historical moments.

Douglass was not always thought of as an autobiographer. At the time of his death in 1895, he was renowned as a black leader and orator, and also known (by some) as the author of *Life and Times*. For around seventy years after his death, *Life and Times* and the earlier *Bondage and Freedom* were considered Douglass's most important autobiographical achievements, at least by the relatively few who read Douglass's autobiographies in the first half of the twentieth century. That judgment was radically revised during the 1960s when Douglass suddenly came to be celebrated as an autobiographer, but mainly as the author of the 1845 *Narrative*, a book he published when he was all of twenty-seven years old and a member of an antislavery organization that he would soon renounce. Douglass lived for another fifty years after publishing the *Narrative*, and during that time he skillfully used autobiography to make his mark on nineteenth-century American culture and beyond. In *The Lives of Frederick Douglass* I hope to make clear why we should take account of a much wider range of

Douglass's autobiographical work, beginning in the early 1840s, when he lectured about his life in slavery for Garrison's Massachusetts Anti-Slavery Society. First, though, I want to take up two interrelated questions: How did Douglass, one of the most admired orators of the nineteenth century, come to be revered as an autobiographer, and how did the *Narrative* emerge as what many regard as his greatest and most representative autobiography? Addressing these questions will help to explain why much of Douglass's autobiographical writings are currently neglected, and why we need to rethink the place of the *Narrative* in Douglass's career.

~ぷ~

In 1995, the Smithsonian Institute Press, in conjunction with the National Portrait Gallery, the National Park Service, and the United States Department of the Interior, published a handsome volume entitled *Majestic in His Wrath: A Pictorial Life of Frederick Douglass*. The book provides a documentary record of Douglass's growing fame in nineteenth-century American culture from 1845, the year of the publication of the *Narrative*, to 1899, the year of the unveiling of Sidney E. Edwards's monumental sculpture of Douglass next to a busy train station in Rochester, New York.[5] Among the fascinating reproductions in the volume are pictures of Douglass dolls of the late 1850s, numerous photographs and drawings of Douglass as a public speaker and diplomat, a replica of a bust of Douglass completed in 1873, an earthenware pitcher engraved with scenes from Douglass's life, and a haunting silver print of the elderly Douglass (c. 1890) working at his desk at his home in Cedar Hill, Washington, DC (which became a National Historic Site in 1972; Figure 1). James Monroe Gregory

FIGURE 1. Douglass at his home in Cedar Hill, Washington, DC. Photographer unknown; c. 1890. Courtesy of the National Park Service, Frederick Douglass National Historic Site, Washington, DC.

wrote in his 1893 *Frederick Douglass the Orator* that Douglass's "influence on the colored race has been greater than that of any other man. . . . They point with pride to his achievements and success; they reverence him because of his sterling qualities and spotless character. They recognize him as their most prominent leader." Waldo E. Martin, Jr., similarly notes in his 1995 foreword to *Majestic in His Wrath:* "The grand narrative of Douglass's life—an American success story whose hero is the epitome of the American self-made man—reveals enormous inspirational and symbolic power."[6] As is clear from the striking images in the volume, that symbolic power was on full display in the nineteenth century.

Since his death in 1895, Douglass has become of even greater symbolic importance as a cultural figure. Shortly after Douglass's death, Booker T. Washington and W. E. B. Du Bois, the most prominent black leaders of the time, each sought to claim Douglass as a model for his own version of black leadership. Washington, the advocate of black self-help, saw in Douglass "the history of American slavery epitomized in a single human experience," whose significance can be found in the "the uplifting influence he exerted, directly and indirectly, upon the young men of his time." Du Bois, on the other hand, viewed Douglass as a more radical race leader who was distrustful of the value of self-help given "the tremendous might and organization of the slave power."[7] There was a similar divide about Douglass during the debates on blacks' freedom struggles of the 1950s and 1960s, with some civil rights leaders regarding Douglass as a model for black militancy and others regarding him as a more moderate figure whose life spoke to the values of nonviolence and integrationism. Prior to that crucially important moment in twentieth-century American history, Douglass continued to keep his hold on the African American imagination. During World War I, the Frederick Douglass Film Company was formed in Jersey City, New Jersey, with the goal of producing films that presented strong images of blacks. In 1926, the black historian Carter G. Woodson helped to establish an annual Negro History Week in February, the month in which both Douglass and Abraham Lincoln were born. During the late 1930s, black leaders in Harlem founded the Frederick Douglass Historical and Cultural League, with the Booker T. Washington-like intent of encouraging black uplift; and during the 1940s black leaders in Ohio founded a similar group called the Frederick Douglass Community Association.[8] What united Washington, Du Bois, and many other African

American leaders of the early twentieth century was their shared belief that Douglass was not only the greatest black leader of the nineteenth century but also a continuing inspiration to those who followed in his wake.

As a number of critics have pointed out, Douglass in his own time played a major role in consolidating and shaping his status as the country's great and most representative black leader through his three major autobiographies.[9] But the fact is that during the nineteenth century, and even decades after his death, Douglass was best known for the sheer power of his oratory. In his preface to the 1845 *Narrative*, the white abolitionist William Lloyd Garrison marveled at Douglass's "natural eloquence," proclaiming that he "never hated slavery so intensely as at the moment" in 1841 when Douglass gave "his first speech" before Garrison's Massachusetts Anti-Slavery Society. In a similar vein, the abolitionist David W. Bartlett declared in his 1856 *Modern Agitators* that "nature intended Douglass for an orator." The *New York Times* asserted in 1872 that Douglass was "the representative orator of the colored race"; and the African American writer Pauline Hopkins described just how moving Douglass could be to those who heard him in the years following the Civil War: "His voice was full, round, rich, clear, and his enunciation perfect. . . . Child as I was, I felt that I could listen to the mellow richness of those sonorous accents forever." Ironically, in his introduction to Douglass's third and final autobiography, *Life and Times*, which Douglass regarded as his magnum opus, the black lawyer George L. Ruffin asserted what had become a commonplace of the nineteenth century, that "Douglass's fame will rest mainly, no doubt, upon his oratory." The sales figures for the two editions of *Life and Times* would appear to bear out Ruffin's claims, for the evidence suggests that Douglass's final autobiography sold fewer than 5,000 copies. Indeed, in the first full-length post-humous biography of Douglass, Charles Chesnutt's *Frederick Douglass* (1899), which drew on Frederic May Holland's *Frederick Douglass: The Colored Orator* (1891) and Gregory's *Frederick Douglass the Orator*, Chesnutt for the most part ignored Douglass's autobiographies, remarking that "it is upon his genius as an orator that his fame must ultimately rest." That judgment was no doubt inspired by W. S. Scarborough, who in his introduction to Gregory's *Frederick Douglass the Orator* compared Douglass to "Themistocles, Pericles, and Demosthenes."[10]

Douglass may have been adulated in the nineteenth century for his oratory, but by the late twentieth century his fame or "genius" had come to rest primarily on his 1845 *Narrative*, a text that has achieved iconic, indeed hypercanonical status as the best and most representative of the many slave narratives published in the ante-bellum United States and as one of the great American autobio-graphies. That Douglass wrote three autobiographies (including several revised versions of those autobiographies) suggests he was well aware that the voice carries only so far and certainly does not survive the speaking body. Thus, in an effort to ensure his posthumous fame, Douglass devoted an enormous amount of time and energy to producing the two editions of his final auto-biography, *Life and Times*, the second edition of which ran to more than 700 pages and was published just three years before his death. Douglass thought of that work as his most significant autobiography, and perhaps would have brought out another edition had he lived another ten years. In contrast, he regarded the 1845 *Narrative* as a relatively minor work, referring to it dis-missively in the 1855 *Bondage and Freedom*, as a "pamphlet," and in *Life and Times* as a "little book," as if he had outgrown an auto-biography that he had written while still legally a slave and a paid lecturer for a white abolitionist organization.[11] The question of how this "little book" should have emerged as Douglass's most admired and widely read autobiography is worth our consideration, for such a reception history can help to reveal what is currently valued in Douglass as an autobiographer, as well as the costs of this particular instance of textual iconicity.

The *Narrative*'s popularity when it was first published in 1845 by Garrison's Massachusetts Anti-Slavery Society is well known, but the extent of that popularity is difficult to gauge. Although scholars believe that the *Narrative* went through nine or more editions, claims for the book's status as a best seller are difficult to support, especially given that mid-nineteenth-century publishers tended to misrepresent the number of reprints and editions. Nonetheless, by all accounts the *Narrative* was the most successful slave narrative published in the United States, garnering admiring reviews from the likes of Margaret Fuller and the minister Ephraim Peabody, and in all likelihood selling around 20,000 copies between 1845 and the early 1850s in the United States and abroad.[12] Harriet Beecher Stowe's *Uncle Tom's Cabin* (1852), by way of contrast, sold approximately one million copies during the 1850s. Douglass's book went out of print in 1853 (the year of its final printing by the Massachusetts Anti-Slavery Society), and although Douglass quotes from the *Narrative* in his later autobiographies (mainly to give the perspective of the younger Douglass as a character in history), the text itself as a publishing event goes virtually unmentioned in Douglass's two subsequent autobiographies and in most other nineteenth- and early twentieth-century accounts of his career. There were some notable exceptions to the overall silence. William Wells Brown, whose 1847 *Narrative* was influenced by Douglass's 1845 *Narrative*, anticipated mid-to-late twentieth-century assessments when he remarked in 1863 that the "narrative of his life, published in 1845, gave a new impetus to the black man's literature. All other stories of fugitive slaves faded away before the beautifully written, highly descriptive, and thrilling memoir of Frederick Douglass." Decades later, Pauline Hopkins, who delighted in Douglass's oratory, offered one of the few positive appreciations of the *Narrative* published between 1870 and 1960. Douglass's *Narrative*, she exclaimed, "was a soul-stirring and thrilling memoir of his life and the heartrending scenes with which he was so closely connected."[13] Still, the sort of praise that Brown and Hopkins offered was rare, and the book remained out of print until 1960, which means that it practically disappeared from American literary history for over one hundred years.

The *Narrative* (and the later autobiographies) were neglected not simply because most nineteenth-century African American writing was neglected until the time of the Civil Rights Movement—a heady moment when Arno Press (of the *New York Times*) and other presses began to reissue "classics" of African American writing. There were histories of African American literature published well before the 1960s, but even in these early to mid-twentieth-century studies, Douglass continued to be celebrated primarily as an orator, a political presence, a newspaper editor, and only occasionally as an author of autobiographies, typically of *Bondage and Freedom* or *Life and Times*—perhaps because these works had no connections to white antislavery organizations, or perhaps simply because they were genuinely regarded as Douglass's most substantial and complex autographical works.

Conceptions of Douglass's place in African American literary history as it was understood in the first half of the twentieth century can best be gauged through the writings of the African

American critic Benjamin Brawley, whose numerous works on African American literature helped to establish the field. In his *The Negro in Literature and Art in the United States*, first published as a sixty-page pamphlet in 1910, expanded into a book in 1918, and then regularly revised and reprinted, Brawley initially (in the 1910 pamphlet) folds Douglass into his chapter on "The Stage, Orators, Readers," and focuses for the most part on Booker T. Washington. In his chapter on "Other Writers," which analyzes slave narratives and black autobiographies, Douglass isn't even mentioned; instead, Brawley discusses Harriet Jacobs's *Incidents in the Life of a Slave Girl* (which he credits to Linda Brent and Lydia Maria Child), John Langston's *From the Virginia Plantation to the National Capital,* and Washington's "incomparable" *Up from Slavery.* In the more substantial book version of 1918, Brawley comments on Douglass's "fervid oratory" in the midst of a long chapter, "A Hundred Years of Striving," which argues that "practically nothing of abiding literary quality was produced up to the beginning of the last century" until Paul Laurence Dunbar began publishing his poetry and fiction.[14] Though Brawley finds much to admire in pre-Dunbar African American writers, the chapter on "A Hundred Years of Striving" basically assesses the aesthetic limitations of Samuel Ringgold Ward, David Walker, George Moses Horton, Frances Ellen Watkins Harper, Josiah Henson, William Wells Brown, William C. Nell, and Douglass. In a more substantial chapter on Douglass and Booker T. Washington as orators, Brawley offers a sketch biography of Douglass that doesn't mention the *Narrative* but focuses instead on his 1852 "What to the Slave Is the Fourth of July?" Brawley's neglect of Douglass as a writer of autobiographies persists into his 1929 *A Short History of the American Negro,* which has a brief section on Douglass that says nothing about the *Narrative* or the later autobiographies and once again concentrates on Douglass the orator.

But there are indications of changes to come in Brawley's assessment of the literary Douglass. In his pathbreaking 1935 anthology, *Early Negro American Writers*, Brawley includes selections from *Bondage and Freedom*, but nothing from the *Narrative*. Significantly, among the sections he chooses to reprint from Douglass's second autobiography is chapter 22, "Introduced to the Abolitionists," wherein Douglass famously claims that white Garrisonian leaders ordered him to describe but not analyze slavery. Readers of that chapter would have come away thinking that Douglass had little regard for the *Narrative*, given that he presents it in his second autobiography as intimately tied to the Garrisonian organization he had come to reject; and one suspects Brawley shared the view that *Narrative* was a limited, flawed, and overly white-influenced work. Having addressed Douglass as a writer in this 1936 anthology, Brawley has fresh things to say about Douglass in his 1937 *The Negro Genius: A New Appraisal of the Achievement of the American Negro in Literature and the Fine Arts*. Although he once again asserts that "Frederick Douglass was essentially an orator," he now for the first time suggests that Douglass's writings, especially the autobiographies, are worthy of greater consideration: "The works of Douglass have never been fully collected. Naturally of most importance is his account of his own career." But as in *Early Negro American Writers*, it is *Bondage and Freedom* and not the *Narrative* that captures Brawley's attention. He states that the *Narrative* was written solely to respond to "those who regarded the amazing young speaker as an imposter," and he suggests that it is a work compromised by its connection to a white abolitionist organization—or by what the critic John Sekora would later term its "white envelope" (see the discussion in Chapter 1 below). Brawley thus underscores the importance of the fact that *Bondage and Freedom,* unlike the *Narrative,* was introduced "by a member of the author's own race," and that the 1881 *Life and Times* was also introduced by "a man of color."[15] Brawley quietly lets those facts speak for the worth of the *Narrative* in relation to Douglass's later autobiographical works.

Brawley was not alone among early to mid-twentieth-century critics in making little of the *Narrative.* In *The Negro Author: His Development in America* (1931), Vernon Loggins condescendingly remarks that the "style of the *Narrative* is childlike in its simplicity," and he conveys his relative disregard for the *Narrative* by emphasizing the achievement of *Bondage and Freedom:* "What [Douglass] did not dare say in the *Narrative* he now says with boldness. The book is in every sense a surer and bigger work than the earlier autobiography." In his excellent 1948 biography of Douglass, the African American historian Benjamin Quarles devotes less than a half-page of his 377-page volume to the *Narrative.* His description of Douglass's first autobiography is worth quoting in full: "The *Narrative* was a worthy addition to the campaign literature of abolitionism. It revealed a readable prose style, simple and direct, with a feeling for words. It was absorbing in its sensitive descriptions of persons and places—even an unsympathetic reader would be stirred by its vividness if unmoved by its passion. No reader, whatever his temperament, got from the *Narrative* the impression that the slaves were reasonably contented, if not happy."[16] Though Quarles admires the *Narrative,* this is hardly the description of a canonical or iconic work. Appreciative of the book's power, he nevertheless views it somewhat conventionally, in the reformist tradition of the slave narrative, as an antislavery work that through its documentary evidence of the horrors of slavery attempts to create in white readers possibilities of sympathetic identification. Adjectives such as "readable" and "simple" seem of a piece with Loggins's condescending characterization, though words like "absorbing" and "passion" look forward to the more positive reassessment that would inform the introduction to Quarles's crucially important 1960 edition of the *Narrative*.

Published by Harvard University Press as part of its newly inaugurated John Harvard Library Series, Quarles's edition was the first reprinting of the *Narrative* since the early 1850s. The republication came at a time of heightened debate in U.S. culture on the Civil Rights Movement, and the figure of Douglass was at the center of that debate. In 1950, the great Douglass scholar Philip S. Foner published the first volume of what would become the five-volume *The Life and Writings of Frederick Douglass* (1950–1975), arguing in the preface that Douglass was "the outstanding leader of the Negro people" and the black protest leader who offered "the clearest articulation of discontent, protest, militant action, and hope of the American Negro."[17] The vision of a Douglass committed to "militant action" helped to inspire civil rights leaders ranging from Stokely Carmichael to Martin Luther King, Jr., although there was an increasing divide among African American leaders about the extent of Douglass's militancy. Was Douglass overly accommodationist, as Malcolm X claimed, or, as suggested by King, inspirational for his ability to draw on American founding principles for the purposes of social reform? With his 1960 edition of the *Narrative*, Quarles attempted to bring Douglass into the civil rights debate in ways quite different from Foner, who chose not to reprint the autobiographies and whose publisher was known for its editions of Marx, Engels, and Lenin. The fact that Quarles was able to enlist Harvard University Press as the publisher of the *Narrative* was significant, for it ensured the volume's respectability and made the implicit case for the aesthetic and cultural worth of Douglass's first autobiography by placing it alongside the major works of such writers as Cotton Mather, Anne Bradstreet, William Gilmore Simms, James Fenimore Cooper, Ralph Waldo Emerson, and Oliver Wendell Holmes.

In his introduction to the John Harvard Library volume, Quarles argues for the value of the *Narrative* by emphasizing its readability, turning the "simplicity" that Loggins had seen as a negative into a virtue. He assures the possibly hesitant reader: "Except for the length of a few sentences and paragraphs, the Douglass autobiography would come out well in any modern readability analysis. It is written in simple and direct prose, free of literary allusions, and is almost without quoted passages, except for a stanza from 'the slave's poet, Whittier,' two lines from *Hamlet*, and one from Cowper. The details are always concrete, an element of style established in the opening line." Quarles asserts that "the most striking quality of the *Narrative* is Douglass' ability to mingle incident with argument." He then moves from the literary to the cultural and political, sounding a bit like Foner: "Aside from its literary merit, Douglass' autobiography was in many respects symbolic of the Negro's role in American life. Its central theme is struggle. The *Narrative* is a clear and passionate utterance both of the Negro's protest and his aspiration." But rather than discuss such aspiration in relation to militancy, Quarles presents the text in Emersonian terms as a freedom document that "hinted at the infinite potentialities of man in whatever station of life, suggesting powers to be elicited." For that reason, he says, the *Narrative* is "an American book in theme, in tone, and in spirit."[18] Echoing an earlier assessment by Ephraim Peabody, published in the July 1849 *Christian Examiner*, which championed Douglass's *Narrative* as a distinctively American work that exemplifies "the native love of freedom in the individual mind," Quarles also looks forward to, or perhaps more accurately helps to lay the ground for, the presentation of the *Narrative* in numerous American literary anthologies as a work that, to cite one such anthology, "excoriated American society for its lapses at the same time that it affirmed its original promise." In the *Narrative*, Quarles perceives a black writer who both represents the race and pushes his readers to move beyond race. Douglass, he says, "became the first colored man who could command an audience that extended beyond local boundaries or racial ties."[19] Crucial to Quarles's introduction, then, and to the sudden emergence of Douglass's "little book" as canonical, is Quarles's characterization of Douglass as a Representative American in the tradition of figures like Franklin and Emerson.

And yet Quarles cannot completely close his eyes to the raced connections between Douglass's abolitionism in the 1840s and blacks' freedom struggles in the 1950s and early 1960s. After all, in proclaiming that the book is about "struggle," Quarles surely has in mind the ongoing struggles of the Civil Rights Movement. But in alluding to those struggles, Quarles seems anxious about compromising the *Narrative*'s universality by presenting it as overly contentious or threatening to whites who might be suspicious of a book driven by "black" politics. There is a recurrent unease or defensiveness in Quarles's introduction that leads him to downplay, or even undercut, Douglass's racial politics. Thus, as if he has in mind future readers of the John Harvard Library's edition of William Gilmore Simms, he concludes his introduction by making the startling suggestion that Douglass in his abolitionist zeal may have been too hard on slavery: "It is always easy to stir up sympathy for people in bondage, and perhaps Douglass seemed to protest too much in making slavery out as a 'soul-killing' institution." Here, Quarles almost seems to be reaching out to those southern whites who had been asserting that black civil rights leaders had been too hard on segregation. Or perhaps he is simply offering reassurances to white readers, in the North and South, that black protest against racial inequities does not necessarily signify the sort of race hate that some whites discerned in the words of Malcolm X and other exponents of black power. As Quarles puts it with specific reference to Douglass: "But if Douglass emerged as the leading Negro among Negroes, this is not to say that the man was himself a racist, or that he glorified in all things black. . . . Douglass did not dislike whites—his close association with reformers in the abolitionist and woman's rights movements, his many friends across the color line, and the choice he made for his second wife indicate that he was without a trace of anti-Caucasianism."[20] (In 1884, two years after the death of his wife, Anna, Douglass married the white Helen Pitts, his former secretary and a women's rights advocate, and was criticized for doing so.)

Quarles's edition of the *Narrative* stirred new interest in Douglass during the 1960s. The mainstream publisher Doubleday brought out its own edition of the *Narrative* in 1963, the year of Martin Luther King's March on Washington. Douglass thus became even more of a focal point for black leaders, who were often in conflict about the meaning of Douglass's legacy. Harold Cruse observed in his 1967 *The Crisis of Black Leadership* that during this time "integrationist and nationalist" leaders alike often found themselves "honoring the same hero" in the person of Douglass, whom Cruse identified as in "a direct line" to "the modern civil rights movement." But was Douglass a militant or an advocate of nonviolence? In a 1963 cover story in the mass-circulation black monthly magazine *Ebony*, Lerone Bennett, Jr., portrayed Douglass as a militant who "favored ballots, if possible, and bullets, if necessary." Stokely Carmichael and Charles Hamilton similarly regarded Douglass as a militant, stating in the introduction to their 1967 *Black Power* that their own political positions were inspired by the "meaningful language . . . of Frederick Douglass, a black American who understood the nature of protest in this society." From a very different perspective, while Malcolm X allowed that "Douglass was great," he maintained that he was a white accommodationist in the tradition of Booker T. Washington, and that instead of learning more about the life of Douglass, he would rather "be taught about people who fought, who bled for freedom and made others bleed," such as the Haitian Revolutionary Toussaint L'Ouverture. Malcolm X also attacked Martin Luther King for his supposed accommodationism, perhaps because, as Eric J. Sundquist remarks, King "remained wedded to Douglass's redemptive embrace of the Fathers." But like Douglass, King regarded the revolutionary founders (as he believed Douglass regarded them) as militants who fought against oppression. Thus King, more than Carmichael, Hamilton, and Malcolm X, was willing to invoke the nation's founding documents as freedom documents, just as Douglass regularly invoked them. As King states about the Declaration of Independence in his 1962 "The Ethical Demands for Integration," "Never has a sociopolitical document proclaimed more profoundly and eloquently the sacredness of human personality. . . . Frederick Douglass stated the same truth in his [1851] lecture on the Constitution of the United States of America."[21]

But even as Douglass remained a focus of debate among African American leaders of the 1960s, he began to emerge as a more mainstream "American" hero for white Americans, perhaps as a direct result of Quarles's edition of the *Narrative*. In 1965, Quarles himself gave a speech at the site of the bridge connecting predominately black Anacostia to the rest of Washington, DC, when it was renamed the Frederick Douglass Memorial Bridge. In 1967 the United States Postal Service issued a Frederick Douglass stamp. One year later, on November 22, 1968, seven months after the assassination of King and on the anniversary of the assassination of John F. Kennedy, *Life* magazine ran a story on black history with a cover photograph of the "Abolitionist Frederick Douglass" (Figure 2). In the story itself, "Rebels, Runaways, and Heroes: The Bitter Years of Slavery," the influential African American historian John Hope Franklin focused on the Douglass who is central to the *Narrative*—slave, runaway, and emerging abolitionist—although he concludes his article with a pronouncement drawn from Douglass's self-representations in his later autobiographical narratives: "Douglass was, in fact, the unofficial president of American Negroes in the years before and immediately after the Civil War."[22]

As indicated by his attention to race, Franklin hardly argued for an assimilated or nonraced Douglass, but a cover article on Douglass in one of the nation's most widely read magazines further contributed to the emergence of Douglass as a major figure in American history who spoke to the contemporary moment. Not surprisingly, there was an upsurge in the late 1960s, continuing to our present day, of Douglass iconography. Schools throughout the Mid-Atlantic and Northeast region, where Douglass did his major antislavery and antiracist work, began taking on his name, as did major thoroughfares. The National Park Service officially opened Douglass's Cedar Hill home to visitors in 1972; and in subsequent years Frederick Douglass Institutes were established in

FIGURE 2. Daguerreotype portrait of Douglass, c. 1850, on the cover of the November 22, 1968, issue of *Life*. Portrait by J. R. Eyerman, from the collection of Robert A. Weinstein. Photo by *Life* magazine/*Life* Premium Collection/Getty Images.

Rochester and Pennsylvania. More recently, Frederick Douglass Circle at the northwest corner of New York's Central Park was dedicated in 2011, and a Frederick Douglass statue was unveiled at the U.S. Capitol in 2013. Indeed, just about the only locale that has vociferously resisted glorying in Douglass is the Eastern Shore of Maryland, which remains uncomfortable about its most famous native. A proposal to build a Douglass statue on the lawn of the Talbot County Courthouse, the county where Douglass lived as a slave, met with fierce resistance from descendants of Civil War veterans in the area, who were concerned that a Douglass statue would overshadow the thirteen-foot-high memorial to Confederate soldiers that has been on display on the lawn since the early twentieth century. After *Washington Post* columnist Courtland Milloy called attention to the controversy in an article of 2006, negotiations proceeded, and the sculpture was at long last presented to the public in June 2011.[23]

Accompanying the past half-century's renewed attention to Douglass has been the apotheosis of the *Narrative* itself. Crucial to the reevaluation of the *Narrative* in post-Brawley and -Loggins scholarship was the reevaluation of the slave narrative as a literary genre, stimulated by Quarles's republication of Douglass's first autobiography and then by such key critical works as Charles H. Nichols's *Many Thousands Gone: The Ex-Slaves' Account of Their Bondage and Freedom* (1963), Stephen Butterfield's *Black Autobiography in America* (1974), and Sidonie Smith's *Where I'm Bound: Patterns of Slavery and Freedom in Black American Autobiography* (1974). In an influential collection of essays, *The Slave's Narrative* (1985), edited by Charles T. Davis and Henry Louis Gates, Jr., the result of such a reevaluation can be discerned in the title of the book's concluding section: "The Slave Narratives as Literature." The literariness of the slave narrative was probably not on the mind of Douglass and others working in the genre during the pre–Civil War years, which can help to explain Douglass's modesty about his own *Narrative* (he probably thought of *Bondage and Freedom* as a work more in the tradition of classic autobiography). But by the 1980s a critical consensus had come to regard Douglass's *Narrative*, as James Olney put it in 1985, as the "greatest" of the slave narratives; such a consensus prompted further reprintings of Douglass's first autobiography, along with an increasing identification of Douglass with the *Narrative* itself. In 1982, the Penguin American Library brought out its first volume of Douglass, an edition of the *Narrative*, which Houston A. Baker, Jr., in his introduction termed a "masterpiece of American literary art."[24] (Penguin wouldn't publish its second Douglass volume, an edition of *Bondage and Freedom*, until 2003.) A recent search of the Books in Print database shows that there are approximately 400 editions of Douglass's *Narrative* in print (books, e-books, and audio recordings), which far outnumber editions of the other autobiographies and collections of Douglass's miscellaneous writings (which typically include the *Narrative* anyway). The *Narrative* truly is everywhere in American literary study: it appears (usually in full) in all of the major American literature anthologies; it serves as the prime example of African American writing in numerous American literature courses; it also serves as the prime example of African American autobiography and the slave narrative for those interested in traditions of autobiography but not in the full range of African American autobiography.[25] Outside of the classroom, it remains the text that, for many, defines the totality of Douglass's career, given that most people who have a sense of Douglass's historical and cultural significance know him either through the *Narrative* or from accounts that draw on the *Narrative*. To put this another way: most people know Douglass from a work that has nothing to say about his life as a free person (fifty years of his adult career) and from a work that Douglass himself sometimes belittled. We need to consider Douglass's lives beyond the *Narrative,* and we need to rethink what it is that we're reading when we read the *Narrative.*

~ఠ~

Douglass certainly thought about his own life beyond the *Narrative.* Shortly after Garrison published the book, Douglass began to revise it. Few know about the 1845 and 1846 Dublin editions, which Douglass had a considerable hand in editing. Why did he revise the Boston text for his British readers? Why are those revisions generally not part of the conversation about the *Narrative* or about Douglass as an autobiographer? At the very least, the Dublin editions suggest the extent to which Douglass regarded the *Narrative* as a fluid text that brought together stories he had been telling about his life in his lectures and then, once in print, became a source for stories about his life that he could tell in new ways in speeches and writings to come. Relatively little attention has been paid to Douglass's autobiographical accounts (in speeches, essays, and letters) during the years immediately following the publication of the *Narrative,* as if he had produced no further autobiographical work until the 1855 *Bondage and Freedom.* But in his 1848 "Letter to My Old Master, Thomas Auld," Douglass takes the characters "Douglass" and "Thomas Auld" in new directions, and he does that as well in *Bondage and Freedom* and *Life and Times.* Shortly after the publication of the *Narrative,* Douglass also began to write and speak about the slave rebel Madison Washington, and those accounts, which had an autobiographical component, had a major impact on his depiction of himself as a black revolutionary in *Bondage and Freedom*. Twenty-six years would pass between the publication of Douglass's second autobiography and *Life and Times*, but during that period he did not stop lecturing and writing in an autobiographical mode. Among his most compelling autobiographical works during this period are his lectures and essays on John Brown and Abraham Lincoln, who have a central place in *Life and Times*. Thomas Auld, whom Douglass wrote about over a forty-year period, is also prominently featured in this late autobiography. There is much to learn about Douglass and the Civil War, Douglass and violence, and Douglass and his white "family" by reading the currently underrated *Life and Times* in relation to a wide range of his other autobiographical writings.

From beginning to end, *The Lives of Frederick Douglass* pays close attention to Douglass's constantly shifting acts of self-representation. Douglass was a contradictory, complex, and performative figure who ultimately baffles efforts to reduce his life to a single story. There is the Douglass who was a model American devoted to uplift in the manner of Benjamin Franklin; the Douglass who was a postnationalist cosmopolitan; the Douglass who fought for the rights of minorities and women from a postracial perspective; and the Douglass who was fully engaged with black culture as an advocate of black nationalism. There is a nonviolent Douglass and a Douglass who celebrated the violence of John Brown and eighteenth- and nineteenth-century black revolutionaries; there is a Douglass who served the U.S. nation loyally after the Civil War and a Douglass who challenged U.S. imperialism by taking the side of Haiti during a tense period of negotiations late in the nineteenth century. In all of his autobiographical essays and lectures, Douglass skillfully crafts an image of himself as a heroic black man and a model for the race whose energy, resolve, and intelligence helped him to rise from his obscure origins in slavery to become one of the great black leaders of the time. Along the way, he used his autobiographies to articulate his and other blacks' quests for freedom in slave and post-slave culture. But identity is never stable in Douglass; it is tied to the contingencies of the historical moment and to the problematics (and challenges) of the autobiographer's art.

To emphasize the large argument and overarching perspective of *The Lives of Frederick Douglass:* Any examination of Douglass as an autobiographer must take account of the centrality of revision and seriality to his autobiographical imagination, which is yet another reason why there are limits to focusing on the *Narrative* as his signal autobiographical achievement. In an important essay on African American autobiography, William L. Andrews writes that "the dynamic principle . . . in the history of Afro-American autobiography is the *revising,* not the canonizing, of traditions, and even texts." Revision was of crucial importance, Andrews observes, because African American autobiographers confronted constantly changing notions of slavery and freedom over the course of the nineteenth century; as a result, their understanding of how to conceive of and represent their own identity was just as constantly changing. Writing for multiple audiences, black autobiographers experimented with a range of strategies for depicting their humanity in a world in which they were regularly under siege; they wrote for something more than critical acclaim. In this context, it is not surprising that Douglass the former slave who became a prominent social reformer and critic—and who regularly addressed white, black, and racially mixed audiences—was a "compulsive revisionist," as Celeste-Marie Bernier puts it, who "retold, revisualised and restaged multiple and kaleidoscopic narrative vignettes of selfhood throughout his lifetime."[26] Given the protean nature of Douglass's writing, we need to rethink our approach to the *Narrative,* which emerged less from revision than from collaboration between Douglass and Garrison's Massachusetts Anti-Slavery Society. The *Narrative*'s current canonical status has deflected attention away from that collaboration. As Andrews suggests, canonization also deflects attention away from the process of revision.

The influential theorist of autobiography Paul John Eakin asserts that autobiography is "a ceaseless process of identity formation in which new versions of the past evolve to meet the constantly changing requirements of the self in each successive present." Douglass scholar Waldo E. Martin, Jr., similarly argues that Douglass's autobiographical writings and oratory enact "his odyssey of self-realization" and display his "evolving self-awareness."[27] The idea that writing about one's self can be a mode of self-discovery has an implicit place in the chapters that follow. But the emphasis of my analysis of Douglass's autobiographical works is more on their performative dimension, the ways in which Douglass revises and crafts those works for audiences at particular historical moments. In the spirit of the black autobiographical tradition described by Andrews, Douglass over the years reconceived aspects of his life history as he responded to changing historical circumstances. In crucial ways, he thought of his life history as making an argument, and arguments generally are developed most effectively when the writer or speaker takes the fullest measure of the rhetorical occasion. There is no writer or speaker of the nineteenth century more skillful in shaping an autobiographical narrative, or any sort of narrative, for actual or imagined audiences than Frederick Douglass.

Finally, a word about historicism. Though I am interested in Douglass as a cultural figure (or construction) in the twentieth-

and twenty-first centuries, the overwhelming emphasis of *The Lives of Frederick Douglass* is on understanding Douglass as an autobiographer in the nineteenth century. The historicist assumption informing my critical approach is that recovering Douglass as best we can in his own time helps us to construct a more vital Douglass for our own—a figure, in other words, that is more than simply a figment of our collective cultural imaginations. Through a method of collage (which regards Douglass's autobiographical writings as part of an ongoing, lifelong project) and prismatic refraction (which attends to the various and sometimes conflicting images of Douglass that emerge from those writings), this study of the lives of Douglass offers a revisionist biography of the man as a social reformer, African American leader, and writer. Douglass himself was aware of the challenges and opportunities of conceiving of his life history as fluid and changeable. Arguably, Douglass continues to seem so elusive because he both understood and invented himself through writings that refuse to rest on a single, unified sense of self. His autobiographical works were often motivated by his desire to rethink accounts produced earlier in his life, sometimes just months, weeks, or days before; such is the nature of the seriality of his autobiographical imagination. Whether in his speeches, essays, letters, or autobiographies, Douglass always conveys some idea of his goals as an autobiographer at the time of production and some recognition of the rhetorical occasion in his self-representations. To return to the 1845 *Narrative*, then, which is where Douglass's autobiographical project famously begins: Here is a work whose hypercanonicity has made it seem as if it has only a scant relation to specific historical and institutional contexts. But what happens to the *Narrative* when we read it in the context of Douglass's work as an abolitionist in Garrison's Massachusetts Anti-Slavery

Society and in relation to his other autobiographical writings of the period and beyond? Do we have a diminished *Narrative* or a somewhat defamiliarized *Narrative* that offers Douglass's first iteration (very quickly to be revised) of his life history? These are the large questions that I take up in the first two chapters of this study.

~✒ 1 ✐~

THE MASSACHUSETTS
ANTI-SLAVERY SOCIETY
NARRATIVE

F IRST PUBLISHED IN MAY 1845 by William Lloyd
Garrison's Massachusetts Anti-Slavery Society, *Narrative of the Life of Frederick Douglass, an American Slave: Written by Himself* has come to be lauded as a slave narrative masterpiece that transcends its time and place. Most readers who now encounter the *Narrative* in paperback editions and anthologies probably rush through the preliminary remarks by the white abolitionists Garrison and Wendell Phillips to get to Douglass himself, and then hear a voice that indeed speaks across the centuries about the triumph of the human spirit over the degradations of slavery. The power of that voice and the compact and moving story of Douglass's rise from slavery to freedom have helped to make the *Narrative* the most widely read slave narrative of the antebellum period, and the one that is generally taken as representative of the genre and of Douglass himself. In his later writings, Douglass described his first book somewhat negatively as a youthful effort that was defined in large part by his relationship with Garrison

and the Massachusetts Anti-Slavery Society. Breaking with Garrison not long after the publication of the *Narrative*, and over the years presenting a number of other accounts of his life history (including two additional book-length autobiographies), Douglass did not want a text that describes only the first twenty-seven years of his long and productive life to stand as his signal autobiographical achievement. Nor did he want a book published by Garrison to define him for his own time and beyond. And yet the evidence suggests that in the spring and summer of 1845 Douglass gloried in the achievement of the *Narrative*, which he regarded as the fruitful culmination of the collaborative work he had been doing with Garrison's antislavery society since 1841.[1] Although Douglass later regretted the text's close association with the Garrisonians, the *Narrative* arguably achieved much of its power precisely because of that association.

Admittedly, in titling this chapter "The Massachusetts Anti-Slavery Society *Narrative*," I am being tendentious in the way of a critic who would call Hawthorne's first novel "The Ticknor, Reed and Fields *The Scarlet Letter*." But my approach is governed by a conviction that there is much to learn by reconsidering Douglass's first autobiography in relation to the institutional and personal networks that helped to bring it into being. Because the *Narrative* has become such an iconic text, we have lost touch with the importance of those networks to nearly all aspects of the *Narrative*. And when historically minded critics actually do consider such influences, they tend to view them negatively. John Sekora set the terms of such an approach when he argued that slave narratives of the antebellum period, including Douglass's *Narrative*, typically present accounts of black lives in slavery as "mandated by persons other than the subject." From this perspective, the 1845 *Narrative* could be seen as the product of a racist cultural process in which "white sponsors [such as Garrison and his associates] compel a black author [such as Douglass] to approve, to authorize white institutional power." To be sure, Sekora believed that the ex-slaves who published their narratives had important things to say about slavery and race in the United States, which he called the "black message." Convinced, however, that there were deep, irresolvable conflicts between black autobiographers and their white abolitionist sponsors, Sekora concluded that it was typically the case that the black message of the slave narrative came "sealed within a white envelope" that muffled its force.[2]

In the wake of Sekora's influential essay, Douglass has been celebrated for crafting a powerful black message that rips apart the Massachusetts Anti-Slavery Society's white envelope. Viewed in this way, Douglass succeeded in writing a great slave narrative in spite of his relationship with this group. More often, however, the *Narrative* is read as if the society simply didn't exist, which takes me back to my opening claim that many readers skip or skim the opening prefaces by the sponsoring white abolitionists, or else see the sponsors' prefaces as condescending and ultimately unsuccessful efforts to keep the great black abolitionist under their control. In this chapter I take a different approach by exploring the *productive* role of Garrison and his antislavery society in the making of Douglass's first autobiography, and thus of the relative convergence, or congruence, of the white envelope with the black message. After all, at the moment of the *Narrative*'s publication, Douglass was a fervent Garrisonian abolitionist who had been working collaboratively with Garrison and his associates for approximately four years. It is a mistake, I think, to read the *Narrative* through the lens of Douglass's later disillusionment or to conceive of its power as existing wholly apart from its Garrisonian context.

Douglass became a lecturer for the Massachusetts Anti-Slavery Society in 1841, which was a crucial moment in Garrison's career. Up to that time, Garrison had been recognized as the nation's leading antislavery reformer. He was the editor of the most influential antislavery newspaper, the Boston-based *Liberator*, which he had founded in 1831, and the leader of the American Anti-Slavery Society and its auxiliary branch, the Massachusetts Anti-Slavery Society, which he had founded in 1833 and 1835, respectively. Garrison promoted a wide range of social reforms, including women's rights. As an antislavery reformer, he opposed the movement to colonize blacks to Africa, called for immediate emancipation, and emphasized the importance of helping the free blacks to rise in the culture. More controversially, he supported nonresistance, or moral suasion, over violence, and insisted that the Constitution was a proslavery document. Thus he opposed political abolitionism (working within the political system or through the electoral process) on the grounds that such work helped to sustain the proslavery nation. Instead, he advocated dis-Unionism, and in his newspaper articles and speeches urged the free states to break from a nation constitutionally committed to upholding slavery. In 1839 and 1840, political abolitionists primarily based in New York, and still members of the American Anti-Slavery Society, challenged Garrison on a number of issues. The New Yorker Gerrit Smith, who would befriend Douglass in the late 1840s, was among the opposition leaders who insisted that the Constitution was an antislavery document and that it therefore made sense to work within the political system to oppose slavery. Leading the break from the American Anti-Slavery Society, Smith founded the Liberty Party in 1840. Garrison maintained hold of the American Anti-Slavery Society, but he was now under fire from those aligned with the Liberty Party and other political and reform organizations who backed political abolitionism and the strategic use of physical resistance (such as helping fugitive slaves to escape from their captors). In an open letter "To the Abolitionists of the United States," published in the February 28, 1840, *Liberator*, Garrison lamented the schism among the abolitionists: "We are no longer an unbroken phalanx." Two months later, in a second open letter, he underscored one of his main beliefs, that slavery "corrupts the State," and precisely for that reason he continued to preach the doctrine of dis-Unionism, declaring again and again during the 1840s: "NO UNION WITH SLAVEHOLDERS."[3]

When Douglass signed on as a speaker for Garrison's Massachusetts Anti-Slavery Society in 1841, just one year after the schism in the antislavery ranks, he embraced Garrison's call for immediate emancipation, championed moral suasion, and shared as well in Garrison's suspicion of political abolitionism. During the four years leading to the publication of the *Narrative*, Douglass began to have doubts about at least two of Garrison's main tenets—moral suasion, which he feared gave too much power to the slave owners, and dis-Unionism, which he thought could lead to the abandonment of the southern slaves—but for the most part he espoused Garrison's views in his lectures and early writings. Although it is tempting to view Douglass as an outlier, rebel, or critic of the man he was working for, and thus as an independent black writer and speaker who had no need for the support of a white antislavery leader and his abolitionist organization, there are good reasons to regard the *Narrative* as the result of a productive collaboration between Douglass and the Garrisonians. In the discussion that follows, I reexamine ideas about Douglass's authorial agency during this period, with the aim not of diminishing him, or presenting him in a subordinate role, but rather of suggesting his skill in negotiating his situation as a valued employee of Garrison's Massachusetts Anti-Slavery Society in order both to write the *Narrative* and then to move on to new ways of telling his life story.

DOUGLASS'S WRITING WORKSHOP

Douglass escaped from slavery in September 1838, at the age of twenty. Shortly after his escape, he married the Baltimore free black Anna Murray in New York City, and then husband and wife made their way to New Bedford, Massachusetts, where Douglass initially worked in the shipyards. As he makes clear in all of his autobiographies, he encountered racism among the white laboring classes; he also encountered racism at the white churches, which led him to join the New Bedford Zion Methodist Church. In April of 1839, he received a preaching license from the African Methodist Episcopal Zion Church, and it was at this time that he subscribed to Garrison's antislavery newspaper, the *Liberator*, the organ of the Massachusetts Anti-Slavery Society and the larger American Anti-Slavery Society, and began speaking to New Bedford blacks about slavery and racism. His attack on the American Colonization Society's program to ship the free blacks to Africa, delivered at a meeting of New Bedford African Americans in March 1839, was noted in the March 29, 1839, issue of the *Liberator*. Douglass continued to speak out against slavery and racism over the next two years. In August 1841, the New Bedford Quaker abolitionist William C. Coffin, who had heard Douglass address an antislavery meeting at the Zion Methodist Church earlier that year, urged Douglass to attend a meeting of the Massachusetts Anti-Slavery Society in Nantucket. Probably on August 10,

1841, Douglass took a boat to Nantucket with Coffin and joined the gathering of the antislavery society. With the renowned Garrison in attendance, Douglass found the courage to rise from his seat and speak to the group about his experiences in slavery. In this triumphal moment, history was made: Douglass was "discovered" by Garrison, and so began his career as an antislavery lecturer on the national and soon international stage. Garrison's organization, which had other black speakers, hired Douglass as a paid lecturer for a three-month trial period; he was so successful that the position was quickly made permanent. The antislavery society helped Douglass with a down payment for a house by the railroad tracks in Lynn, Massachusetts, which he purchased in the fall of 1841, and his speaker's salary allowed him to manage his mortgage payments. With a new home, a growing family (his third child was born in March 1842), and a packed lecture calendar, Douglass was suddenly thriving as Garrison's most sought-after black speaker, and there is every indication that he was thrilled with this new role.[4]

However, looking back on his experiences as a Garrisonian lecturer from the vantage point of his 1855 *My Bondage and My Freedom*, published four years after he had publicly broken with Garrison, Douglass presents Garrison as something of a crafty seducer who in August 1841 had lured the innocent Douglass into his organization, not only to assume a kind of ownership over him, but also to feed on him (almost in the way of a vampire) in order to recharge his flagging energies. As Douglass tells the story in *Bondage and Freedom*, right after he spoke at the antislavery meeting in Nantucket, "Mr. Garrison followed me, taking me as his text; and now, whether I had made an eloquent speech in behalf of freedom or not, his was one never to be forgotten by those who heard it. Those who had heard Mr. Garrison oftenest, and had known him longest, were astonished." Nearly fifteen years after the fact, Douglass suggests that Garrison appropriated the black speaker, making Douglass into a "text" or subject of a lecture that mainly served to glorify Garrison. And things get worse in the 1855 account. The naïve Douglass signs on as a speaker for the Massachusetts Anti-Slavery Society and "entered upon this new life in the full gush of unsuspecting enthusiasm." The "unsuspecting" hints at the betrayal to come; and indeed, in an oft-quoted passage, Douglass asserts that he was viewed by the white abolitionists, as he was viewed by his slave masters, as "a *'chattel'*—a *'thing.'*" As Douglass attests in 1855, the abolitionists of Garrison's organization ordered their "chattel" simply to describe his experiences in slavery while letting the Garrisonians "take care of the philosophy." Douglass writes in 1855 that he wanted not just to "*narrate* wrongs; I felt like *denouncing* them," but that such denunciations were regarded as beyond his purview as an escaped slave for hire. According to Douglass in 1855, the Garrisonians even believed that displays of rhetorical eloquence would undercut his value to the organization. They therefore asked him to retain "a *little* of the plantation manner of speech."[5] One comes away from reading about Douglass's time with the Garrisonians, as he describes it in *Bondage and Freedom,* with a sense that it was fortunate that he was able to break from Garrison as early as 1847, by starting up his own newspaper, the *North Star,* and that it might have been an even better thing had he been able to break from Garrison sooner.

But if Douglass had left Garrison and the Massachusetts Anti-Slavery Society before 1845, we probably would not have the *Narrative,* which Douglass published through Garrison's organization, and maybe not even *Bondage and Freedom,* which reworks and extends the *Narrative.* Here it's worth underscoring, as

I discuss in Chapter 3, that Douglass and Garrison had come to hate each other by the early 1850s, and that Douglass's 1855 remarks on the early to mid-1840s Garrison cannot fully be trusted. Contra Douglass's account in *Bondage and Freedom*, all of the available evidence suggests that during the years when Douglass was a paid lecturer for Garrison (1841–1845), he was energized by the cause and by his association with Garrison. During those years, Douglass was a committed black Garrisonian who shared the Massachusetts Anti-Slavery Society's views on the main tenets of Garrison's philosophy, such as the importance of moral suasion and the belief that the Constitution was a proslavery document. Douglass and Garrison traveled and spoke together on numerous occasions, with Douglass participating in all of the society's major activities, ranging from the tours linked to the group's 1843 Year of One Hundred Conventions to the 1844 meeting of the American Anti-Slavery Society which endorsed Garrison's principles of abolitionism. Moreover, the evidence suggests that Douglass, who claimed otherwise in 1855, was offered what appears to have been carte blanche to denounce and analyze U.S. slave culture on his own. For if, as Douglass alleged in *Bondage and Freedom*, the Garrisonians were expecting Douglass and other black speakers to offer firsthand testimony about slavery while leaving the analysis to the white leaders, Douglass managed to do a great job of skirting those demands. In his extant lectures from 1841 to 1845, Douglass typically spoke as a Garrisonian abolitionist and was profoundly analytical.

To highlight just a few of the topics that Douglass addressed in his extant pre-*Narrative* speeches: Again and again Douglass, like Garrison, pointed to the hypocrisy of the northern and southern churches, which would become a major motif of the *Narrative*. He also spoke on abolitionist petitions, on the party system, and on whites' antiblack prejudices in the North and South. There simply is not a surviving lecture in which Douglass speaks *only* as an escaped slave who is authenticating the horrors of slavery. In 1842 Garrison began to print Douglass's letters in the *Liberator,* another clear indication that he saw Douglass as fully capable of analyzing slavery and the larger political system, whether he was writing in support of the fugitive slave George Latimer in 1842 or reporting on political and reform conventions. As articulated in a letter to Garrison of October 27, 1844, which Garrison printed in the November 1844 *Liberator,* Douglass regarded his main mission as an antislavery speaker to contribute to "the enlightenment of the public mind," which is not what one would expect from someone viewed as a mere chattel of an antislavery organization.[6] In this long letter to Garrison, Douglass describes a Liberty Party convention in New Bedford, discussing the strengths and limits of the party while at the same time denouncing Henry Clay and his fellow Whigs, along with James Polk and his fellow Democrats. Garrison would continue to print Douglass's letters on slavery and politics long after the publication of the *Narrative;* Douglass's analytical letters were one of the admired features of the newspaper.

Still, it may well be true that, at least from Garrison's sometimes paternalistic perspective, Douglass best served the Massachusetts Anti-Slavery Society as an escaped slave who could eloquently tell the story of his life in slavery. It is here that things get complicated. Were Douglass's and other ex-slave lecturers' stories, as Douglass suggested in 1855, simply created to specifications dictated by Garrison and his colleagues? Douglass biographer William McFeely writes that "Douglass . . . and other black antislavery speakers were always treated as visiting artists in a production of which the white Bostonians never dreamed of losing the direction"; and Sekora claims that "Garrisonians sometimes alleged that their black agents had no stories until the abolitionists gave them one—sponsors assumed in advance that they knew what slave lives should contain."[7] Drawing on Douglass's 1855 assessment of the Garrisonians, McFeely and Sekora convey what has become a widely held belief that Garrison regarded his black speakers and writers as subordinates whose job was to forward the agenda of his antislavery society. In that context, Douglass's autobiographical speeches and writings of the period would have to be regarded as constrained, even tainted, by the very society that was "directing" his antislavery work in the first place.

But there is another way of thinking about the relationship between Douglass and the Massachusetts Anti-Slavery Society with respect to the stories he told about his life in slavery: that the organization, by asking Douglass to describe his life history, gave exigence to his life history and thus served as a kind of writing workshop for the *Narrative* to come. The society provided Douglass with forums in which people wanted to hear about his life in slavery and whose responses helped him to think about the strengths and limits of the different ways he was telling his story.[8] So we might think of Douglass's *Narrative* as emerging from a series of storytelling possibilities in which Douglass was given actual audiences (always important to the development of one's writing and speaking) and a set of assumptions about abolitionism which empowered him as a writer and speaker. If Douglass found it difficult to speak at that first Garrisonian meeting in Nantucket "without hesitation and stammering," as he writes in *Bondage and Freedom*, just a month later he was lighting up the stage at a Garrisonian antislavery meeting in Rhode Island. As Nathaniel P. Rogers, the editor of the Concord, New Hampshire, *Herald of Freedom* testified in a column of December 3, 1841, Douglass, whom he terms "the fugitive Othello," is "an extraordinary man" and a "speaker [who] has few equals."[9]

It is as an admired and empowered speaker *within* the Massachusetts Anti-Slavery Society that Douglass began to try out aspects of his autobiographical story. Around the time that Rogers was extolling Douglass as a speaker, Douglass offered his first extant remarks on his slave master Thomas Auld. The story that he told his audience in October 1841 about Auld's cruelty to Douglass's cousin Henny is later retold in the *Narrative* and in all of his subsequent autobiographies: "I have seen this pious class leader cross and tie the hands of one of his young female slaves [Henny], and lash her on the bare skin and justify the deed by the quotation from the Bible, 'he who knoweth his master's will and doeth it not, shall be beaten with many stripes.'" Douglass in his early 1840s lectures regularly worked with the trope of the separation of black families, which would become central to the opening chapters of the *Narrative,* where he describes his own separation from his mother and siblings. "Oh, my friends," he proclaims in the same speech on Auld, "you cannot feel the slave's misery, when he is separated from his kindred."[10] In subsequent speeches he refers again to Auld's beating of his cousin, and he shares more about his life, all the while working on ways of drawing in his listeners so that they might feel the misery of the slave. Appealing to sympathetic feeling, Douglass and his compatriots found, was a highly effective way of motivating whites to engage with antislavery reform.

Perhaps the most exemplary of these life-story previews can be seen in Rogers's article on Douglass's lecture of February 11, 1844, "Southern Slavery and Northern Religion," published in the *Herald of Freedom* at the very moment (according to a letter from

Garrison to Parker Pillsbury of February 23, 1844) Douglass had begun working on the *Narrative*. Rogers is once again enthralled by Douglass, and in his transcriptions we see the broad outlines of the *Narrative* emerging not apart from but within the framework of a speech delivered under the aegis of the Massachusetts Anti-Slavery Society. As would be true of the *Narrative*, Douglass in this lecture, Rogers reports, "began by a calm, deliberate and very simple narrative of his life. . . . He did not remember his mother, I think he said, and never knew who was his father." In the *Narrative*, Douglass describes (or imagines) the sad fate of his grandmother, who was allegedly sent out to die when she was too old to be a productive member of the slave owner's household; in the 1844 lecture, Douglass tries out that story on his audience, working on the pathos that would become central to the account in all versions of his autobiography. Rogers summarizes Douglass's remarks: "She, by the way, had reared twelve children of her own, for the market—all sold and gone from her—and she now blind and alone." The key scene in which Douglass physically resists Edward Covey is also tried out in this speech: "He [Douglass] was sent to a slave-breaker, when some 16 or 17 years old—his master not being able to manage him. An attempt at breaking him once brought on a struggle between him and the Jockey. The result of it was such that the Jockey did not care to repeat it, while his care for his reputation, as a successful breaker, kept him from getting help to manage a slave boy." In the *Narrative*, Douglass describes the various ways he learned to read and write; in the 1844 lecture Douglass similarly tells of "his *schooling*—the beginning of the wife of his master's relative to teach him letters, and the stern forbidding of it, by her husband, which Frederick overheard—how he caught a little teaching here and there from the children of the streets." If there is a

significant difference between the speech and the *Narrative*, it re-
sides in the differences between oral and written forms of com-
munication, for Rogers's visceral response to the lecture is unlike
the typical response to the *Narrative*. He states that Douglass
"closed his slave narrative, and gradually let out the outraged
humanity that was laboring in him. . . . It was the volcanic outbreak of human nature long pent up in slavery and at last bursting
its imprisonment. It was the storm of insurrection. . . . He reminded me of Toussaint among the plantations of Haiti."[11]

In perceiving Douglass as an American version of the great
Haitian revolutionary leader, the white Rogers may have been
confessing to some of his own anxieties about rebellious slaves,
or he may have heard something in Douglass's voice that most
readers would fail to discern in the text published a year later.
For now, the point that needs to be emphasized is that Douglass
from 1841 to early 1845 tried out his life history on Garrisonian
audiences, saw what worked most effectively, and proceeded
accordingly with his writing. The role of these lectures in the development of Douglass's 1845 Massachusetts Anti-Slavery Society *Narrative* cannot be overstated. In subsequent speeches he
tried out other aspects of his life; and then, in his May 6, 1845,
"My Slave Experience in Maryland," which he delivered in New
York City, he began to use the completed book as a source for
the autobiographical portions of his lectures, discussing Colonel Lloyd's domineering character, Austin Gore's killing of
Demby, Mrs. Giles Hicks's killing of Douglass's cousin, and other
people and events as presented in the soon to be published *Narrative*.[12] Drawing on the recently completed work as his source for
the lecture, even as he took liberties in adapting material for this
particular occasion, Douglass initiated the process of revising the
Massachusetts Anti-Slavery Society *Narrative*, which would lead

to, among other things, the Dublin editions of 1845 and 1846, his great public letter to Thomas Auld of 1848, and eventually the publication of *Bondage and Freedom* in 1855 and *Life and Times of Frederick Douglass* in 1881 and 1892.

BLACK AND WHITE ENVELOPE

An emphasis on the productive influence of Douglass's close connections with Garrison and his antislavery society encourages a rethinking of Douglass's agency or "freedom" as author of the *Narrative*. On the one hand, he was an employee of the Massachusetts Anti-Slavery Society and to a certain extent was under the paternalistic constraints of white reformers; on the other hand, he shared in the society's main beliefs, and thus those "constraints" may have empowered him. Still, questions remain: What are we to do with a canonical text that so clearly served the aims of Garrison's antislavery organization? And what are we to do with a text that may well have needed some editorial assistance? After all, Douglass was a first-time author who lacked a formal education. One possibility would be to ignore the role of editors and institutions in the emergence of the *Narrative,* as if such considerations would be an insult to Douglass. That is precisely what Benjamin Quarles, the great twentieth-century champion of the *Narrative,* chose to do when he first wrote about the text, asserting in his 1948 biography: "Douglass' story was the product of his own pen; he needed no abolitionist 'hack' to edit his writings."[13] But as we learn from the recently published first volume of Douglass's correspondence, Douglass was pleased to acknowledge the role of his abolitionist editors at the Massachusetts Anti-Slavery Society. In a flawlessly written letter published in the

November 1842 *Liberator*, Douglass states, "I can't write to much advantage, never had a day's schooling in my life, nor have I ever ventured to give publicity to any of my scribbling before; nor would I now, but for my peculiar circumstances." Those circumstances are that he is working and writing for Garrison, who no doubt edited the letter for publication. For we see in a surviving manuscript letter of September 10, 1842, to Garrison's associate Maria Weston Chapman that Douglass needed editing. In a single paragraph he has "worte" for "wrote," "qustion" for "question," "caurse" for "cause," and "distruction" for "destruction," along with such phrasings as "I was interupted [*sic*] for be out of order." Straightforwardly, and self-aware, Douglass wrote to Chapman the following year, when submitting a piece to an abolitionist gift book she edited, "you will confer a favor on me by correcting any mistakes which may occur in it." There are no extant records about the role of Chapman, Garrison, and others in the editing of the *Narrative*, but Garrison biographer Henry Mayer may well be correct in saying that Garrison, the publisher of the *Narrative*, "saw it through the press in a labor that posterity has not fully credited."[14]

Of course Garrison did much more than see the book through the press. As the publisher of a slave narrative, he supplied the standard "paratexts" of the antebellum slave narrative—the various documents by white editors, publishers, and supporters typically printed at the opening and close of slave narratives, which served to legitimate the black text for white readers. The critic Gérard Genette has usefully defined paratexts as the verbal and pictorial features of a volume—title, epigraphs, frontispieces, prefaces, appendices, and the like—that aim *"to ensure that the text is read properly."*[15] Such paratextual materials in the typical antebellum slave narrative can be regarded metaphorically, in

Sekora's terms, as the "white envelope" conveying the "black message"; and it is certainly true that Garrison as the editor of the paratexts accompanying the *Narrative* did what he could to ensure that the book was read "properly" as a contribution to antislavery reform in the terms promoted and defined by the Massachusetts Anti-Slavery Society. Thus, with respect to Sekora's conceit, many recent readers regard Garrison as having sought to create a white envelope that closed off any sense that he and Douglass were in conversation, or that Douglass had his own message apart from that of Garrison's organization. In this negative schema, Douglass, at the very least, has been partly throttled by Garrison, and the "truer" autobiographies are the 1855 and 1881/1892 versions that he published on his own with introductions by black friends and intellectuals.[16] But does such a view of a lack of collaboration or dialogue hold up under close examination of the paratexts?

To be sure, Douglass's collaborative relations with Garrison and the Massachusetts Anti-Slavery Society are not immediately apparent from the opening paratexts of the *Narrative;* at first glance, the white envelope appears to be sealed shut. The title of the volume, *Narrative of the Life of Frederick Douglass, an American Slave: Written by Himself,* which may have been supplied by Garrison, arguably presents Douglass as a chattel (his primary identity within Garrison's organization); the author credit, "Written by Himself," affirms the capability of the slave author but does not actually name Douglass as author (that information is supplied in small font on the copyright page); and the publisher credit under the title and author, "Boston: Published at the Anti-Slavery Office," is in font around the same size as the "Written by Himself." Even with the bold frontispiece image of Douglass looking intellectual, defiant, black, and free (Figure 3), which Douglass very

FIGURE 3. *Narrative of the Life of Frederick Douglass, an American Slave* (Boston: Anti-Slavery Office, 1845), frontispiece. Image reproduction courtesy of the Williams College Archives and Special Collections, Williamstown, Massachusetts.

much liked (no doubt because it made him look like a man capable of authoring and editing the volume), the title page makes clear that the *Narrative* was both produced by and in the service of Garrison's Massachusetts Anti-Slavery Society.

Consistent with such a presentation, Douglass's first-person narrative is preceded by testimonials from two white abolitionist leaders of the society—Garrison himself, who supplies a relatively long preface, and his associate Wendell Phillips, who offers a more intimate letter to Douglass. Much has been made of the condescending, paternalistic, and even racist aspects of Garrison's preface, such as his praise of Douglass as "[c]apable of high attainments as an intellectual and moral being—needing nothing but a comparatively small amount of cultivation to make him an ornament to society and a blessing to his race." Garrison's paternalism comes through as well in his account of Douglass's speech at the August 1841 Nantucket meeting of the Massachusetts Anti-Slavery Society, which emphasizes how important that speech was, not just for the antislavery society or Garrison, but for Douglass himself, "as it brought him into the field of public usefulness." Garrison recounts how Douglass in that first speech "proceeded to narrate some of the facts in his own history as a slave," which is precisely what the Garrisonians want him to continue to do until slavery is abolished. Then Garrison moves to the nub of the matter, portraying himself as the teacher of a black man who was uncertain about taking on "a vocation so anomalous" as antislavery lecturer. Encouraging Douglass "to make a trial" as a lecturer for his organization, Garrison describes how Douglass, with his help, found his institutional identity, vocation, and purpose as a worker for the group that is now publishing his *Narrative,* noting that "ever since that [trial] period, he has acted as a lecturing agent, under the auspices either of the American or the

Massachusetts Anti-Slavery Society." Approvingly (and paternalistically), Garrison remarks that within the organization Douglass "has borne himself with gentleness and meekness, yet with true manliness of character." But by the end of the preface, Douglass himself seems to have disappeared, for Garrison in his concluding paragraph makes no mention of Douglass and instead sets forth his own political agenda (which was probably Douglass's as well), proclaiming in the closing sentence what he had been proclaiming in his writings and speeches since the early 1840s: "Come what may—cost what it may—inscribe on the banner which you unfurl to the breeze, as your religious and political motto—'NO COMPROMISE WITH SLAVERY! NO UNION WITH SLAVEHOLDERS!' "[17]

Using his preface to focus on Douglass's role in the Massachusetts Anti-Slavery Society from 1841 to 1845, which Douglass does not address in the first-person narrative that follows, Garrison frames Douglass's journey from slavery to freedom mainly in relation to Garrison's organization. The evidence suggests that Douglass would come to resent that framing, arguably as soon as late summer or fall of 1845. But was he resentful in May 1845? That's what remains unclear. For as condescending as Garrison's remarks can seem long after the fact, there is considerable truth to his claim that Douglass initially needed the Massachusetts Anti-Slavery Society and indeed thrived under Garrison's tutelage while sharing many of Garrison's political beliefs. In significant ways, the paternalistic Garrison tells a story about a productive relationship between Douglass and the antislavery society that in large part captures the reality of the situation circa May 1, 1845, the date that Garrison signed to his preface. Moreover, there is a surprisingly close fit between much of Garrison's preface and the story that Douglass tells about his life in the *Narrative*, starting with the fact that Douglass's first-person narrative culminates in precisely what Garrison celebrates at the beginning of his Preface: the triumphal speech at the Nantucket antislavery meeting in August 1841.[18] Douglass may have had his own stories that he wanted to tell, but as even Douglass suggests, through the very structure of his first-person narrative, at least one of those stories is about his excitement at becoming a Garrisonian abolitionist. And, very crucially, another is about how he learned at the Nantucket meeting that what he had to say about his life in slavery could have an impact on abolitionists such as Garrison.

Garrison's preface speaks to that impact, for as paternalistic as Garrison sounds in parts of it, he clearly responds to (rather than simply appropriates) Douglass's first-person narrative. As a result, there is a synchronicity of perspectives between the white envelope (the paratexts, but especially Garrison's preface) and the black message (Douglass's own narrative), not only because Douglass at this time was a black Garrisonian but also because Garrison's preface was in considerable ways influenced by what he had learned from reading either the draft or typeset version of Douglass's narrative. The white envelope may not be so white after all. For example, in his preface Garrison the moral suasionist conceives of Douglass as in the American revolutionary tradition, comparing him to Patrick Henry. In the *Narrative*, Douglass says that when he and his fellow slaves attempted to escape from William Freeland's plantation, they "did more than Patrick Henry, when he resolved upon liberty or death." This is just one of a number of places where Douglass suggests connections between himself and the American revolutionaries within a narrative that can be read, as Wendell Phillips notes in his letter of endorsement following Garrison's preface, as a "declaration of freedom" in the tradition of the Declaration of

Independence.[19] By honoring Douglass as a Patrick Henry figure, Garrison shows that he is a good reader of Douglass.

There are numerous other instances of Garrison responding in his preface to what Douglass writes in his autobiography. Garrison refers to Douglass not only as a revolutionary leader but also as "consecrated . . . to the great work of breaking the rod of the oppressor, and letting the oppressed go free!" In this way he argues for Douglass's exceptionality in the antislavery struggle. At key moments in the *Narrative*, Douglass conveys a similarly exceptionalist belief that he has been chosen by God to take up the "severe cross" and "sacred cause" of being a black leader, and indeed when he is first sent to Baltimore he describes himself as benefiting from "a special interposition of divine providence in my favor." Garrison uses his preface to argue for Douglass's (and blacks') equality with whites, asserting that blacks' lack of what he terms "high attainments" has more to do with condition than biology. Invoking the Irish reformer Daniel O'Connell, whom Douglass would meet later that year, Garrison shares an anecdote about a white man who "was cast away on the shore of Africa, where he was kept in slavery for three years" and, when rescued, was found to be "imbruted and stultified." Garrison somewhat crudely says that this example "proves at least that the white slave can sink as low in the scale of humanity as the black one," with the corollary being, as Douglass argues in his first-person narrative, that blacks such as Douglass, if given the opportunity, are capable of raising themselves as high on the scale of humanity as the most successful whites. Throughout his narrative, Douglass documents numerous assaults on blacks' humanity, perhaps even prompting Garrison's image of "imbruted" by writing about himself under the slave breaker Covey as "transformed into a brute!" Garrison was also moved by what he terms

Douglass's "most thrilling" apostrophe to the sailboats on the Chesapeake, which he hails in the preface as indicative of the "living spirit of freedom" and spiritual strength of Douglass and other blacks under slavery.[20] That apostrophe remains one of the most admired moments in all of Douglass's autobiographies.

Finally, there is much in Garrison's preface about the rhetorical effectiveness of Douglass's narrative of his life in slavery. Garrison testifies to Douglass's abilities not just in providing fresh perspectives on slavery from the experience of a former slave (precisely what Garrison hired Douglass and other black speakers to do), but also in moving readers (including Garrison) to "an unutterable abhorrence of slavery and all its abettors" and thus to a renewed "determination to seek the immediate overthrow of that execrable system." In his letter to Douglass printed right after Garrison's preface, Phillips similarly praises Douglass for the skill with which he bears witness to the evils of slavery, focusing on the importance of his account of slavery in a border state like Maryland, "where we are told slavery appears with its fairest features." Phillips concludes his letter by lauding Douglass for having the courage to put his thoughts into print, even at the risk of becoming vulnerable to fugitive slave hunters: "The whole armory of Northern Law has no shield for you. I am free to say that in your place, I should throw the MS. into the fire."[21] In Phillips's formulation, the black man is bolder and in certain ways more independent than his white sponsors. As paternalistic as they may be, Garrison's preface and Phillips's letter convey the enormous respect that both men have for one of the de facto leaders of their organization. Garrison and Phillips may have been Douglass's teachers, but in their prefaces they suggest that they are his students as well.

THE FRUIT OF ABOLITION

Garrison's preface and Phillips's letter point to ways of reading what Garrison terms Douglass's "own narrative" as part of a larger collaboration with the abolitionists of the Massachusetts Anti-Slavery Society. That said, even if the *Narrative* works with many of the assumptions of the Garrisonians, Douglass, as in his speeches and letters, does much more than narrate his history and authenticate his experiences as a slave. He displays his ability to analyze the events he describes, portraying slavery in the United States as a powerful cultural force that makes resistance on the part of the slaves a daunting prospect. At the same time, he presents himself as a sort of black Benjamin Franklin, an exemplar of self-reliance whose hard work, energy, and creativity help to lift him from slavery to freedom. As he would in all of his book-length autobiographies, he depicts himself in spiritual terms as a black leader who shares traits with Moses, Jeremiah, and Christ, and in political terms as a black leader who shares traits with the American revolutionaries. And in this first autobiography, which is both constrained and enabled by his white sponsors, Douglass reveals some of his confusions about his personal identity (especially with respect to family and race), his indebtedness to the black slaves (and not just to the Garrisonians) for his knowledge about slavery, his hesitations about Garrisonian moral suasion, and, in ways that aren't directly related to the burden of black Garrisonian leadership explored in the *Narrative*'s closing scene, his more private spiritual longings. And he does all of this with a rhetorical artistry that suggests, at least retrospectively, he is more than ready to move on from his Massachusetts Anti-Slavery Society sponsors. Indeed, in the context of his subsequent autobiographies, the *Narrative* would come to assume the status of an urtext—the work that Douglass would regularly draw on and revise precisely because he had come to read his life history very differently from the Garrisonians. But that was in the future. Douglass's Garrisonianism, which took the form of a collaborative and sometimes questioning engagement from within, informs the *Narrative* and helps to make it the compelling text that it is.

The opening chapter points to the productive tensions between the *Narrative*'s Garrisonian frame and Douglass's more personal perspectives. There is nothing in this chapter about Douglass's representative leadership, nothing about his heroic rise from slavery to freedom, and nothing about his alliance with the Massachusetts Anti-Slavery Society. Instead, there are confessions of dislocation and confusion. In the manner of the many slave narratives opening with the phrase "I was born," Douglass begins: "I was born in Tuckahoe, near Hillsborough, and about twelve miles from Easton, in Talbot county, Maryland." He knows that his father is white but is unsure of exactly who he is; he barely knows his mother and thus cannot grieve when he learns of her death; he's not even sure of his age. Anticipating (or influencing) Harriet Beecher Stowe's efforts to link white readers to black slaves by showing how slavery undermines the family, Douglass crafts this understated opening so that he sounds more like an orphan out of a Charles Dickens novel than an escaped slave narrating his life history for an antislavery organization. His anger about slavery and racism remains beneath the surface (there are no declamations against slavery in the opening paragraphs), and it is only at the end of the first chapter that he depicts one of the "bloody scenes that often occurred on the plantation," describing how he watched his master Aaron Anthony whip his Aunt Hester in a disturbing scene that more than hints at rape.[22] Through the circular structure of the chapter, which moves from birth to rape, Douglass from the perspective of his child self enacts his discovery of how he came into being, showing how his very existence depended (so this dramatic moment suggests) on the rape of his mother (a blood relative of Hester) by a slave master who may well have been Anthony.

In this opening chapter of the Massachusetts Anti-Slavery Society *Narrative*, Douglass is highly personal, provocative, complex, and transgressive. He transgresses Victorian conventions of sexual representation in order to do his job as a Garrisonian. Urged by Garrison and his associates to describe the horrors of slavery, Douglass shows that rape was integral to the system. Douglass has been criticized for the gender politics of the unsettling scene with Hester, particularly for the ways he assumes a voyeuristic relation to the unclothed black female body.[23] But the whipping of his aunt was not an easy moment for Douglass to describe, as he self-consciously acknowledges when he suggests his complicity in this gruesome moment: "I was doomed to be a witness and a participant." Terming himself a "doomed" "participant," Douglass begs the question of how he could not report on what he observed, as awful as it was (or precisely because of how awful it was). In collaborative fashion, Garrison registers some of Douglass's anguish about the scene and its larger implications by remarking approvingly in his preface, as someone who is continuing to learn from Douglass, that among the many dark aspects of slavery revealed in Douglass's narrative are "concubinage, adultery, and incest." As Douglass elaborates in the opening chapter, as if in conversation with Garrison, precisely because of the pervasiveness of rape on the plantation, race has become an unstable category in the American South (and by extension in U.S.

culture). He remarks: "If the lineal descendants of Ham are alone to be scripturally enslaved, it is certain that slavery at the south must soon become unscriptural; for thousands are ushered into this world, annually, who, like myself, owe their existence to white fathers, and those fathers most frequently their own masters."[24]

In the opening chapter, then, Douglass makes clear that the whipping of Aunt Hester was in certain respects just another horror in the quotidian reality of slavery. As Aliyyah I. Abdur-Rahman observes, by including this scene Douglass sought to "transform individual readers into a galvanized community of first-hand witnesses to slavery's *everyday* terror."[25] Again, this is precisely what the Garrisonians enjoined him to do. It is worth noting that Douglass's accounts of the violence done to blacks do not stop with descriptions of violations to his Aunt Hester, his cousin Henny, and the few other black women mentioned in his narrative. Douglass reports on victimized black men as well. In a shocking incident early on in his narrative, the "artful, cruel, and obdurate" overseer Gore, a man of "savage barbarity," shoots the male slave Demby dead in cold blood, and Douglass describes how "his mangled body sank out of sight, and blood and brains marked the water where he had stood." He offers an account of an unnamed male slave who is "killed with a hatchet," the death resulting from his owner "knocking his brains out." He tells of how Colonel Lloyd's old slave Barney, who is entrusted with Lloyd's beloved horses, is "frequently whipped"; and on one occasion, as part of what Abdur-Rahman terms the *"scopic terror"* of slavery, Douglass as a slave boy watches the whipping of Barney as he earlier watched the whipping of Hester: "I have seen Colonel Lloyd make old Barney, a man between fifty and sixty years of age, uncover his bald head, kneel down upon the cold, damp ground, and receive upon his naked and toil-worn shoulders more than thirty lashes at the time." He also recounts how Anthony's son Andrew brutalized Douglass's own brother: he "threw him on the ground, and with the heel of his boot stamped upon his head till the blood gushed from his nose and ears." And of course he eventually offers an extended narrative of his own brutalization by Covey, who beats him so severely that "the blood ran freely."[26]

Douglass's copious examples of the myriad forms of violence inflicted on the slaves serve the Garrisonian end of challenging proslavery idealizations by providing firsthand testimony from an escapee who is still legally a slave. Following the powerful first chapter, in which the horrifying scene with Aunt Hester mostly speaks for itself, Douglass brings together firsthand testimony with analysis, which, on the evidence of his published letters and speeches, Garrison had always encouraged him to do, as he describes not only his own childhood on Colonel Lloyd's "businesslike" slave plantation but also the masters' practice of depriving slaves of food, clothing, and sleep, and the slaves' recourse to theft and deceit in order to survive. He also addresses what could be termed the slaves' false consciousness, remarking on how some slaves take pride in the wealth of their masters. In various ways, the pre-Baltimore opening chapters show how slavery functions as a total institution in which the whites' power over blacks is nearly unlimited—and certainly not constrained by law.[27]

Douglass the analytical observer becomes much more of a participant when he is sent to Baltimore to live with Hugh and Sophia Auld. Although the *Narrative* is indebted to such traditionally American autobiographies as Franklin's in tracing Douglass's eventual escape to freedom by dint of hard work, there is an equally powerful effort on Douglass's part to represent himself as a spiritual leader who, in the manner of Moses, has been chosen by God. As Garrison notes in his preface, Douglass underscores the role of the providential in the description of the critical moment when he is chosen from all the young slaves to be sent from Maryland's Eastern Shore to Baltimore, where he will soon have opportunities for education and exposure to abolitionist thought that will be crucial to his emergence as a black leader. The "good spirit" of God may be watching over him, but Douglass's exemplification of Franklinian forms of uplift, self-making, and possessive individualism remains central to the limning of his identity in subsequent chapters.[28] In scenes that have become well-known, Douglass, like Franklin, uses imitation, trickery, and hard work to teach himself to read and write after Hugh Auld forbids his wife, Sophia, to continue with her teaching. By reporting on how he acquired such knowledge mostly on his own, even as a slave, Douglass demonstrates, against the grain of the emerging racist science of the period, the capacities of black intelligence.[29] At the same time he demonstrates precisely what the appreciative Garrison states in his preface: that blacks are fully capable of self-improvement if they have the same opportunities as whites.

Douglass's move to Baltimore is crucial to what Douglass calls his "pathway from slavery to freedom," a phrase suggestively pointing to the teleological structure of the *Narrative,* which is intent on showing how Douglass got from his starting point in the Eastern Shore, with all of the stasis implied by his hiding place in the closet, to the end point in Nantucket, where he becomes a black abolitionist speaker in Garrison's antislavery organization. As my phrasing here suggests, the overarching structure of the *Narrative* can be termed Garrisonian, in the sense that all of the key events, from the opening to the closing chapter, acquire their fullest meaning when viewed in relation to the telos: Douglass's taking up of the "severe cross" that, in the closing paragraphs of his narrative, signifies his coming into being as an abolitionist leader in Garrison's organization. For good reason, abolitionists have a significant place in Douglass's story. As is well known, after teaching himself to read and write with the help of "the little white boys" of Baltimore, Douglass at around age twelve gets hold of a copy of a popular antislavery miscellany, *The Columbian Orator*, and reads the "Dialogue between a Master and a Slave," in which a slave refutes proslavery arguments and convinces his master to free him. Reading this and other selections in *The Columbia Orator* leads Douglass to view slave masters as "a band of successful robbers, who had left their homes, and gone to Africa, and stolen us from our homes."[30] Just as importantly and not often remarked upon, his new skill in reading leads him, at the same time and in the same chapter, to the abolitionists.

Douglass thus places the role of the abolitionists in the development of his political consciousness at the center of the *Narrative*, and as critical as well to the overarching account of his journey from slavery to freedom, In a key passage in chapter 7, which no doubt was dear to Garrison's heart, Douglass describes his efforts to learn more about the people whom Baltimore's white leaders regularly blame for creating slave dissatisfaction and resistance. Douglass writes:

> Every little while, I could hear something about the abolitionists. It was some time before I found what the word meant. It was always used in such connections as to make it an interesting word to me. If a slave ran away and succeeded in getting clear, or if a slave killed his master, set fire to a barn, or did any thing very wrong in the mind of a slaveholder, it was

spoken of as the fruit of *abolition*. Hearing the word in this connection very often, I set about learning what it meant. . . . After a patient waiting, I got one of our city papers, containing an account of the number of petitions from the north, praying for the abolition of slavery in the District of Columbia, and of the slave trade between the States. From this time I understood the words *abolition* and *abolitionist*, and always drew near when the word was spoken, expecting to hear something important to myself and fellow-slaves.[31]

One could imagine Douglass telling this story at a meeting sponsored by the Massachusetts Anti-Slavery Society, even if some Garrisonian purists would have wanted Douglass to challenge the idea that violent slave resistance ("killed his master, set fire to a barn") is "the fruit of abolition." Still, it is Douglass's discovery of abolitionism that leads to the major acts of resistance that follow, including his turn to violence when he resists the slave breaker Covey.

Given how much of the *Narrative* is in accord with the vision set forth in Garrison's preface, the depiction of the actual physical rebellion against Covey—the moment that Douglass presents as "the turning-point in my career as a slave"—is surprising for its violence.[32] The rebellion against Covey remains central to all of Douglass's subsequent autobiographies, even as he revises details and reshapes the telling in relation to his evolving political identity and circumstances. Douglass's willingness to challenge Garrisonian strictures against violence could be taken as a quietly subversive motif of the *Narrative*. And yet the fact that Garrison and Phillips both link Douglass to American revolutionaries suggests their willingness to consider the role of violence in resisting arbitrary and cruel authority, perhaps (to underscore my argument about the collaborative nature of the *Narrative*) because Douglass's riveting account had persuaded them to do so.[33]

In a passage that Garrison celebrates in his preface, Douglass sets up the scene of his rebellion by delivering his great (and oft-cited) apostrophe to the freely gliding boats on the Chesapeake, seeing in the boats themselves a lesson about freedom in nature: "You move merrily before the gentle gale, and I sadly before the bloody whip! You are freedom's swift-winged angels, that fly round the world; I am confined in bands of iron! O that I were free! . . . Could I but swim! If I could fly! . . . O God, save me! God, deliver me! Let me be free! Is there any God? . . . There is a better day coming." Alternating between hope and despair, Douglass in this apostrophe writes his own divine individuality into being. He then challenges his (Garrisonian) readers to consider the effects of nonviolence on that individuality by describing what happened when he passively took his whippings from the "'nigger-breaker'" Covey: "I was broken in body, soul, and spirit. . . . behold a man transformed into a brute!" After a particularly savage beating, Douglass finally decides to act. Covered with blood, he treks for several hours to the St. Michaels house of his master, Thomas Auld, the son-in-law of the now deceased Aaron Anthony. Once there, he displays his bloody body to Auld, and of course to the reader as well: "From the crown of my head to my feet, I was covered with blood. My hair was all clotted with dust and blood; my shirt was stiff with blood. My legs and feet were torn in sundry places with briars and thorns, and were also covered with blood."[34] With this picture of himself as a sort of black Christ, Douglass gives both Auld and his (Garrisonian) reader the opportunity to sympathize with a suffering black slave. The unresponsive Auld orders Douglass back to Covey; the responsive reader has been set up to applaud the violence to come.

Still, in the context of the Garrisonian moral-suasionism he has not yet renounced, Douglass takes care to present that violence in his Massachusetts Anti-Slavery Society *Narrative* as a form of self-defense by representing himself as refusing to inflict physical harm on Covey once he has him under his control. Douglass will revise this key scene in his later autobiographies.[35] But the buildup to this moment—including the slave Sandy Jenkins's offering of a useless root that he promises will magically ward off Covey's punishments—attempts to teach readers of 1845 and beyond that without resorting to violence, Douglass might not have survived his year with Covey. Surprisingly for someone who still claimed to be a moral suasionist, Douglass in this fight scene seems to be discovering the joys of black violence. Claiming that he doesn't know "whence came the spirit," he "seized Covey hard by the throat," taking immediate pleasure in discerning Covey's surprise and fear at his resistance. When Covey's assistant Hughes joins the fray, Douglass writes with brio about how "I watched my chance, and gave him a heavy kick close under the ribs. This kick fairly sickened Hughes, so that he left me in the hands of Covey." Encouraged by his success with Hughes, Douglass "seized him [Covey] with both hands by his collar, and brought him by a sudden snatch to the ground." There ensues a long wrestling match in which Douglass mostly parries Covey's assaults, until a stalemate is achieved and Covey releases Douglass with the hope that the encounter will remain secret so that he can preserve his "unbounded reputation for being a first-rate overseer and negro-breaker." Emphasizing his self-control at the end of the encounter, Douglass nonetheless offers a boastful warning about what he has learned by fending off Covey: "the white man who expected to succeed in whipping, must also succeed in killing me."[36] Working against the political grain of his sponsors, Douglass at this moment in his Massachusetts Anti-Slavery Society *Narrative* resembles the black heroic slaves he will be celebrating in the late 1840s and 1850s after his break from Garrison.

Douglass's account of his resistance to Covey takes place in a long chapter that does not end with Douglass's triumph as a black fighter but instead quickly moves to Douglass as a black leader who seeks to conspire with his fellow black slaves. This thematic strand of the *Narrative* is also not so easily tied to Garrisonianism. As Douglass tells the story, after Thomas Auld hires him out to William Freeland, Douglass begins running an informal Sabbath school for his fellow slaves and at first conceives of the school as a form of Franklinian uplift. "I taught them," he says, "because it was the delight of my soul to be doing something that looked like bettering the condition of my race." Though Douglass can sound elitist here and at other moments in the *Narrative* when he talks about the slaves, his depiction of his time at Freeland's reveals the important role that the black slaves themselves played in his journey from slavery to freedom. Earlier in his narrative, Douglass had credited the slave songs he heard on Lloyd's plantation with offering him "my first glimmering conception of the dehumanizing character of slavery. I can never get rid of that conception. Those songs still follow me, to deepen my hatred of slavery, and quicken my sympathies for my brethren in bonds." Though he initially doesn't understand the "deep meaning of those rude and apparently incoherent songs," he retrospectively acknowledges how important they were to stimulating his hatred for slavery. All of which is to say that Douglass's story of his efforts to help the "society of my fellow-slaves" at the Freeland plantation moves from uplift to something more revolutionary—an escape plot—that seems to have been inspired by the slaves themselves. Uncharacteristically, Douglass conveys an indebtedness to his fellow slaves that is rooted in communalist feeling. "We loved each other," he remarks of the group of slaves while in the midst of their plotting at Freeland's. And he adds: "I believe we would have died for each other. . . . We were one."[37] Though the plot fails, perhaps because of the betrayal of one of their compatriots (probably Sandy), Douglass was sufficiently inspired by the memory of his plotting with his fellow black slaves to revise and extend this scene in *Bondage and Freedom*.[38]

With the failure of the escape, which Garrison in his preface depicts solely in relation to Patrick Henry's revolutionary credo of "liberty or death," the focus returns to the Garrisonian narrative of Douglass's journey from slavery in the Eastern Shore to assuming a leadership role as a black speaker in the Massachusetts Anti-Slavery Society. Increasingly important to the final chapters, which are set mainly in Baltimore and New Bedford, are the abolitionists. As was true for Douglass's earlier time in Baltimore, the Douglass who is sent back to the Aulds in Baltimore discerns the presence of the abolitionists. For instance, when Hugh Auld protests after Douglass is brutally beaten at a Fell's Point shipyard, he is dismissed by his fellow whites as someone who is sympathetic to abolitionism. Douglass explains, "Anything done to resist racism on the part of Hugh or anyone else is seen as abolitionist. The watchwords of the bloody-minded in that region, and in those days, were 'Damn the abolitionists!' and 'Damn the niggers!' "[39] Hugh is hardly an abolitionist, but if acting from the heart to protest brutality against a black person makes one an abolitionist, then abolitionism must be a very good thing.

Nevertheless, after making his protest, Hugh reverts to form, clamping down on Douglass by refusing to let him keep any of his earnings for fear that he would run away. But Douglass does run away, with the help of the abolitionists.

The abolitionists who initially help Douglass are not specifically linked to Garrison; there's a strong black abolitionist component as well, even as the black activists in Baltimore remain invisible. And yet by the end of the *Narrative* it can seem that all abolitionist roads lead to Garrison's Massachusetts Anti-Slavery Society. Deliberately leaving out details of his flight north so as not to compromise the possibility of other slaves making their escape, Douglass reports on how he reached New York with the assistance of white and black abolitionists alike, though he names only the blacks David Ruggles and James Pennington, who at the time were among the leaders of the New York Vigilance Society. Abolitionism, as Douglass presents it here, is about human kindness across the color line, and not about racial hierarchies or even specific organizations; thus he credits the (black) abolitionists for helping him to overcome his initial suspicion of white people. He says of the charitable Mr. and Mrs. Nathan Johnson, who initially take him in at New Bedford: "They proved themselves quite worthy of the name of abolitionists." Describing his new home of New Bedford as clean, temperate, and well-ordered (contra the accounts he'd heard of the free North from white southerners), Douglass nevertheless finds it difficult to obtain a job at the shipyards because of the same antiblack racism he had experienced among the white laborers at Fell's Point. But he supplies a footnote on the successful efforts of the abolitionists to help change this situation: "I am told that colored persons can now get employment at calking in New Bedford—a result of anti-slavery effort."[40] Here, abolitionism is not only about helping the plight of the enslaved blacks in the South but also the free blacks of the North. That is precisely the vision of abolitionism that Douglass embraces when he takes on the Garrisonian cause.

Douglass concludes his narrative with an account of his triumphal speech at the August 11, 1841, Nantucket antislavery meeting described by Garrison in his preface. Douglass discovers the Garrisonians and, in turn, Garrison discovers Douglass. The *Narrative* thus comes full circle, as Douglass at the very end assumes the identity of the black abolitionist for the Massachusetts Anti-Slavery Society that Garrison had celebrated in his prefatory remarks. In the penultimate paragraph of his first autobiographical narrative, Douglass reports that he subscribed to Garrison's *Liberator* about four months after arriving in New Bedford. Douglass's enthusiasm for the newspaper, as recounted at the conclusion of his life history, offers an unconditional endorsement of Garrisonian abolitionism: "The paper came, and I read it from week to week with such feelings as it would be quite idle for me to attempt to describe. The paper became my meat and my drink. My soul was set all on fire. Its sympathy for my brethren in bonds—its scathing denunciations of slaveholders—its faithful exposures of slavery—and its powerful attacks upon the upholders of the institution—sent a thrill of joy through my soul, such as I had never felt before!"[41] There is nothing about how the young Douglass is "unsuspecting" and naïve in being inspired by the Garrisonians, and nothing about Garrisonian paternalism. Instead, Douglass offers an impassioned affirmation of the Garrisonians' genuine sympathy for black people.[42]

Douglass then moves from his reading of the *Liberator* to his great moment of speaking at the antislavery convention in Nantucket. In the *Narrative*, as opposed to his later autobiographies, the journey that Douglass travels from slavery to freedom has its telos—its fundamental fulfillment—in his epochal first meeting with the Garrisonians. Douglass concludes with a description of the immediate consequences of that meeting: his decision to take up the "severe cross" of his new vocation as a black Garrisonian leader. "I spoke but a few moments, when I felt a degree of freedom," Douglass recalls, "and said what I desired with considerable ease. From that time until now, I have been engaged in pleading the cause of my brethren—with what success, and with what devotion, I leave those acquainted with my labors to decide." In temporal terms, the concluding scene of 1841 leads directly to Garrison's preface of 1845, where he sketches out Douglass's swift growth as an antislavery reformer from his electrifying first speech to the publication of the *Narrative*.[43] With its description of a meeting organized by a specific antislavery organization at a specific historical moment, the closing paragraphs of Douglass's narrative leave the reader with a time-bound and not particularly universal sense of a black man who has traveled from slavery to freedom in order to assume the mission—consecrated by Garrison and God—of working as an escaped slave for the Massachusetts Anti-Slavery Society cause. The "envelope" and the "message" are in sync in celebrating what has to be taken as the principal "fruit of abolition" in Douglass's own life up to May 1845: the publication of the Massachusetts Anti-Slavery Society *Narrative*.

$2.75 PER DOZEN

But then there's the appendix. In a departure from the typical closing paratext accompanying the slave narrative—testimonies from whites or advertisements by the publisher—the Massachusetts Anti-Slavery Society *Narrative* concludes with an appendix by Douglass himself. Dated April 28, 1845, from Lynn, Massachusetts, and thus predating Garrison's preface, the appendix is an alternately angry and comical assault on proslavery religion, culminating with Douglass's parody of "Heavenly Union"—a hymn that was popular in the South but not exclusive to southern churches. As discussed in the next chapter, Douglass's Dublin editor and collaborator, Richard D. Webb, found the appendix's attack on Christian churches so aggressive that he asked him to revise and condense it for British readers of the *Narrative*. Douglass acceded to that request. But if we were looking for early indications that Douglass while still in Massachusetts and still aligned with Garrison sought to analyze and critique U.S. slave culture on his own terms, we need look no further than this appendix.[44]

Douglass begins in an analytical mode: "I find, since reading over the foregoing Narrative that I have, in several instances, spoken in such a tone and manner, respecting religion, as may possibly lead those unacquainted with my religious views to suppose me an opponent of all religion. To remove the liability of such misapprehension, I deem it proper to append the following brief explanation." As he would in his later autobiographical writings, he positions himself in temporal and historical terms as having already moved beyond the persona he created for the autobiographical narrative, which concludes in 1841. The more mature, reflective Douglass of 1845 now offers retrospective explanations for his criticisms of Christianity in America, employing a diction ("liability," "misapprehension," "append") considerably different from that used to represent the younger Douglass in the opening chapters of the *Narrative*. He states that his criticisms are of "the *slaveholding religion* of this land, and with no possible reference to Christianity proper." But as his analysis of Christianity and slavery develops over the several pages of the appendix, it becomes increasingly clear that precisely because he regards slavery as a national problem, he views the failure of most Christian churches to speak out against slavery as a national problem as well. So Douglass moves from the particular to the general in ways that convey his anger at the vast majority of churches that remain silent about such acts as the selling of "my sister, for purposes of prostitution." That silence, he says, reveals much of what one needs to know about the complicity of the "Christianity of America" in the practice of slavery. Accordingly, he concludes the appendix by denouncing "the religion of this land, that which is revealed in the words, deeds, and actions, of those bodies, north and south, calling themselves Christian churches, and yet in union with slaveholders."[45] In the main autobiographical section of the *Narrative*, the only churches that he criticizes are the Methodist churches in the Eastern Shore to which Thomas Auld and Edward Covey belong. Here, in the appendix, Douglass moves beyond the geographical and temporal boundaries of that narrative to condemn those who have anything to do with churches or Christian institutions that refuse to speak out against slavery. That would include the churches and Christian institutions of most of his white northern readers.

In some ways it is surprising that Garrison included the appendix in the *Narrative*, even though he regularly attacked proslavery churches himself, for the voice that Douglass assumes in it jars against the voice of his autobiographical narrative. Garrison's willingness to print the appendix suggests that he admired Douglass's critical voice and was willing to offer him considerable freedom to express himself as a writer and speaker in the service of the Garrisonian cause. To underscore the large argument of this chapter, then, there is much in the 1845 Massachusetts Anti-Slavery Society *Narrative* that points to collaboration and mutual respect between Garrison and Douglass, even if there are tensions as well. Nevertheless, the voice that Douglass adopts in this appendix, as is true for the voice that he adopts in many of his lectures of late 1845 and 1846 (and beyond), differs from the voice in the autobiographical section of the *Narrative*, suggesting that Douglass the paid lecturer and writer for Garrison's society was continuing to develop his rhetorical skills and would be increasingly difficult for that organization to control.

Still, the Garrisonians would seek to control their prized speaker for a while longer, or at least retain control of the *Narrative*. In the appendix, Douglass to a certain extent exerts his ownership over the *Narrative* with a strong closing voice comparable to the strong voice of Garrison in the Preface. But in the pages of Garrison's *Liberator*, which Douglass continued to read, the *Narrative* was regularly featured—through advertising, reviews, and excerpts—as a major work coming out of the Massachusetts Anti-Slavery Society that was as much about the society as Douglass.

From the time of the first significant mention of the *Narrative* in the May 9, 1845, issue of the *Liberator*, Garrison and his editors presented Douglass's autobiography as a contribution to the work of the Massachusetts Anti-Slavery Society. They also presented it as a narrative by a black man who did what black men were supposed to do for the Garrisonians: provide testimony about the horrors of slavery. Because it was such an effective and popular volume, the *Narrative* provided Garrison and his associate editors with an opportunity to recruit new subscribers to the newspaper and new members to their society. To that end, Garrison ran a number of excerpts in the *Liberator*. The first excerpt, which accompanied the first announcement of the publication of the *Narrative*, however, was not by Douglass but by Garrison himself. In the issue of May 9, 1845, just days before the official publication of the *Narrative*, Garrison or his managing editor printed Garrison's preface to the *Narrative* in its entirety. The *Narrative* and Garrison's preface were announced in this way: "It will give our friends as much pleasure to hear as it does us to announce, that a 'NARRATIVE OF THE LIFE OF FREDERICK DOUGLASS,' written by himself, is in press, and will be published in a few days. . . . In addition to the interest contained in the incidents, and the pleasure to be derived from the perusal of the many noble, manly and eloquent passages of the narrator, the value of the work is greatly enhanced by a Preface from the pen of Mr. GARRISON, and a brief though animated and thrilling Letter to the author, in anticipation of his publication, from WENDELL PHILLIPS."[46] There follows Garrison's preface, dated May 1, 1845, which builds to a rousing celebration of the Massachusetts Anti-Slavery Society cause.

Over the next several months, Garrison offered substantial excerpts from the *Narrative*, all framed by the editors of the *Liberator*. The issue of May 23, 1845, printed Douglass's reflections on the slave songs and a section on how he taught himself to read and write; the issue of May 30, 1845, printed Douglass's famous apostrophe to the sailboats on the Chesapeake and his lament for his blind, frail grandmother; and the issue of June 6, 1845, printed Douglass's analysis of why the slave masters allow their slaves to drink during holiday times (the slaves' drunkenness dissipates their insurrectionary energies). Garrison chose not to print an excerpt from Douglass's dramatic resistance to Covey (perhaps because he regarded Douglass's resort to physical force as a challenge to his moral-suasionist philosophy), and he did not print the scene about the whipping of Aunt Hester (perhaps because of its graphic nature). In an effort to highlight the *Narrative*'s power of sentiment, Garrison or one of his editors remarked on Douglass's description of his ill-used grandmother: "he whose eye does not moisten in contemplating it must possess extraordinary command over his feelings." And when introducing the first full excerpts from the *Narrative*—on the slave songs and Douglass's efforts to learn how to read and write—the editor proclaimed: "Great God! how awful is the pressure brought to bear on the human intellect and heart by slavery! What a lifting of the veil this is, to convince the skeptical that it is impossible to exaggerate the horrors and enormities of that impious system!"[47] Lifting the veil of slavery is exactly what the Garrisonians hoped Douglass would do when they first signed him on as a lecturer.

Garrison's publication and marketing of the *Narrative* made Douglass into a celebrity who was ever more vulnerable to fugitive-slave hunters. At the urging of the concerned Garrison, Douglass agreed to undertake a lecture tour of the British Isles beginning in late August 1845. As they worked on arrangements, Garrison and his editors continued their vigorous marketing of the *Narrative* by reprinting positive reviews and offering testimonials to Douglass's authorial skills and character, emphasizing, for example, his "spirit and power," along with his "strength of mind and purity of heart." They conveyed their excitement about the *Narrative*'s commercial success, with Garrison or one of his editors predicting "a sale of at least twenty thousand in this country, and equally great in Europe." Though the *Narrative* probably failed to achieve such sales until its republication in 1960, Garrison's organization did what it could to promote the "neat volume occupying 125 pages." The *Liberator* ran regular ads for the book, reported on Douglass's speaking schedule and speeches, and printed positive reviews and responses, including a letter from an enthusiastic reader who was so moved by the *Narrative* that she decided to send Garrison $5 for publicity purposes. (There's no mention in the letter of sending anything for Douglass.) In the issue of June 20, 1845, the editors announced: "Our anti-slavery friends will be pleased to learn that the first edition of the Narrative of Frederick Douglass has nearly all been disposed of, and that the author has a cheap edition in progress of publication, which will be ready for sale in a few days." That cheap edition, as publicized in the issue of August 29, 1845, a day after Douglass arrived in Liverpool, was newly available from the Massachusetts Anti-Slavery Society "at the extremely low price of twenty-five cents," and for those who wanted to buy in bulk from the society's office, it was available for "$2.75 per dozen."[48]

In short, in the pages of the *Liberator* the *Narrative* was in some respects a commodity coming more from Garrison's Anti-Slavery Office than from Douglass himself. This is not to say that the collaborative relationship between the author and publisher broke down in the immediate wake of the publication of the *Narrative*. Douglass continued to speak under the aegis of the Massachusetts Anti-Slavery Society with Garrison and his associates, and he was pleased that the Garrisonians sold his autobiography, along with subscriptions to the *Liberator,* at their meetings. Still, given how aggressively Garrison and his associates exerted their control over the *Narrative* in the *Liberator,* it is not surprising that Douglass would soon want to frame and sell his own version of the book. What Garrison would not have been able to predict was that just five months after he published the *Narrative*, and even as he was working to market it, Douglass while in Ireland would attempt to take it back.

∞ 2 ≪

TAKING BACK THE *NARRATIVE*

The Dublin Editions

WHEN DOUGLASS ARRIVED in Liverpool on August 28, 1845, he was heralded as the author of *Narrative of the Life of Frederick Douglass* and as a renowned lecturer for the organization that was his publisher. For many, Douglass was the *Narrative* and the *Narrative* was Douglass, and both the *Narrative* and Douglass were Garrisonian. However, from the very start of his travels, tensions developed between Douglass and the white Garrisonians watching over him; these tensions augured the break between Garrison and Douglass that some say occurred in 1851 (when Douglass publicly rejected Garrison's idea that the Constitution was a proslavery document), and that others say occurred in late 1847 (when Douglass began publishing his own antislavery newspaper against Garrison's wishes), but that arguably occurred even before Douglass returned to the United States. During his nearly twenty-one months abroad, Douglass actively attempted to take back the *Narrative* (and himself) from Garrison by working with the Irish abolitionist and publisher Richard D. Webb to bring out new, revised editions of the *Narrative* and by assuming an increasingly cosmopolitan voice indicative of his more capacious transatlantic identity. By the time Douglass returned to the United States in May 1847, he had pretty much gone his own way, apart from the Massachusetts Anti-Slavery Society, despite professing allegiance to Garrisonian principles until 1851.

My Bondage and My Freedom has generally been taken as Douglass's second full autobiography, which it is. But between the 1845 publication of the first edition of the *Narrative* and the 1855 *Bondage and Freedom*, Douglass gave speeches and published letters and essays that offered revised accounts of his life history, extending that history, as he would in each of the major autobiographies, to his present situation. When Douglass spoke about his life in speeches delivered in the United States shortly after the publication of the *Narrative,* he typically drew on the incidents included in the *Narrative.* But in the lectures that he gave during his tour of the British Isles, he began telling different and newer stories, focusing in particular on an incident that occurred on the *Cambria,* the British Cunard steamship he took from Boston to Liverpool in August 1845. Defying a mobbish proslavery group on the *Cambria,* Douglass spoke on his own terms to the passengers who wanted to hear his antislavery message. For Douglass the storyteller, the *Cambria* incident quickly assumed an importance comparable to his rebellion against the slave breaker Edward Covey. As is clear from the many references in his speeches, he increasingly saw his response to the mob on the *Cambria* as the moment when he emerged as an independent figure in the antislavery movement.

Consistent with his new sense of independence, Douglass became personally involved in revising the *Narrative* shortly after his arrival in Ireland. Over the next six months, he would oversee the publication of two Dublin editions (1845, 1846), which, among other things, reworked the prefatory materials and appendix. Douglass scholars in Ireland and elsewhere have called for a greater attention to these Dublin editions,[1] and in 2011 Cambridge University Press published a facsimile of the 1845 Dublin edition, providing a text much as readers would have seen it in Britain later that year and early in 1846. The more substantially revised second Dublin edition remains hidden away in the archives. Despite the 2011 facsimile, these two post-Garrison Dublin editions of the *Narrative* continue to be marginalized in Douglass studies, which seems content to keep the *Narrative* fixed and locked in its publishing context of May 1845. Consider, for example, the arguments made by the textual scholars who brought out the standard edition of the *Narrative* for Yale University Press's *Frederick Douglass Papers* in 1999. Although the editors include a record of the changes Douglass and Webb made to the *Narrative* in late 1845 and 1846, they regard those revisions as corruptions because they "adapt the text to the British audience and away from the primary American context." The editors thus claim that their text—derived from the May 1845 edition—is authoritative because it has "no taint of adaptation to a secondary audience."[2] But from late 1845 through mid-1847, Douglass's British readers *were* his primary audience, and if anything was tainted in Douglass's eyes, it was the first American edition, which failed to give him a full editorial voice. It's not that we should abandon the 1845 U.S. edition, but the two Dublin editions can help us to see how Douglass conceived of his autobiography as a work in progress in need of regular updating and rearticulation. Clearly, Douglass himself did not regard the 1845 Boston edition as iconic.

Just prior to the outset of his British tour, the day before the ship docked in Liverpool, Douglass responded to a proslavery mob on board the *Cambria*. As explored in depth below, his repeated and varied proferrings of this story, which eventually made its way into the 1855 *Bondage and Freedom*, signaled that something crucial had happened in Douglass's life beyond what he recounts in the 1845 Boston *Narrative*, and beyond even what Garrison recounts in his preface. A more autonomous and self-reliant Douglass has emerged with new stories to tell that don't necessarily have anything to do with his life as a slave or his participation in the Massachusetts Anti-Slavery Society. In making the *Cambria* story his own during his first few months overseas, and telling it in a variety of ways, Douglass demonstrated to himself and others that he had little need for the Garrisonians who insisted on watching over him. Displaying his newfound independence and his almost uncanny promotional instincts in using the *Cambria* incident to publicize his talents as a black leader and speaker, Douglass provided a compelling warrant for creating a new Dublin edition of the *Narrative* that existed apart from the Massachusetts Anti-Slavery Society. Among the highlights of that edition, which went to press less than two months after his arrival in the British Isles, was the addition of a preface authored by Douglass and informed by the transatlantic voice that he initially tried out on the *Cambria* and then developed during his first few months in Ireland.[3]

THE *CAMBRIA* RIOT

Garrison and his associates set up Douglass's initial itinerary for his tour of the British Isles and purchased a first-class ticket for him on the *Cambria*, departing mid-August 1845. They also purchased a ticket for James N. Buffum of Lynn, Massachusetts, a carpenter and loyal Garrisonian whose job was to report on Douglass's activities to Maria Weston Chapman, secretary of the Massachusetts Anti-Slavery Society. For a time, Douglass and Buffum seemed genuinely to like each other, and in the account Douglass would write up for *Bondage and Freedom*, he praises Buffum for joining him in "the second cabin," or steerage, when he was denied access to his first-class cabin on deck, even though (as he doesn't say in his autobiographical writings) their relationship had frayed by the time they got to Dublin.[4] Still, Buffum offered his full support for Douglass after he chose to defy the proslavery mob on the *Cambria*.

As Douglass describes the *Cambria* incident in *Bondage and Freedom* and in his earlier speeches on the subject, the ship was somewhat like the American ship of state, divided between proslavery and antislavery people, including the famous antislavery Hutchinson family singers from New Hampshire. Near the end of the voyage, the English captain Charles H. E. Judkins and some of the passengers asked Douglass to talk about his experiences as a slave and to address the larger problem of slavery in the United States. Without consulting Buffum, Douglass began to speak about the horrors of slavery, but was quickly shouted down by proslavery people who called him a liar. Douglass countered by reading from southern slave laws that treated blacks as chattel with no human rights. In response, the proslavery group became increasingly aggressive in trying to silence him, going so far, Douglass claims in *Bondage and Freedom*, "as to threaten to throw me overboard." The situation remained tense until Captain Judkins warned that he would put the most rowdy proslavery people in irons. It's not clear if Douglass continued to talk about slavery while on board, but upon his arrival in Liverpool he passed along stories of the ruckus to local newspapers, which criticized the proslavery passengers' efforts to suppress his speech.

As he writes in *Bondage and Freedom*, "This incident of the voyage . . . brought me at once before the British public."[5] Over the next twenty-one months he regularly adduced the *Cambria* incident as one of the key moments of his evolving life history, emphasizing both his bravery in facing down his opponents and the supportive role played by the British captain and the numerous British passengers on board ship. Douglass used the events on the *Cambria* to suggest that he had new allies in addition to those linked with the Massachusetts Anti-Slavery Society, and that he wanted to address them, too. This is the Douglass who would move very quickly to make the *Narrative* a more transatlantic text under his own editorial control.

And yet it would be mistaken to overstate the extent of Douglass's political distance from Garrison at this early moment in his British tour. Douglass's first account of the incident, after all, which he wrote up in Dublin just a few days after arriving in Liverpool, appeared in a letter to Garrison printed in the September 26, 1845, issue of Garrison's *Liberator*. In the letter, Douglass adopts an aggressive tone consistent with his attack on proslavery religion in the *Narrative*'s appendix, but otherwise quite different from that of the persona who tells his life history in his first autobiography. He states ironically: "Yes, they actually got up a MOB—a real American, republican, democratic, Christian mob,—and that, too, on the deck of a British steamer. . . . I declare, it is enough to make a slave ashamed of the country that enslaves him." He offers a detailed recounting of the events, pointing out that before addressing the passengers on board he humbly asks the captain for permission to speak; that a Connecticut passenger named Mr. Hazzard initially calls out in response to Douglass's talk, "That's a lie"; that Douglass's recitation of southern slavery laws further enrages the proslavery group;

and that a slaveholder from Cuba remarks, "O, I wish I had you in Cuba!" Douglass presents himself as heroic for standing up to what he terms an "AMERICAN MOB ON BOARD OF A BRITISH STEAM PACKET," and equally heroic is the English captain who comes to the rescue. Among the fascinating details that Douglass shares about the incident is the role of the *Narrative* itself. Douglass brought along copies of the *Narrative* with the hope of selling them abroad and using the proceeds to help fund his British tour. He also brought them along because his fame at the time was tied to that book. He says about activities aboard ship just before the captain asks him to speak: "We had anti-slavery singing and pro-slavery grumbling; and at the same time that Governor Hammond's Letters were being read, my Narrative was being circulated."[6] In a shipboard competition between two texts published in 1845—the slaveholding former governor of South Carolina James Hammond's *Two Letters on Slavery in the United States* and Douglass's *Narrative*—it is the *Narrative* that captivates the attention of the majority of the passengers. By mentioning the *Narrative*, Douglass implicitly suggests his continued connection to Garrison in a letter in which he appeals to Garrison as a sympathizer. But that connection would begin to fray when Douglass turned on the Garrisonians in Great Britain— Chapman in particular—even as he continued to send Garrison letters about his travels, in part because he couldn't resist the audience that Garrison offered him in the *Liberator*.

But he also couldn't resist the audiences that he addressed during his British tour. No doubt helping to hasten Douglass's break from Garrison and the Garrisonian associates who were watching over him was the great pleasure Douglass took in speaking to large gatherings in Ireland, Scotland, and England without being under the sponsorship of the Massachusetts

Anti-Slavery Society. Douglass was hosted by a number of British antislavery organizations, only some of which were aligned with Garrison. In his speeches of late 1845 and 1846, Douglass presented the *Cambria* incident as having guided him toward transatlantic alliances that transcended the political sectarianism of U.S. antislavery organizations. To that end, he gave the English captain and an Irish passenger named Gough increasing importance in his evolving accounts of the incident, while emphasizing that it was the British passengers who were eager to hear him speak about slavery. In a lecture delivered in Cork, Ireland, on October 23, 1845, Douglass rehearses the facts as he shared them with Garrison and would eventually present them in *Bondage and Freedom*. He offers special praise for the English captain, Judkins, who "invited me to address the passengers on slavery." As if this opportunity were foreshadowing his British tour, he states that even at the risk of violence, "I wanted to inform the English, Scotch, and Irish on board on Slavery." (Throughout his British travels, he would play down the conflicts between the English, Scotch, and Irish as if they were a single united audience.) As described in the October 27, 1845, issue of the *Cork Examiner,* Douglass's speech about the incident concludes with a striking temporal collapse of the event that is the focus of his lecture—the fracas on the *Cambria*—with the dramatic scene of the lecture itself: "The Captain threatened the disturbers with putting them in irons if they did not become quiet—these men disliked the irons—were quieted by the threat; yet this infamous class have put their irons on the black. (Mr. Douglass showed the slave-irons to the meeting.)"[7]

In his accounts of the *Cambria* incident in speeches delivered in Ireland later in 1845, Douglass toned down his praise for the captain and made the hero of the event the Irishman Gough.

Douglass first emphasized Gough's role in a talk delivered in Limerick, Ireland, on November 10, 1845; by the time he referred to the incident in a speech delivered in Belfast on December 5, 1845, Gough had taken on heroic stature. Douglass again describes how his reading aloud of the southern slave code prompts a southerner to threaten to throw him overboard, but in this telling there suddenly steps forth "an Irishman—a man of gigantic size—of the name of Gough; and Mr. Gough, looking down upon this man with his glass in his eye, and coolly surveying the discreet gentleman who would be one of an indefinite number to throw him (Mr. Douglass) overboard, hinted that two might possibly play at that game—(loud cheers)—and that two might possibly be thrown overboard. (Cheers.) That had a very good and salutary effect upon the young man." By emphasizing the solidarity that exists between himself, the English captain Judkins, the Irishman Gough, and the unnamed British passengers, Douglass shifts dramatically from the first newspaper account of the *Cambria* incident that he published in Garrison's *Liberator,* now transforming the story to flatter his supporters across the British Isles. The *Cambria* would remain one of Douglass's stock stories during his lecture tour about his life beyond the United States. As reported in the Scottish newspaper *Advertiser* on April 11, 1846, shortly after Douglass spoke in Paisley, "Mr. Douglass concluded by giving a graphic description of his voyage across the Atlantic in the *Cambria* which drew from his audience the most rapturous applause."[8]

In nearly all of Douglass's stories about the *Cambria*, the *Narrative* has pride of place. Describing what he calls "the *Cambria* riot" in his Belfast lecture of December 5, 1845, for example, Douglass credits the circulation of the *Narrative* on board the *Cambria* for having stimulated the passengers' interest in

Douglass and slavery. He tells his audience that he had brought onto the ship "a number of copies of his narrative; and, through these, the greater number of the passengers soon became well acquainted" with the black abolitionist author. Just as on the *Cambria*, he then displayed copies of his *Narrative* that he hoped to sell to those gathered at Belfast's Independent Meetinghouse.[9] But by the time Douglass delivered this speech in early December 1845, his auditors were learning about his life as a slave not from the Boston edition of the *Narrative* that had been on board the *Cambria* but from an edition that had recently been published in Dublin. In significant ways, then, the 1845 Boston edition had become part of Douglass's historical past.

THE BOOKS GO OFF GRANDLY

The story of the first Dublin edition of the *Narrative* takes us back to Douglass's arrival in Liverpool in late August 1845. From Liverpool, Douglass and Buffum made their way to Dublin, where they initially lodged at the homes of the antislavery Irish Quaker Richard D. Webb, who was a printer by trade, and his brother James, moving back and forth from one Webb to the other. As Douglass traveled on speaking tours, he and Buffum also stayed at hotels and at the residences of antislavery sympathizers, including the Jennings family of Cork, who put them up for several weeks. Isabel Jennings, the cosecretary of the Cork Ladies Anti-Slavery Society, reported to Maria Weston Chapman that "Frederick won the affection of every one of us."[10] Though Douglass received initial funding from Garrison's organization and additional funding from a number of antislavery British organizations, along with regular gifts of meals and lodging, he nonetheless needed money for expenses. Having profited from sales of the *Narrative* on the *Cambria,* Douglass concluded that continued sales would help to keep him as independent as possible from one or another sponsoring antislavery organization.

Meredith McGill has shown how the traffic in texts during the antebellum period—the unregulated reprintings that occurred because of the lack of an international copyright agreement—could sometimes empower authors by offering new opportunities for textual circulation and profits untethered by contractual agreements.[11] Douglass's *Narrative* offers an excellent case in point. Published by Garrison in Boston in May 1845, the *Narrative* was available to resourceful printers and in fact circulated in extracts and pirated editions in the northeastern United States (which is how one of Douglass's critics, A. C. C. Thompson, encountered it; see the discussion below). More important, the lack of a copyright agreement meant that Douglass could do what he wanted with the *Narrative* once in Britain. Almost immediately upon arriving at the Dublin home of the printer Richard D. Webb, he and Webb began working on a new edition. Douglass wrote Garrison from Dublin on September 16, 1845, without any evident concern about copyright issues: "You will see James [Buffum] and myself are still in Old Ireland. Our stay is protracted in consequence of the publication here of my narrative. I need hardly say we are happy, when I tell you our home is the house of Mr. R. D. Webb."[12]

Richard Webb was a friend of Garrison's and an active member of the Hibernian Anti-Slavery Society, a predominately Quaker Irish antislavery group that had been at the forefront of the campaign to abolish slavery in the British West Indies. Garrison had met Webb in 1840 at the World Anti-Slavery Convention in London, and at the time Webb had offered lodgings to the black

Garrisonian Charles Lenox Remond. Webb initially respected Remond, but soon came to regard him as "a big spoiled child."[13] Unaware of Webb's disdain, Remond returned to Massachusetts carrying Webb's coauthored "Address of the Irish People to Their Countrymen and Countrywomen in America," signed by 60,000 Irish supporters, which urged Irish Americans to embrace the antislavery cause. In January 1842, Remond and Garrison presented Webb's "Address" to a meeting of the Massachusetts Anti-Slavery Society in Boston's Faneuil Hall, where it was enthusiastically received. Douglass was among those in the assemblage cheering the display of Irish solidarity with abolitionism.

Douglass no doubt greatly admired Webb, the man whom he had to some extent "met" in 1842, but during the fall of 1845 and winter of 1845–1846, Douglass and Webb were not a happy household. Though Webb publicly spoke well of Douglass and maintained a political friendship with him for many months (he genuinely admired the work that Douglass was doing for the antislavery cause), privately he groused about the man as he had earlier groused about Remond. He expressed his displeasure in a letter to Maria Weston Chapman: "F. Douglass was a very short time in my house, before I found him to be absurdly haughty, self-possessed, and prone to take offence." Perhaps Webb was unprepared to interact with "self-possessed" black men keen on asserting their will and distrustful of white supervision. And yet Douglass, whom Webb described in the same letter as "the least likeable and the least easy of all the abolitionists with whom I have come into intimate association," may well have been hard to deal with as he reveled in his celebrity. Webb was particularly bothered by Douglass's treatment of Buffum, a kind and loyal person whom Douglass nonetheless perceived, with reasonable cause, as a spy working for Chapman (and Garrison). "How

Buffum has put up with the conduct from one for whom he has done so much," Webb confided to Chapman, "is past my comprehension."[14] But post-*Cambria,* the more independent Douglass increasingly resented that officers of the Massachusetts Anti-Slavery Society believed he needed to be trailed from one place to the next; and his suspicion of the society would flare early in 1846 when he learned that Chapman had accused him of embezzling funds.[15] For now, Buffum had the paternalistic Webb's sympathies as a person who, like himself, had to "put up" with a black man he was trying to help.

Despite the tension between Webb and Douglass, the two men worked on the first Dublin edition of the *Narrative* during September 1845, and Webb managed to produce 2,000 copies by late September. Webb printed the books at a set price plus the cost of shipping, and then it was Douglass's job to sell them. The changes that Douglass and Webb made to Garrison's 1845 edition are small but striking, focusing on the title page, illustration, epigraph, prefaces, and appendixes, the very paratexts (as described by Genette) which offer guidance to the reader about how to read a published work.[16] They also lightly revised Douglass's prose in order to make it more accessible to British audiences. Without consulting Douglass, Webb replaced the bold engraving of the author on the Boston edition with a new engraving by H. Adlard, which presents Douglass, out of character, as a sort of meek-looking British dandy—and relatively light-complected besides (Figure 4).[17] (Douglass was angered by this change and would insist on a different image for the next Dublin edition.) In a calculated effort to appeal to female readers, Webb or Douglass, or both working together, added a stanza from John Greenleaf Whittier's "Expostulation" (1834), which from its opening line— "What! mothers from their children riven!"—directs attention

FIGURE 4. *Narrative of the Life of Frederick Douglass, an American Slave* (Dublin: Webb and Chapman, 1845), frontispiece. Image reproduction courtesy of the Williams College Archives and Special Collections, Williamstown, Massachusetts.

to the domestic tragedy of slave mothers being separated from their children. At Webb's insistence, Douglass changed the appendix of the U.S. edition to a "Postscript," and then cut back on the bitterly ironic excoriation of proslavery U.S. Christian churches because Webb feared British readers would take the May 1845 version of the appendix as an attack on British churches as well. Douglass would retain that revised version in the second Dublin edition. The condensed postscript was followed by an antislavery appeal titled "To the Friends of the Slave," in which Harriet Martineau and other British abolitionists requested donations for the American Anti-Slavery Society and the Female Anti-Slavery Society. The first Dublin edition concluded with a "Critical Notices" section featuring five glowing reviews from U.S. newspapers of Garrison's edition of the *Narrative*.[18]

The most significant change in the paratexts came with the front matter, arguably the most important component of what John Sekora terms the "white envelope" of the slave narrative.[19] Garrison's Boston edition begins with prefaces by Garrison and Phillips that frame (and arguably "enclose") the entire *Narrative;* the first Dublin edition begins with a new preface by Douglass himself, which not only pushes back against the prefaces by the white abolitionists, which are retained, but updates the *Narrative* by making Garrison and Phillips part of its earlier history. Garrison's preface is now called "Preface to the American Edition" and Phillips's prefatory letter retains its date of April 22, 1845, and so it, too, is linked to a prior moment in the *Narrative*'s history. Garrison is no longer needed to authenticate or legitimate the text. Instead, the post-*Cambria* Douglass offers his own account of the publication of the *Narrative* in Boston and then links the new edition to his current travels in Great Britain. He claims that 4,500 copies of the Boston edition have been sold between the time of its publication in May and his departure for England in August, with the implied hope that this new edition would be similarly popular. He then turns to his current travels in the British Isles, declaring that he has three large goals: to keep his distance from fugitive-slave hunters (he is still legally a slave); to "increase my stock of information" as part of an overall project of "self-improvement"; and to offer "public exposition of the contaminating and degrading influences of Slavery" in order to shame the United States "out of her adhesion to a system so abhorrent to Christianity and to her republican institutions."[20] By referring to his own goals for the British tour, Douglass presents himself right from the start as an antislavery worker who is not limited to a particular nation or antislavery organization. That point is underscored by the title page, which now gives the publisher information as "Dublin: Webb and Chapman, GT. Brunswick-Street," instead of "Boston: Published at the Anti-Slavery Office."

Mainly, though, Douglass in this new preface assiduously emphasizes that it is he, not Garrison, who is the editor of the volume. For after elaborating on his reasons for traveling to Britain, he provides an overview of the paratexts of the Dublin edition, urging his readers to peruse not only Garrison's earlier preface and Phillips's letter, but also the "notices of my Narrative extracted from American newspapers, which will be found at the end of the book." He concludes the preface by reprinting an account of the August 1845 farewell meeting held for him at Lynn, Massachusetts, along with the meeting's resolutions wishing him and Buffum "successful issue of their journey" and testifying "to the fidelity with which he [Douglass] has sustained the various relations of life, and to the deep respect with which he is now regarded by every friend of liberty throughout our borders." By choosing to print the resolutions as part of his preface, Douglass appropriates a printed account that otherwise might have seemed yet another act of white legitimation. A testimonial to Douglass from the Dublin-based Hibernian Anti-Slavery Society immediately follows the cover page (and appears just before Douglass's preface), praising Douglass for his "Anti-Slavery mission to Great Britain and Ireland"; but the testimonial is set in exceptionally small type so the eye could miss it.[21] Even so, it contributes to the overall presentation of Douglass in this new edition of the *Narrative* as an active agent in the larger Anglo-American antislavery movement and not as a factotum of the Massachusetts Anti-Slavery Society. The ensuing remarks by Garrison and Phillips now seem to be praising a provincial Douglass of the historical past and not the cosmopolitan figure of late 1845.

Douglass was thrilled with this new edition of the *Narrative* and took special pride in the sales that accompanied his lectures. "My Narrative is just published," he informed Garrison from Dublin in late September, "and I have sold one hundred copies in this city." In a speech delivered in Limerick in November 1845, he recounts how he wrote the *Narrative* as a response to those who said "that he was not a slave," and then giddily calls attention to its impressive sales: "There were 6500 copies of the work sold from the time of its publication May last till the first of August." Douglass probably included in this inflated figure the sales of the new Dublin edition of the *Narrative*, which he offered at this talk for a half crown each. The correspondent for the Limerick *Reporter*, who transcribed Douglass's lecture for his newspaper, conveyed Douglass's views on the propriety of such salesmanship at his lectures: "As the lectures were free, the sale of his book was the only means of bringing him from town to town, and as he did not wish to make money, but to have the means of exposing American slavery, and enlisting against it the feelings of the people of

the country, he found the sale of his work which he had got reprinted since he came over to be quite sufficient for his purpose."
Douglass may have been understating his desire for sales (and
money) and the extent to which he was dependent on such profits
for his British travels. In his private letters, he remained exuberant
about selling books. He writes Webb from Belfast in December
1845 about his most recent antislavery meeting: "Well all my
books went last night at one blow. I want more[.] I want more." In
a subsequent letter sent to Webb from Belfast, he explains that,
for a planned second edition, he has gathered letters of endorsement from leading clergy who have attended his lectures, such as
Presbyterian minister Isaac Nelson of the Belfast Anti-Slavery Society, who would call the *Narrative* a "literary wonder" in the
appendix of the second Dublin edition. Douglass asks Webb if it
might not be a good strategy to use such letters as a way of
selling the remaining thousand copies of the Dublin *Narrative*
that Douglass now wants Webb to ship him. His excitement about
the quick sales of the first thousand copies is palpable: "The books
go off grandly."[22]

THE SECOND DUBLIN EDITION

Douglass was energized by his residence in Ireland, and not just
because the *Narrative* sold so well. He met the legendary Irish
nationalist Daniel O'Connell in late 1845, spoke with him at a
rally in Dublin, where O'Connell himself introduced Douglass
as "the black O'Connell in the United States," and was moved by
O'Connell's and other Irish patriots' decades-long efforts to
achieve a greater independence and voice for the Irish people.
O'Connell's willingness to work politically within existing insti-

tutions to bring about the repeal of the 1801 Act of Union, which had shut down Ireland's Dublin-based parliament, may have been one of the inspirations for Douglass's turn to political abolitionism in the late 1840s and early 1850s. A number of Douglass's speeches delivered in Ireland also conveyed his sense of common cause between U.S. slaves and the Irish working poor. Ignoring the occasional racist insult from those who were suspicious of a black speaker, Douglass affirmed his belief that the Irish en masse did not exhibit racial prejudice. As he reported in a letter from Dublin published in the *Liberator:* "One of the most pleasing features of my visit, thus far, has been a total absence of all manifestations of prejudice against me, on account of my color."[23]

Despite his professed admiration for the Irish people, Douglass initially had relatively little to say about the sufferings brought on by the potato famine. In October 1845 he spoke at Cork's Temperance Institute under the aegis of Ireland's renowned temperance leader, Father Theobald Mathew, and subsequently gave a number of other lectures on temperance because he believed, as he reported in a February 1846 letter to Garrison, that "the main cause of the extreme poverty and beggary in Ireland, is intemperance." That Douglass naïvely thought that temperance pledges could alleviate Irish "beggary" does not mean that he was oblivious to the increasingly dire situation facing the Irish poor. As he remarked to Garrison on the sufferings he observed in Dublin early in 1846: "I speak truly when I say, I dreaded to go out of the house. . . . The spectacle that affected me most, and made the most vivid impression on my mind, of the extreme poverty and wretchedness of the poor of Dublin, was the frequency with which I met little children in the street at a late hour of night, covered with filthy rags, and seated upon the cold stone steps, or in corners, leaning against brick walls, fast asleep, with none to look upon them, none to care for them." Such was his concern about the children in particular that Douglass began to make ministering visits to "the huts of the poor in [the] vicinity." During such visits, he reported to Garrison, he saw "much here to remind me of my former condition," and thus much to remind him yet again that "the cause of humanity is one the world over." Still, by the end of this extended letter, which Garrison published in the March 27, 1846, *Liberator,* Douglass blames much of Irish poverty on the "drunkenness . . . rife in Ireland." In short, the man who in the late 1830s was brutalized by Irish workers at Baltimore's Fell's Point had no problem in casting at least some of the blame for the poverty exacerbated by the famine on the Irish workers themselves. It was not until his return to the United States in 1847 that Douglass fully grasped the severity of the blight that had struck the potato crop, writing the black abolitionist editor Thomas Van Rensselaer about the need to send "a ship-load of grain into Ireland . . . [to] succor the afflicted and famine-stricken millions of that unhappy land." Eight years later, in *Bondage and Freedom,* Douglass would convey an even greater understanding and solidarity when he revised his account of the slave songs that he had first described in the *Narrative* to include the Irish: "I have never heard any songs like those anywhere since I left slavery, except when in Ireland. There I heard the same *wailing* notes, and was much affected by them. It was during the Famine of 1845–6."[24]

Although Douglass sympathized with the Irish poor, and eventually came to understand the causes of the famine, during his 1845–1847 travels in the British Isles he found his greatest sense of community with the antislavery elites he met in Ireland, Scotland, and especially England. An Anglophile at heart, Douglass lived well while abroad, and to some extent exemplified what

Elisa Tamarkin has identified as one of the attractions of abolitionist work during this period: the pleasurably sociable days and
nights of sharing lecture podiums and meals with like-minded
people devoted to the cause.[25] But there were tensions as well,
both personal and political. The Garrisonians, for instance, were
suspicious of the British and Foreign Anti-Slavery Society, which
was aligned with the American and Foreign Anti-Slavery Society,
the group that had broken from Garrison's American Anti-Slavery
Society in 1840. Various antislavery organizations lay claim to
Douglass, ranging from the Irish-based Hibernian Anti-Slavery
Society to the British and Foreign Anti-Slavery Society to the
Garrisonians themselves, and Douglass did his best to avoid becoming entangled in the increasingly tense conflicts between the
Irish and the English, as well as between different antislavery organizations. He could maintain a degree of independence from
all of these groups in part because he had funds coming in from
his new edition of the *Narrative*. And he wanted "more" with a
second edition.

Work on a second Dublin edition began in late 1845 or early
1846, with back and forth between Douglass and Webb on how
to proceed. In a letter of January 1846, Douglass responded to a
letter from Webb that is no longer extant, remarking that "I have
recieved [*sic*] the Books, and your letter of 10th ultimo. I have ad-
dopted [*sic*] your advice as to how I might correct and amend the
narrative." Douglass gave his own advice for the second edition,
such as the importance of finding a new frontispiece and adding
to and rearranging the appendix. In an intriguing letter written
later in January, Douglass even suggested the possibility of making
cuts to the *Narrative:* "I think it will look much better a little
shorter besides" (in fact the second Dublin edition is longer). And
then he complained to Webb about his failure to supply him with

additional copies of the first Dublin edition: "It is a great loss to me to be without my narrative as I am dependant [*sic*] on it for all my support in this country."[26]

Douglass's complaint about not having enough copies of his autobiography to sell at antislavery meetings spoke to the persistent tension between the two men. For even as Webb continued to work with Douglass on his Dublin editions, he shared his frustrations with Maria Weston Chapman about Douglass's "insolence . . . such as I was not prepared to meet with from any abolitionist," which he blamed on "the flattering and petting [Douglass] met with in Ireland." But he probably should have blamed Chapman for Douglass's "insolence," for she had been one of the people who had insisted on having Buffum watch over Douglass, and she made no secret of her belief that Douglass could not be trusted with money from antislavery organizations. In a letter to Webb of early 1846, Chapman accused Douglass not only of regarding himself as more important than the American Anti-Slavery Society but also of embezzling funds from the group—a letter that Webb (as he frankly told Chapman) read aloud to Douglass. In his response to Chapman's letter, Webb agreed with her on one main point—that Douglass was "much less devoted to the cause and much more to himself than I took him to be"—even as he remained unconvinced, from his point of view as a printer for hire who was regularly paid by Douglass, about her scurrilous allegation that Douglass was a thief: "In his money transactions he had been more than honourable." On the charge that Douglass could not be trusted with money, the good-hearted Buffum, too, shared his thoughts with Chapman, telling her that "Frederick is not satisfied with a reference you made in one of your letters to R. D. Webb, *that he would* be likely to be influenced by the great temptations in this country and especially that of money—which [he] says that he has given you no reason to entertain—he is *quite sensative* [*sic*] on that *point.*"[27] Angry at Chapman, Douglass may have also taken Webb's reading aloud of the letter as more accusatory than exculpatory.

Despite their steadily deteriorating relationship, Webb and Douglass completed their work on the second Dublin edition of the *Narrative* early in February 1846, and Webb printed it later that month. In a letter to Chapman, Webb announced the publication while conveying a touch of envy at Douglass's financial success, both with the *Narrative* and with the funds that were coming his way from various British antislavery organizations. The letter also makes clear that Webb continued to have a hand in the revisions: "In the last edition of Douglass' Narrative just published I made some addition to the Address to the Friends of the slave and put in some new names. The first edition is nearly sold and he cannot have made less than 750 dollars by it. . . . In Belfast they paid D's bill at the hotel for nearly a month & made him a present of about 200 dollars beside." Although antislavery groups helped to support him, Douglass, contra Webb, continued to state that most of his funding came from sales of the *Narrative.* Nowhere was Douglass more pointed about that than in a letter he wrote Chapman from Kilmarnock, Scotland, on March 29, 1846. Responding to her allegation that he had taken money from antislavery organizations, he insisted that he was managing to get by in Great Britain on profits from the *Narrative:* "I brought with me three hundred, and fifty dollars, money which I had saved from the sale of my narrative. For means to sustain me while here I have relied—and still rely mainly upon the sale of the narrative."[28] In economic and other terms, the *Narrative* in its revised form had become central to Douglass's independence from the woman who embodied everything that he found wrong with Garrison's Massachusetts Anti-Slavery Society.

The second Dublin edition of the *Narrative*, which, as the critic Patricia J. Ferreira observes, has been "little more than a footnote in Douglass's literary accomplishments," is the edition over which Douglass had the most editorial control and thus the edition that he probably would have argued, at least in 1846, should be taken as authoritative.[29] Douglass approved of a new engraving of himself on the frontispiece, modeled on that of the 1845 Boston edition, in which he looked blacker and more forceful; he expanded his preface, keeping it in its place before the letters from Garrison and Phillips; he worked with Webb to make additional style changes for British readers; and he and Webb added new reviews to the critical notices in the appendix and then moved those notices so that they preceded the fundraising plea, "To the Friends of the Slave," which now concluded the volume. In his expanded preface to the second edition, Douglass brings his life history up to the present moment by adding a full paragraph on his British travels, mentioning his successful meetings in Dublin, Cork, Belfast, Glasgow (where he wrote the expanded preface), and elsewhere, and making sure to note the connection between those meetings and sales of his *Narrative:* "An edition of 2000 copies of my Narrative has been exhausted." Presenting himself as a transatlantic antislavery leader, he expresses his "great hopes" that his continued travels in Great Britain will have an impact on "thousands and tens of thousands of the intelligent and philanthropic." And in the new final paragraph of his expanded preface, he mentions one other change to the second edition: "It gives me great pleasure to be able to add, in an Appendix to the present edition, an attempted Refutation of my Narrative, lately published in the 'Delaware Republican' by Mr. A. C. C. Thompson. My reply will be found along with Mr. Thompson's letter."[30]

The letter exchange between one A. C. C. Thompson of Delaware and Frederick Douglass is the most important addition to the second Dublin edition; and it is more than simply a new paratext. It can also be read as an updated "life" of Douglass that makes the figure of Douglass in the 1845 *Narrative* seem historically distant from the transatlantic Douglass of 1846. Like the shouting Connecticut passenger on board the *Cambria*, Thompson, whose full name was Absalom Christopher Columbus Americus Vespucious Thompson, charged that Douglass was a liar, and Douglass rebutted the charge. That is the simple story of their exchange. To sketch out the more complex story: Thompson, who had lived on a farm near Edward Covey's and knew many of the people described in the *Narrative*, claimed that Douglass misrepresented Maryland's Eastern Shore slaveholders and moreover could not possibly have written the *Narrative* because he was an illiterate slave. His letter thus raised questions of authenticity, which Douglass had become skilled in refuting, but even more importantly (from Douglass's perspective) his letter extended the *Narrative* into the present moment, making it more fully alive. Thompson presented Covey, the Aulds, Colonel Lloyd, and others as living figures, not just characters in a text, whose lives could be commented on beyond the frame of the *Narrative*. For good reason, then, Douglass avowed that he was overjoyed to read Thompson's letter. Conveying that joy is one of the rhetorical achievements of Douglass's response to Thompson, and it is crucial to note that, as with the various *Cambria* accounts, the voice of that response is different from the more measured and conciliatory voice that Douglass uses in the *Narrative* to describe his life as a slave. Douglass's feisty and ironic response to Thompson, included in this new edition of the *Narrative*, thus presses the reader to regard the first-person voice of Douglass's narrative portion of the book as an artful rhetorical construction best suited to the Garrisonian publication context of 1845. In 1846, a different sort of Douglass was needed to take on Thompson.

Publication context is crucial to the several stagings of the epistolary exchange between Thompson and Douglass, starting with the moment when Thompson published his letter in a late 1845 issue of the *Delaware Republican*. It was then reprinted in the Albany *Patriot*. Douglass's response first appeared in the February 27, 1846, *Liberator* and was reprinted in other antislavery newspapers. By pulling the letters out of their newspaper contexts and resituating them in the appendix of the second Dublin edition of the *Narrative*, Douglass positioned the letters to speak directly to the main body of the *Narrative*, while presenting an exchange between a proslavery white and an antislavery black that was completely under his editorial control. (Indicative of his control, Douglass revised his letter for the exchange printed in the appendix while keeping Thompson's as it first appeared in the *Delaware Republican*.) Douglass famously recounts in the *Narrative* how he was inspired by the selection in *The Columbian Orator* titled "Dialogue between a Master and a Slave," in which a slave talks his master into granting him his freedom, but in the *Narrative* there isn't much dialogue at all between master and slave. Now, in this new Dublin edition, there is a dialogue, albeit in the appendix. Though still legally a slave, Douglass in this exchange assumes an aggressive rhetorical posture that looks forward to his powerful response as a free man to Thomas Auld in his 1848 "Letter to His Old Master" (see Chapter 5).

Exerting his editorial control as a form of mastery, Douglass introduces and contextualizes the appendix's epistolary exchange in a paragraph added to the expanded "Preface to the second Dublin edition." As Douglass says about Thompson's letter in the concluding sentence of the preface: "He agrees with me at least in the important fact, that I am what I proclaim myself to be, an ungrateful fugitive from the 'patriarchal institutions' of the Slave States; and he certifies that many of the heroes of my Narrative are still living and doing well, as 'honored and worthy members of the Methodist Episcopal Church.'"[31] With this phrasing, Douglass shrewdly undermines, or parodies, one of the key conventions of the antebellum slave narrative—the authenticating testimony of the white editor or publisher—by making Thompson, not Garrison or Phillips, the initial authenticator of his story. Moreover, by placing a sampling of Thompson's comments *before* Garrison's and Phillips's testimonials, Douglass comes close to grouping Thompson with the authenticating white abolitionists who follow.

Announced in the preface and then printed in the revised appendix, with additional prefatory remarks, Douglass's exchange with Thompson to some extent not only oddly legitimates but also frames the second Dublin edition of the *Narrative*. In his remarks on the exchange in the appendix, Douglass again rehearses the publication history of Thompson's letter, his "pleasure" at being able to present it to his readers in this new edition of the *Narrative*, and his belief that, rather than refuting Douglass's story, Thompson's various allegations "are valuable as a confirmation of the main facts of my Narrative, while the denials are only such as might be expected from an apologist of slavery."[32] Douglass then prints Thompson's letter under the title it had in the *Delaware Republican*, "Falsehood Refuted," and it is a strange letter indeed, though absolutely riveting in its placement at the end of the *Narrative,* coming right after Douglass's denigrating characterizations of slaveholders like Aaron Anthony, Edward Lloyd, Thomas Auld, and Edward Covey, whom Thompson assures us in his letter are all good people (and alive and well). In a letter notable for its lack of rhetorical skill, Thompson accuses Douglass of "Falsehood" even as he concedes that Douglass has accurately described the thick network of social relations in Maryland's Eastern Shore.[33]

To highlight some of the more striking aspects of Thompson's letter: He says that it is "with considerable regret" that he must appear before the public, but that after reading what was apparently a pirated edition of Douglass's *Narrative,* titled *Extract from a Narrative of Frederick Douglass, an American Slave, written by himself,* he has no choice but to defend his "shamefully traduced" friends and give "a true representation of the character of these gentlemen." He proclaims that Colonel Lloyd, whom Douglass depicts as separating slaves from their families, is "a kind and charitable man"; that the overseer Gore, whom Douglass depicts as killing the slave Demby in cold blood, is "a worthy member of the Methodist Episcopal Church"; that the overseer Covey, whom Douglass depicts as a brutal slave breaker, is "a plain, honest farmer, and a tried and faithful member of the Methodist Episcopal Church"; and that Thomas Auld, whom Douglass depicts as mean and cold-hearted, is "an honorable and worthy member of the Methodist Episcopal Church; and only notable for his integrity and irreproachable Christian character." What Thompson does not refute is that these men were either slave owners or overseers or that Douglass was a former slave. But he wonders about Douglass's ability to write his own narrative without the help of white abolitionists, for he insists that the young

Douglass he knew, Frederick Bailey, "was an unlearned, and rather an ordinary negro" who could not possibly have written the *Narrative* (such a charge means skipping over Douglass's description of how he learned to read and write). Like the proslavery passengers on the *Cambria,* he asserts that Douglass and other abolitionists are guilty of "glaring falsehoods" when they claim that slavery separates mothers from their children or does anything harmful to blacks. As he declares in paternalistic proslavery fashion: "I was raised among slaves, and have also owned them, and am well aware that the slaves live better and fare better, in many respects, than the free blacks." Although Thompson fails to corroborate some of the specifics of Douglass's representations of individual slave owners and overseers, he does offer support for Douglass's main contention, that slavery, as Thompson concedes at the end of his letter, is a "great evil." But it is an evil, Thompson says, that "*falls not upon the slave,* but on the owner," who can become overwhelmed with the responsibilities of caring for so many people under his authority, even as he bears the brunt of slanderous attacks from abolitionists like Douglass. Thompson thus concludes his letter by championing the colonizationist agenda of "removing the blacks from the country," presumably by shipping them to Africa.[34]

Douglass initially responded to Thompson in a January 22, 1846, letter to Garrison from Perth, Scotland, which was published in the February 27, 1846, *Liberator.* The letter begins:

> *To the Editor of the Liberator:*
> DEAR FRIEND—
> For the sake of our righteous cause, I was
> delighted to see, by an extract, copies in the
> Liberator of 12th Dec. 1845, from the Delaware

Republican, that Mr. A. C. C. Thompson, No. 101,
Market-street, Wilmington, has undertaken to
invalidate my testimony against the slaveholders,
whose names I have made prominent in the narrative
of my experience while in slavery.[35]

For the appendix to the second Dublin edition of the *Narrative*,
Douglass begins the letter somewhat differently:

> REPLY TO MR. A. C. C. THOMPSON
> Sir,
> For the sake of the abolition cause, I was
> delighted to see by an extract copied into the
> "Liberator" of 12 Dec. 1845, from the "Delaware
> Republican," that a Mr. A. C. C. Thompson, No.
> 101, Market-street, Wilmington, has undertaken to
> invalidate my testimony against those slave-holders,
> whose names I have made prominent in the humble
> Narrative of my experience in slavery.

Douglass makes a number of revisions to the appendix version
of the letter, but the main revision, right at the outset, involves
ridding the letter of any expression of solidarity with Garrison;
thus he drops the salutation to his "Friend" Garrison, along
with the consensual appeal to "our righteous cause," and addresses Thompson directly. There is also a downplaying of the
Narrative, which here becomes Douglass's "humble" early text
before he achieved an even greater celebrity in Great Britain.
He remarks in a sentence useful for thinking about Douglass
beyond the 1845 Massachusetts Anti-Slavery Society *Narrative:*
"Frederick the Freeman is a very different person from Frederick
the Slave."[36]

In the overall letter, Douglass takes pains to emphasize that "Frederick the Freeman" is both a writer and an editor. Addressing his editorial decision to include the letter exchange in the appendix of the *Narrative*'s second Dublin edition, Douglass says that he initially chose to publish his response to Thompson in a newspaper other than the *Delaware Republican* because he knew that that newspaper, whose unstated "motto is, 'we don't allow niggers in here,'" would never give him a "hearing" in its opinion columns, and instead would "advertise me as a fugitive slave." For good reason, then, he responded to Thompson in the *Liberator*. But now Douglass takes full editorial control of the exchange, placing Thompson's letter in the appendix in order to corroborate the first-person narrative that preceded it and to stage a dialogue between a "master" and "slave" more than four years after the *Narrative*'s closing scene of Douglass's triumph at Garrison's anti-slavery meeting in Nantucket. Douglass uses the letter, both in the *Liberator* and in the second Dublin edition of the *Narrative*, not only to respond to the accusation that he is a liar, but also to develop antislavery arguments from the perspective of being free and empowered "on this side of the Atlantic." As he did on the *Cambria*, he discusses slave laws and slave codes, showing how the southern legal system, like the *Delaware Republican*, works to silence blacks, making it impossible to bring charges against even the most tyrannous of white masters. In that context, Douglass's placement of his response to the slaveholders' friend in the appendix to the *Narrative* has an even greater urgency. Having talked back to his accuser and established his authority as writer and editor, Douglass again emphasizes that he is a very different person from the slave Thompson saw with Covey and others a mere seven years ago. As he remarks to Thompson (and the reader), in a sort of concession: "if any one had told me

seven years ago, that I should ever be able to *dictate* such a Narrative, to say nothing of *writing* it, I should have disbelieved the
prophecy."[37]

And it is with the image of a free Douglass "on this side of the
Atlantic" that Douglass concludes his letter to Thompson, suggesting that just as he would have disbelieved a prophecy about
his ability to write the *Narrative,* he would have similarly disbelieved a prophecy about the man he would become over just the
last few months:

> I feel myself a new man. Freedom has given me a new
> life. The change wrought in me is truly amazing. If
> you should meet me, now you would scarcely know
> me. You know when I used to meet you near Covey's
> wood-gate, I hardly dared to look up at you. If I should
> meet you where I now am, amid the free hills of Old
> Scotland, where the ancient "Black Douglass" once
> met his foes, I presume I might summon sufficient
> fortitude to look you full in the face. It may be that,
> wearing the brave name which I have assumed, might
> lead me to deeds which would render our meeting
> not the most agreeable. Especially might this be the
> case, if you should attempt to enslave me.[38]

With his threat of violence, Douglass in this astonishing passage prompts the reader to imagine a new scene in the autobiography: Douglass using force to resist a fugitive slave hunter
(or simply someone as arrogant and annoying as Thompson).
Emphasizing the "now" in Scotland, where he wrote the first
version of the letter, Douglass situates himself in 1846 as a
freedom fighter both in word and in deed. Douglass, the name the
former Frederick Bailey had taken from Sir Walter Scott's *The*

Lady of the Lake, then links himself to Scottish history in a different way by imagining himself in the tradition of Sir James Douglas of Scotland (c. 1286–1330), who fought for Scottish independence. Through this linkage, he once again suggests his growing distance from the moral-suasionist imperatives of Garrison. Douglass would continue to argue for the legitimacy of antislavery violence in his speeches and essays of the late 1840s and 1850s, particularly in his celebrations of the slave rebel Madison Washington, who in 1853 would become the subject of his autobiographically inflected novella of black rebellion, *The Heroic Slave* (see Chapter 3).

Douglass closes his letter to Thompson: "Believing that you are condemned out of your own mouth, I subscribe myself, FREDERICK DOUGLASS." The revised and expanded appendix of the second Dublin edition then offers two additional sections following the letter exchange: "Critical Notices" and "To the Friends of the Slave." The "Critical Notices" section raises the number of adulatory reviews and testimonials from five (in the first Dublin edition) to ten. The first Dublin edition contains reviews only from the United States and only of the May 1845 Massachusetts Anti-Slavery Society edition; the five additional reviews, from England, Scotland, and Ireland, respond to the first Dublin edition of late 1845 and are suggestive of the new transatlantic reach of the *Narrative*. The reviewer for *Chambers's Edinburgh Journal*, for instance, remarks on how Douglass is currently "in Great Britain, lecturing on the subject of slavery"; and the Reverend Isaac Nelson of Dublin not only celebrates the *Narrative* as a "literary wonder," as we saw earlier, but also hails Douglass as "an intellectual phenomenon . . . in the republic of letters."[39] The Douglass of these additional five British reviews has no explicit relation to Garrison or to Garrisonian abolitionism. The second Dublin edition concludes with "To the Friends of the Slave" (a shorter version of the appeal had preceded the "Critical Notices" in the first Dublin edition), the revised placement of which allows Douglass to keep the focus on the *Narrative* until the very end. Significantly, in the call for donations to the American Anti-Slavery Society and the Boston Female Anti-Slavery Society, Harriet Martineau and the other cosigners (all women) state that those who give at least ten shillings and ten pence will receive subscriptions to the *National Anti-Slavery Standard*. There is no mention of the *Liberator* and no mention of the man who published the Boston edition of the *Narrative*.

A NARRATIVE OF HIS PREVIOUS LIFE

Douglass and his *Narrative* (in various editions) continued to circulate in the British Isles, and there is considerable evidence that he continued to prosper from book sales linked to his lectures. In a letter of February 2, 1846, to the Garrisonian and Massachusetts reformer Edmund Quincy, Webb predicted that Douglass "will pocket 2500 dollars in twelve months time" from the sales of the second Dublin edition, in part because he was so good at marketing it. After Douglass addressed an antislavery meeting in London in May 1846, for example, the chairman of the meeting appealed to the crowd (in ways no doubt coached by Douglass): "Frederick Douglass has left a wife and four children in America, and I wish to state that he has published a little book, entitled *The Narrative of Frederick Douglass*, which may be had at the door, and by the sale of which he and his wife are supported."[40]

As Douglass had hoped, the funds from sales at such public gatherings allowed him to live abroad without feeling overly in-

debted to a particular antislavery organization, which further contributed to his ongoing development as an independent thinker,
speaker, and antislavery leader. When Garrison arrived in London
in July 1846 for a three-month tour of England, there was every
sense that Douglass was no longer his protégé but instead the
celebrity who brought Garrison in tow to antislavery meetings.
Webb wrote to Maria Weston Chapman about the two together:
"Frederick Douglass . . . looks stately & majestic—with an air
that makes Garrison a mere baby beside him."⁴¹ Garrison joined
Douglass in the "Send Back the Money" campaign—the effort
to persuade Scottish Presbyterian churches to return funds they
received from churches in the U.S. South—and on August 18,
1848, the two men, along with British abolitionist George
Thompson, visited the gravely ill English antislavery reformer
Thomas Clarkson. Garrison reported to his antislavery associates
about the pleasures of traveling with Douglass, whom he described in letters of August 1846 to Webb and Quincy, respectively, as the speaker who was "rapturously received" and "drew
forth a perfect storm of applause." He also noted how Douglass
managed to market his new editions of the *Narrative* at their public
meetings. "In a pecuniary point of view," he remarked to his
wife, Helen, in a letter of September 1846, "he is doing very well,
as he sells his Narrative very readily, and receives aid in donations and presents, to some extent." That same month Garrison
wrote British abolitionist John B. Estlin that Douglass "is chiefly
dependent upon the sale of the Narrative, but I believe he is at
this time receiving a small stipend from the Edinburgh friends";
and he wrote Webb shortly after a lecture in Sheffield: "It was a
most animating spectacl[e,] and a more delightful meeting I
have not yet seen in England. . . . F. D. sold on the spot, a considerable number of his Narrative."⁴²

Garrison's letters about Douglass are genuinely warm, but they assume that Douglass would continue to serve the Garrisonian cause as a lecturer and contributor to his newspaper. However, soon after Garrison returned to the United States in October 1846, Douglass's English supporters began working to secure his freedom and raise funds for a printing press that would enable him to start up his own newspaper. With the help of a contribution from John Bright, Anna and Ellen Richardson purchased Douglass's freedom from Hugh Auld on December 12, 1846. That same month, Douglass met Julia Griffiths, who in 1849 would cross the Atlantic to live with Douglass's family and serve as his newspaper's managing editor. Richardson and Griffiths were among a number of British women reformers who were taken with Douglass during his visit, and Estlin was not alone in expressing his concerns to his U.S. abolitionist friend Samuel May about the propriety of Douglass's relationships with white women: "You can hardly imagine how he is noticed,—*petted* I may say by *ladies*. . . . My fear is that often associating so much with white women of education & refined taste & manners, he will feel a 'craving void' when he returns to his own family." Estlin's concerns aside, Douglass by all accounts was delighted to see "my dear Anna" and "my two bright-eyed boys" when he returned to Lynn in late April 1847.[43]

On April 4, 1847, Douglass once again boarded the *Cambria* at Liverpool for the voyage that would take him to Boston sixteen days later. Shortly before his departure, his English friends sponsored a "Soirée" at the London Tavern in Douglass's honor. Among those in attendance were the British abolitionists Thompson, Estlin, William Howett, and Joseph Griffiths. Julia Griffiths wrote "The Farewell Song of Frederick Douglass" for the occasion. Charles Dickens sent his regrets, which were printed in the *Report of Proceedings at the Soirée Given to Frederick Douglass, London Tavern, March 30, 1847.* The *Report of Proceedings* was published by R. Yorke Clarke and Company of London, which was also the publisher of the London editions of Douglass's *Narrative.* The *Report* shows how Douglass continued to be closely tied to the *Narrative,* though by this point in his travels the editions he was best known for were published by Webb and Clarke, and not Garrison. At the dinner, Douglass was celebrated in his own right as an antislavery leader, with few references to an institutional affiliation with Garrison or anybody else; the prefatory remarks on the proceedings state simply that people were there "to testify their high estimation of the character and talents of Mr. Frederick Douglass, and of his eminent services to the Anti-slavery cause."[44]

As chairman of the evening's events, Thompson offered an opening speech of appreciation, proclaiming that those who have read Douglass's *Narrative* "will know how he at last achieved the great object for which he had been sighing for many years—that he took leave of the house of bondage." But he goes on to term Douglass's 1845 book "a narrative of his previous life," a work published before Douglass had an impact on the antislavery movement in Great Britain and before he had achieved a greater cosmopolitanism and independence. Thompson points to that greater independence by reminding those at the soirée that Douglass had arrived in Great Britain "accredited" by Garrison and other U.S. abolitionists, but that he has done much more than simply represent a specific abolitionist group's way of thinking; instead, he has traveled widely, worked with numerous organizations, and "awakened a larger amount of attention to the question of slavery than has ever been awakened in the same time by the individual labours of any other person in this country." With his "mission . . . fulfilled" in the British Isles, Douglass can now return to the United States and take up the "labors which lie before him in his native country."[45] As Thompson suggests, Douglass would have new stories to tell as he continues to work for the antislavery cause. But would he continue to work with Garrison?

In his speech addressed to those gathered at London Tavern, and implicitly to the antislavery public in the United States and Great Britain, Douglass offers a tribute to Garrison, whom he calls "my beloved, my esteemed, and almost venerated friend." But then he pointedly refers to "the noble Gerrit Smith," the political abolitionist whom Garrison despised, and who in the early 1850s would help Douglass to fund his newspaper. And he thanks his British friends for purchasing his freedom, knowing that most Garrisonians remained opposed to such purchases for the way they appeared to legitimate the slave trade. Challenging those in the Garrisonian wing who objected to the sale, even though Garrison himself generously supported Douglass's decision to allow the purchase to go forward, Douglass asserts: "I feel that there has been no noble principle sacrificed in the transaction. . . . If there is anything to which exception may be taken it is in the *expediency* and not in any principle involved in the matter." He concludes with rousing words of thanks to his British friends that underscore his growth over his twenty-one months abroad: "I came here a slave, but I go back free."[46]

And he went back as well with funds for a printing press. The concluding pages of the *Report of Proceedings* link Douglass's new freedom with his opportunity to become an editor of his own newspaper. Though Garrison would express his surprise and annoyance that Douglass so quickly upon his return would start up the *North Star,* in the *Report* there is no mystery at all about Douglass's intentions. The "British Testimonial of Esteem for Frederick Douglass, and of Sympathy for the American Slave," printed on the *Report*'s penultimate page and signed by twenty-one supporters, notes that "a subscription is in progress for the purpose of presenting MR. FREDERICK DOUGLASS with a Steam Printing Press." Once again the *Cambria* has a key role in Douglass's development as a writer and editor, for his British supporters assert that the *Cambria*'s unwillingness to sell a cabin ticket on the main deck to Douglass, a free man who is "immensely superior in refinement and intellect, to any one of the passengers whose disgusting prejudice caused his exclusion," demonstrates the need for a newspaper that will lead the fight against slavery and racism from a black point of view. With his uncommon refinement and intellect, Douglass, his British supporters declare, "is peculiarly fitted to engage in the editorship of a paper."[47]

In helping to fund the *North Star*, Douglass's British supporters were also helping him to continue the process of breaking from Garrison. The final page of the *Report of Proceedings* consists of a full-page ad for the third English edition of the *Narrative*, published by Clarke, the publisher of the *Report*. The ad is graced with four of the ten testimonials that Douglass selected for the second Dublin edition, including the praise from Reverend Isaac Nelson. There is nothing in the advertisement about Garrison or the Massachusetts Anti-Slavery Society. In fact, the London editions, which Douglass was not involved with as an editorial consultant, dropped Garrison's preface and most of the other paratextual materials in favor of printing just the narrative itself, along with a speech by Douglass that he delivered at Finsbury Chapel, Moorfield, on May 22, 1846 (sections of which Douglass himself would print in the appendix to *Bondage and Freedom*).

Despite the growing friction over his plans for a black news-paper, Douglass remained aligned with Garrison's antislavery organization after his return to the United States on April 20, 1847. He spoke and wrote for the group, and in October accompanied Garrison on a lecture tour to western New York, Pennsylvania, and Ohio. Garrison took ill during the tour, and while he recuperated in Cleveland, Douglass headed back to Rochester to begin publishing the *North Star*, which he initially coedited with the Pittsburgh black abolitionist Martin Delany. In a private letter to his wife, Helen, which he wrote while recuperating in Cleveland, Garrison expressed his disappointment, indeed his sense of betrayal, at Douglass's founding of an antislavery newspaper that he viewed as directly competing with the *Liberator*. Garrison's complaints to his wife blend the personal and political: "Is it not strange that Douglass has not written a single line to me or to any one, in this place, inquiring after my health, since he left me on a bed of illness? It will also greatly surprise our friends in Boston to hear that, in regard to his project for establishing a paper here, to be called 'The North Star,' he never opened to me his lips on the subject, nor asked my advice in particular whatever. Such conduct grieves me to the heart. His conduct . . . has been impulsive, inconsiderate, and highly inconsistent. . . . Strange want of forecast and judgment!"[48] But as the published proceedings of the farewell dinner in London make clear, Douglass was hardly secretive about his plan to use funds from his British supporters to establish a newspaper. In this letter to his wife, Garrison sounds a bit like Maria Weston Chapman and others of the Massachusetts Anti-Slavery Society who were watching over Douglass in Great Britain. Douglass was angered by that supervision and he no doubt felt angry about Garrison's quick condemnation of his decision to establish a black newspaper. Given their recent history as collaborators, Douglass may have also felt the burden of Garrison's condemnation, experiencing some guilt. But when Garrison publicly attacked him in the pages of the *Liberator* during the early 1850s, any remaining guilt turned to anger, and by 1855, in *Bondage and Freedom*, Douglass was describing Garrison as a sort of antislavery slave master who insisted on telling his black speakers what they could or could not do. Douglass remarks in the 1855 autobiography: "I could not always obey."[49]

In the inaugural December 3, 1847, issue of the *North Star*, Douglass affirmed the importance of establishing an African American newspaper in which "he who has *endured the cruel pangs of Slavery* is the man to *advocate Liberty*." For the first two years of his editorship he mostly championed the tenets of Garrisonian abolitionism, while emphasizing (as Garrison did) the importance of helping the free blacks to rise in the culture. Like Garrison, he was also devoted to the cause of women's rights. Douglass included the slogan "RIGHT IS OF NO SEX" on the masthead of the *North Star*, and from the outset he used his paper to promote the women's rights convention at Seneca Falls, New York, the first of its kind, which convened on July 14, 1848. Douglass was among the small group of men attending the convention organized by Elizabeth Cady Stanton, Lucretia Mott, and other prominent women's rights advocates, and during the 1850s he would continue to attend women's rights conventions and argue for the cause. But as a public social reformer who felt marginalized by a culture that regarded black men as unworthy of the rights of white men, Douglass during the 1840s and 1850s (and beyond) also took it upon himself to perform manhood in ways that (from the perspective of our own historical moment) might seem suspect or even regrettable for the way he appeared to privilege male leadership and (as in his account of the rebellion against Covey) the fighting male body. But there was a compelling logic to his efforts to make claims for black manhood in the terms of the larger white culture, starting with the fact that there was a long tradition of linking soldiery to citizenship. In an effort to forward his arguments in favor of African American citizenship, for example, the generally pacifistic black Garrisonian William C. Nell published two tracts during the 1850s celebrating the "black patriots" who had fought in the American Revolution and the War of 1812. He even included praise for such black rebels of the Americas as the Haitian revolutionary Toussaint L'Ouverture and the South Carolina conspirator Denmark Vesey. As Nell makes clear, moral suasion has its limits; historically, whites and black alike in quest of freedom from oppressors have chosen violent resistance.[50] Douglass had begun to think in similar terms during the mid-to-late 1840s.

Though he founded the *North Star* at a time when he avowed a commitment to Garrisonian principles of moral suasion, Douglass moved fairly quickly toward advocating violence as a proper response to slavery. He announced his break from Garrison in 1851, as a logical corollary of his outrage at the Fugitive Slave Law of 1850, which he believed violated what he had come to regard, contra Garrison, as the antislavery spirit of the U.S. Constitution. Still, Douglass's ideological break with Garrison had blurry edges. Both leaders were pragmatists who were capable of adjusting their principles to the demands of the moment. Garrison the moral suasionist, for instance, not only published a slave narrative in which a slave's violent response to a slave master is presented as the turning point of that slave's life (Douglass's resistance to Covey), but in the pages of the *Liberator* he never failed to offer his after-the-fact support for black resistance to slavery. Thus he had positive things to say about David Walker, Nat Turner, the rebels of the *Amistad* and the *Creole,* and (during the 1850s) the many whites and blacks who fought back against those attempting to enforce the fugitive slave law. Douglass, too, remained conflicted on black violence. To be sure, in his early years as a Garrisonian moral suasionist he expressed his hesitancy about violence, but while with Garrison in Pendleton, Indiana, in 1842, he had fought back against proslavery attackers; in his *Narrative* he had displayed his recourse to violence against Covey; and in a remarkable speech delivered in Scotland in March 1846, he warned of the possibility of black violence in the manner of a David Walker or Nat Turner. He says about the white slaveholder: "I will not let him know the deadly enemies that continually surround him when pursuing the run-away, nor the unseen hands that are raised to strike him the deadly blow. I will not tell him the evils that hover over his path, nor ease the terrors I know rankle in his breast; I would rather show him that even when surrounded by those whom he thinks he has subdued and humbled, he is yet in the midst of death, and that the negro crouching at his feet, has it in his heart to level him with the dust."[51]

With its imagery of death and dust, and its sheer anger, the speech is one of Douglass's boldest statements about black violence, and it's notable that he voiced these sentiments while still nominally a Garrisonian. In 1853, seven years after delivering this speech and two years after breaking with Garrison, Douglass made slave violence the subject of *The Heroic Slave,* his only work of fiction. In the novella, Douglass uses the license of a fiction writer to reimagine the history of the rebellion on the U.S. slave ship *Creole* in 1841, the year Douglass became a Garrisonian abolitionist. As I argue in the next chapter, the novella is informed by Douglass's autobiographical investment in the life and heroic deeds of Madison Washington, the leader of the *Creole* rebellion who fights back against slavery in the way of a "Black Douglass." A fighting black Douglass has an important place in *Bondage and Freedom* as well.

❧ 3 ❧

HEROIC SLAVES

Madison Washington and
My Bondage and My Freedom

ANGERED BY THE ENGRAVING that Richard D. Webb used as the frontispiece to the first Dublin edition of the *Narrative* (Figure 4), Douglass had Webb change the dandyish image of a smiling Douglass for the second edition. But that didn't stop the Manchester-based Garrisonian Wilson Armistead from using a version of the engraving to illustrate a chapter on Douglass in his 1848 *A Tribute for the Negro*. In a review of Armistead's book in the *North Star*, Douglass again voiced his objections to the image, stating that the engraving in Armistead's book "has a much more kindly and amiable expression, than is generally thought to characterize the face of a fugitive slave." He then remarked on the larger problem of whites' representations of black people: "It seems to us next to impossible for white men to take likenesses of black men, without most grossly exaggerating their distinctive features."[1] As if to provide further evidence for Douglass's concerns about white misrepresentations, just a few months later the Massachusetts Unitarian minister Ephraim Peabody, in an admiring review of recent slave narratives by Douglass and several others, suggested that the slave authors' skills as writers could be credited to their "mixed blood" (with the implication that white blood is essential to authorship), and he chided Douglass for mistaking "violence and extravagance of expression and denunciation for eloquence." In his response to Peabody, Douglass ignored the comment about racial mixing and remarked with resignation about the critique of his supposedly overaggressive rhetoric: "This is undoubtedly well intended, and worthy of all consideration; yet we by no means admit the entire soundness of the ground on which it is based."[2] That ground, of course, was the perspective of a white man who, despite his antislavery predilections, remained anxious about black men.

As Douglass learned in his first decade as an antislavery lecturer and writer, African Americans faced distinct challenges when they chose to represent black lives in a white racist culture. Douglass addressed those challenges directly in the paratexts of his second autobiography, the 1855 *My Bondage and My Freedom*, which has a visually engaging title and dedication page, a preface by the publisher that incorporates a letter from Douglass about whites' misrepresentations of blacks, a daguerreotype of Douglass as a proud and imperious-looking black man (Figure 5), an introduction not by a white Garrisonian but by the black intellectual James McCune Smith, and an appendix that offers a selection of Douglass's speeches from 1846, the year after he published the Boston edition of the *Narrative*, to 1855. In the letter to his publisher with which he begins the volume, Douglass insists that he would have preferred having someone else write his life history, but then he abandons the false modesty and explains why he decided to write this second autobiography on his own:

> I see . . . that there are special reasons why I should
> write my own biography, in preference to employing
> another to do it. Not only is slavery on trial, but un-
> fortunately, the enslaved people are also on trial. It is
> alleged, that they are, naturally, inferior; that they are
> *so low* in the scale of humanity, and so utterly stupid,
> that they are unconscious of their wrongs, and do
> not apprehend their rights. Looking, then, at your
> request, from this stand-point, and wishing every-
> thing of which you think me capable to go to the
> benefit of my afflicted people, I part with my doubts
> and hesitation, and proceed to furnish you the de-
> sired manuscript.

Douglass's letter is immediately followed by Smith's "Introduction," which presents Douglass as "a Representative American—
a type of his countrymen," who, has "raised himself by his own
efforts to the highest position in society." But as Smith makes
clear, Douglass is also a black man and a former slave. Working
against the grain of whites' assumptions about blacks' inferiority
and savagery, Smith concludes his introduction by underscoring
what Douglass (in a belated rebuke to Peabody) says about himself in *Bondage and Freedom:* that he got "his energy, persever-
ance, eloquence, invective, sagacity, and wide sympathy," not
from his white slave owner (and father), but from the "negro
blood" of his black mother.[3]

With the help of Smith and his own letter to his publisher,
Douglass framed his second autobiography in relation to the
historiographical issue of how to represent and interpret a black
life—a life that happened to be his own. Two years earlier he
had addressed similar issues about black representation in his

FIGURE 5. *My Bondage and My Freedom* (New York: Miller, Orton and Mulligan, 1855), frontispiece. Image reproduction courtesy of the Williams College Archives and Special Collections, Williamstown, Massachusetts.

1853 novella, *The Heroic Slave*. An imaginative retelling of the *Creole* slave rebellion of 1841, the novella was the culmination of Douglass's interest in the leader of the rebellion, Madison Washington, a black man who had come to the nation's attention just three months after Douglass first spoke to Garrison's Massachusetts Anti-Slavery Society at Nantucket. By late 1841 and 1842, Washington and Douglass were both regularly featured on the pages of Garrison's *Liberator*. Douglass was fascinated by what he read about Washington during his early years as a Garrisonian, and his interest was not short-lived. Soon after publishing the *Narrative*, he began lecturing on Washington while working on the Dublin editions of the *Narrative*. Upon his return to the United States, Douglass continued to lecture on Washington as he moved toward the political abolitionism that led to his formal break with Garrison in 1851. He published *The Heroic Slave*, a novella in part about interracial friendship, at a time when Garrison had begun maligning his reputation, and he commented on Washington again in the late 1850s and during the Civil War. In his writings and lectures about the leader of the *Creole* rebellion, Douglass drew on a variety of sources in an effort to produce a compelling representation of a militant black hero for a culture that he thought had not given Washington his due. In addition, Douglass used Washington to reflect on his own life, and (especially in the novella) used his life as a "source" for Washington. In surprising ways, *The Heroic Slave*, Douglas's principal work on the *Creole* rebellion and his only work of fiction, can be thought of as one of the lives of Frederick Douglass.

In a pioneering reading of *The Heroic Slave* published in 1982, Robert B. Stepto was the first to discuss parallels between Douglass and Washington suggestive of Douglass's autobiographical investment in the hero of the *Creole* rebellion: "Douglass might very possibly have been attracted to Washington's story because it in some measure revises his *own* story. Both Washington and Douglass began their escape attempts in 1835, and both gained public attention as free men in the fall of 1841." Eric J. Sundquist also notes "resonant autobiographical overtones" in Douglass's 1853 novella.[4] Though I'm wary of pushing autobiographical parallels and resonances too hard, I will be offering considerable evidence that Douglass was inspired by Washington during the 1840s (when he was avowedly committed to Garrisonian non-violence); that he saw the *Creole* rebellion as an important test case for thinking about the role of black violence in the anti-slavery movement; and that he saw parallels between his and Washington's life histories that spoke to his ongoing concerns about black (self-)representation. In *The Heroic Slave*, Douglass depicts key moments in the life of a heroic slave through a complex mélange of biography, autobiography, and fiction.[5] He works with a similarly complex mélange in *Bondage and Freedom*.

In the opening of the novella, Douglass addresses the historiographical challenge of writing about Washington by asserting that the chronicler of an African American hero will necessarily have to draw on "marks, traces, possibles, and probabilities." Douglass begins his own life history in the *Narrative* by declaring that "I have no accurate knowledge of my age, never having seen any authentic record containing it."[6] Even in his autobiographical writings, Douglass assumed the role of biographer, historian, and to some extent fiction writer when exploring the uncertainties of his own life. Because *The Heroic Slave* was published two years before *Bondage and Freedom*, Sundquist and William McFeely describe the novella as a "bridge" (Sundquist) or "way station" (McFeely) that charts Douglass's move away from Garrison and toward a more militant revolutionary politics in his second full autobiography.[7] I would suggest that all of Douglass's autobiographical works, including the *Narrative* and *Bondage and Freedom,* can be regarded as "bridges" or "way stations" that look forward to the next autobiographical iteration; such is the nature of the seriality of his autobiographical writings. But *The Heroic Slave* can also be read in its historical moment of 1853 as a *culmination* of Douglass's thinking about black (auto)biography, black revolutionism, and the possibilities of interracial friendship, even as it looks forward to (and influences) Douglass's next major autobiographical work.

As Douglass observed in a number of his writings and speeches about the *Creole* rebellion, Washington received considerable assistance from white abolitionists, both when he made his way to Canada after escaping from slavery in Virginia and when he later chose to return to Virginia in an attempt to rescue his wife. Though Douglass came to be suspicious of Garrison and his colleagues, he developed friendships with a number of white abolitionists in the British Isles, and soon after returning to the United States in 1847 became good friends with the white antislavery leader Gerrit Smith. Based in Peterboro, New York, around a hundred miles east of Rochester, Smith was a wealthy philanthropist who had embraced the antislavery movement during the 1830s and then broken with Garrison in 1840 over such key issues as moral suasion and the question of whether abolitionists should work within the established political system. In 1840, Smith founded the antislavery Liberty Party, arguing for the importance of the electoral process in bringing about social change. And he argued as well that those participating in the antislavery struggle had the moral right to use violence to fight back against the violence of slavery. During the 1840s, he donated money to antislavery causes while offering financial assistance to a number of free blacks. Douglass believed that Smith, whom he first met in 1848, treated him and other blacks as equals in ways that the Garrisonians did not. Smith also offered Douglass considerable financial support for his newspaper. Significantly, *The Heroic Slave*, a novella that includes a character who is friendly with Smith, was serialized in *Frederick Douglass' Paper*, which Smith helped to fund. Given Douglass's vexed relationship with Garrison and his more affirmative bond with Smith, it is not surprising that the politics of interracial friendship would become an especially important concern of both *The Heroic Slave* and *My Bondage and My Freedom*.[8]

Unlike the first two chapters, which focused on versions of Douglass's first autobiography during the 1845–1846 period, this chapter ranges widely over twenty years of Douglass's writings. I examine Douglass's responses to the *Creole* rebellion while a Garrisonian abolitionist and then turn to the historiographical, political, and (auto)biographical issues that Douglass takes up in both *The Heroic Slave* and *Bondage and Freedom*. For about twenty years, Madison Washington served as a focal point for Douglass's thinking about race, nation, interracial friendship, and black revolution. In certain respects Washington had a role in guiding Douglass from Garrison's moral-suasionist Massachusetts Anti-Slavery Society to Smith's politically radical and militant Liberty Party, and thus in guiding him toward his second autobiography, which is dedicated to Smith and expresses considerable hostility toward Garrison. It is no wonder that Douglass sometimes saw his life history as not only parallel with Washington's, but merged. Though Douglass doesn't mention Washington in *Bondage and Freedom*, his second autobiography tells a Washington-inflected story of his own emergence as a black revolutionary freedom fighter. That story begins in 1841, when Douglass the Garrisonian read about Washington the revolutionary in Garrison's newspaper, the *Liberator.*

THE SPIRIT OF FREEDOM

We do not know exactly what Douglass read in order to tell the story of the *Creole* rebellion in his lectures, essays, and novella, but he certainly would have read most if not all of the pieces published in the *Liberator.* As he remarked in the 1845 *Narrative,* he began reading the *Liberator* in 1839, shortly after he arrived in New Bedford, in order to get "a pretty correct idea of the principles, measures, and spirit of the anti-slavery reform." The *Liberator,* he avowed in his 1845 autobiography, "became my meat and my drink."⁹ Ironically, it was in the *Liberator,* the bastion of Garrisonian moral suasion, that Douglass first came to understand that a black man who resorted to violence could be regarded as a heroic slave.

To review the facts of the *Creole* rebellion as they were reported in the *Liberator* and a number of other newspapers across the nation: In October 1841, the American slaver *Creole* set sail from Hampton Roads harbor in Richmond, Virginia, with a white crew, several slave owners and traders (and their families), numerous boxes of tobacco, and 135 slaves who were being transported to New Orleans for public sale. A week into the voyage, Madison Washington and eighteen other slaves rose up against the masters, killing one of the slave owners and seriously injuring the captain. Two of the slaves were killed as well. After gaining control of the *Creole,* the rebels compelled the crew to take the ship to

Nassau, New Providence, in the British Bahamas, knowing that slavery was no longer legal in the British empire. The white sailors expected British authorities to come to their aid; they were therefore shocked when they realized that those in charge in Nassau were sympathetic to the rebels and had no interest in getting back into the business of remanding fugitive slaves. Though the leaders of the rebellion were detained by British authorities for several months, eventually all were set free and most probably chose to remain in Nassau.

The *Creole* rebellion occurred two years after the more famous rebellion aboard the Cuban slaver the *Amistad* and a few months after the Supreme Court ruled in favor of freeing the *Amistad*'s leader, Joseph Cinqué, and his fellow rebels, who had been imprisoned in Connecticut jailhouses since July 1839. The *Creole* got less attention than the *Amistad* because the rebels escaped to the British Bahamas and thus were not available for newspaper interviews and other forms of publicity. Still, there was considerable interest in the case. The *Creole* was an American slaver, after all, and southerners were disturbed by the specter of black revolt (and the loss of human property), while antislavery northerners saw in both the *Amistad* and *Creole* uprisings clear indications of blacks' human desires for freedom. The *Creole* rebellion also exacerbated tensions between the British and the United States during a time when President John Tyler's secretary of state, Daniel Webster, was negotiating the boundary issues central to what would become the Webster-Ashburton Treaty of August 1842. Sympathetic to the legal rights of the slave owners, Tyler and Webster were outraged by Britain's failure to return the slaves to their owners and came close to breaking off negotiations. In an effort to make the case for remanding the rebels, the U.S. consul at Nassau, John F. Bacon, took testimony from the officers and crew of the *Creole* early in November 1841; and in an effort to help the ship's owners recover their losses through insurance claims, the officers and crew retold their story later that month to a notary public in New Orleans. The crew's New Orleans testimony, known as the "Protest," first appeared in the December 3, 1841, issue of the New Orleans *Advertiser* and then was reprinted in a number of newspapers, North and South, including the *Liberator*.

By reprinting the "Protest" in the December 31, 1841, *Liberator*, Garrison chose to share with his readers one of the most violent accounts of the *Creole* slave revolt. In a group deposition similar to what was compiled by U.S. consul Bacon and later printed in the 1842 Senate Documents of the 27th Congress, Madison Washington is described as the leader of rebels who were willing to kill whites and blacks alike. According to the whites' testimony in the "Protest," after one of Madison's co-conspirators wounded the captain with a shotgun blast, "Madison then shouted, 'We have begun and must go through. Rush, boys, rush aft, and we have them!' and calling to the slaves below, he said—'Come up, every one of you! If you don't lend a hand, I will kill you all, and throw you overboard.'" Douglass would eventually depict a heroically militant Washington in his 1853 novella, but in 1841, when he was a Garrisonian moral suasionist, he may well have been disturbed by the rebels' actions as portrayed in this account. The killing of the officer Hewell, for instance, is particularly brutal, at least as recalled by the white sailors in their "Protest": "He [Hewell] advanced, and they fell upon him with clubs, handspikes and knives. He was knocked down and stabbed in not less than twenty places; but he rose, got away from them, and staggered back to the cabin, exclaiming 'I am dead—the negroes have killed me!'"[10]

Were Washington and his fellow plotters brutal savages, as the "Protest" suggests, or freedom fighters? A week after publishing the "Protest," Garrison reprinted an article from the New York *Evangelist* titled "The Heroic Mutineers" that directly addressed the question of how to read the white officers' version of the black rebellion. Proclaiming that the *Creole* rebellion reveals "the nature of slavery—its deleterious influence, and the absolute necessity of its abolition," the anonymous writer says of the "Protest" itself: "The Protest is from the officers and crew of the Creole, given before a Notary Public, in New-Orleans, and cannot be supposed to represent in too favorable colors the conduct of the mutineers." For this anonymous writer, the mutineers were heroes, and no one was more heroic than the "one who wore a name unfit for a slave, but finely expressive for a hero, [who] seems to have been the master spirit—that name was Madison Washington!" Presenting Washington as the "splendid exemplification of the true heroic," the writer praises his "astonishing presence of mind and decision of character," and depicts him as an American revolutionary committed to "liberty or death." Crucially, and in ways that would have appealed to Garrison (and Douglass), the writer is also impressed by what he learned from the New Orleans "Protest" about how the "generous" Washington and his fellow rebels "exercised complete self-control over their passions," refusing to kill whites once they gained control of the ship.[11]

In addition to articles focused on the depositions of the white sailors, Garrison printed articles that drew on abolitionists' oral history about Washington. According to this history, Washington had made his way to Canada sometime after escaping from slavery in Virginia in the late 1830s, and then decided to return to Virginia in search of his wife. Garrison published a compelling article based on such oral testimony in the June 10, 1842, *Liber-*

ator. In "Madison Washington: Another Chapter in His History," an anonymous writer refers to Washington as "the leader of the 'Immortal Nineteen,' who fought for and obtained their liberty on board the Creole," while asserting that this was "but one chapter in the history of Madison Washington," and that a "new clue to the character of this hero of the Creole has just been furnished us." Eighteen months before the revolt, the writer reveals, Washington was living in Canada at the home of Hiram Wilson, a white man opposed to slavery, and had come "to love and rejoice in British liberty." But because he missed his wife, whom he loved more than freedom, Washington decided to return to the United States. With the help of Lindley Murray Moore, another white antislavery reformer, Washington passed through New York on his way to Virginia. There are gaps in the story, but the end result is that Washington, in "attempting to liberate his wife, was himself reenslaved. . . . So Madison, we suppose, was captured, and as a dangerous slave, sold for New-Orleans, and shipped with his 134 fellow sufferers."[12]

"Madison Washington: Another Chapter" points to issues that would become important to Douglass when he began to speak and write about Washington: the sense of Washington's life as having "chapters" (which Douglass would make into a structuring element of *The Heroic Slave*); the challenge to the biographer to use his or her historical imagination in relation to different kinds of sources; the importance of interracial friendship (the whites Wilson and Moore offered lodgings and money); and the idea that Washington's heroism can be understood in a variety of contexts, including a domestic one. William L. Andrews and others have dismissed the article as storytelling that to some extent pandered to sentimental readers. As Andrews remarks, "Clearly, a romantic dimension to Washington's story was something the

Liberator wanted to read into the scanty facts it had amassed about his pre-*Creole* past."[13] But the *Liberator* was doing more than simply inventing a Washington who would appeal to a wide range of readers; it was engaged in historical recovery based on stories told by whites and blacks who had met Washington, such as the Canadian Wilson, the Rochester abolitionist Moore (also mentioned in an April 1842 *National Anti-Slavery Standard* article about Washington), and the wealthy black abolitionist Robert Purvis, who claimed to have met Washington in 1841 as he passed through Philadelphia on his way from Canada to Virginia. In 1849, Douglass remarked in a speech that he had learned additional details about Washington from Purvis; and in 1889 Purvis told the full story of his meeting with Washington to a reporter for the Philadelphia *Inquirer*. According to this later account, Purvis met Washington at his Philadelphia home the same day he received a portrait of Cinqué that he had commissioned from the artist Nathaniel Jocelyn. Purvis attempted to dissuade Washington from returning to his wife, but Washington was so inspired by the portrait of the leader of the *Amistad* rebellion that he went ahead with his risky mission.[14] Whether the story of Washington's return for his wife came from Wilson, Moore, Purvis, or some other source, it circulated in antislavery newspapers and in conversation, and was considered by Douglass and many others to be part of Washington's history.

~❦~

Douglass's initial, though somewhat oblique, response to that history came in August 1843, when he attended the National Convention of Colored Citizens in Buffalo. Though the *Creole* wasn't directly debated by the delegates, the rebellion had an important place in the convention's main lecture, Henry Highland Garnet's "Address to the Slaves of the United States of America," one of the most rousing calls for slave resistance in the history of African American oratory. Adducing Lord Byron's famous injunction from *Childe Harold's Pilgrimage* (1812–1818) that "if hereditary bondsmen would be free, they must themselves strike the blow," Garnet instructed the slaves (who of course were not in attendance): "IT IS YOUR SOLEMN AND IMPERATIVE DUTY TO USE EVERY MEANS, BOTH MORAL, INTELLECTUAL, AND PHYSICAL, THAT PROMISE SUCCESS." Mainly Garnet focused on the physical, invoking a heroic genealogy of black rebels who had done precisely what he was now calling on U.S. slaves to do: "choose LIBERTY OR DEATH" by rising up against the masters. After extolling Haitian revolutionary Toussaint L'Ouverture, South Carolinian plotter Denmark Vesey, the "patriotic Nathaniel Turner [who] followed Denmark Veazie," and "the immortal Joseph Cinque, the hero of the Amistad," Garnet offered his most extensive praise for Madison Washington and his fellow rebels of the *Creole:*

> Next arose Madison Washington, that bright star of freedom, and took his station in the constellation of freedom. He was a slave on board the brig Creole, of Richmond, bound to New Orleans, that great slave mart, with a hundred and four others. Nineteen struck for liberty or death. But one life was taken, and the whole were emancipated, and the vessel was carried into Nassau, New Providence. Noble men!

Garnet concluded his talk with a rousing call to the slaves of the U.S. South: "Let your motto be Resistance! Resistance! Resistance!"[15] The lecture was then taken up by a committee of delegates charged to decide on whether to endorse it as convention policy. By a single vote, the committee chose not to make such an endorsement. Among those voting against the lecture was Frederick Douglass.

Given that Douglass just two years later in the *Narrative* was willing to depict his own resistance to Edward Covey, we might ask why the hesitation about resistance in 1843. One answer is that Douglass at this time was a Garrisonian moral suasionist who was loyal to Garrison and aware that even though the *Liberator* celebrated and defended black rebels, including Washington, Garrison himself did not endorse violence. Another answer is suggested by Douglass's comment on Garnet's speech, as recorded in the minutes of the convention:

> Frederick Douglass, not concurring with certain points in the address, nor with the sentiments advanced by Mr. Garnit [*sic*], arose . . . to reply to Mr. Garnit. Mr. Douglass remarked, that there was too much physical force, both in the address and the remarks of the speaker last up. He was for trying the moral means a little longer; that the address, could it reach the slaves, . . . while it might not lead the slaves to rise in insurrection for liberty, would, nevertheless, and necessarily be the occasion of an insurrection; and that was what he wished in no way to have any agency in bringing about, and what we were called upon to avoid.

Douglas's reference to "the moral means" puts him in Garrison's camp, but his concerns about an insurrection speak to other issues as well, such as his awareness as a fugitive slave of the overwhelming odds against mounting a successful slave rebellion—

a perspective he develops in the *Narrative* when he remarks on how carefully the whites watch over the slaves, to the point that the slaves believe there is "at every ferry a guard—on every bridge a sentinel—and in every wood a patrol."[16] In other words, there is something "autobiographical" about his opposition to the sentiments of the free black Garnet.

Still, despite his vote, Douglass probably found Garnet's speech inspirational, for the "Address to the Slaves" resonated with much of what Douglass was already saying as a Garrisonian lecturer. In his second extant speech as a paid lecturer for the Massachusetts Anti-Slavery Society, approximately two years before he voted against Garnet's speech, Douglass warned his audience at Hingham, Massachusetts: "the slaves are learning to read and write, and the time is fast coming, when they will act in concert, and effect their own emancipation, if justice is not done by some other extraneous agency." Two years after the Buffalo conference, and just days before the publication of his *Narrative*, Douglass was moving toward an even more radical position on black violence. He proclaimed in a speech delivered in New York City in May 1845: "You say to us, if you dare to carry out the principles of our fathers, we'll shoot you down. Others may tamely submit; not I. You may put the chains upon me and fetter me, but I am not a slave, for my master who puts the chains upon me, shall stand in as much dread of me as I do of him."[17] Several months after that speech, Douglass, the man who would not submit to chains, began to speak extensively about Madison Washington, the man who had escaped from chains, celebrating him, as Garnet had celebrated him, as a model for black heroic action. He celebrated him as well as a man not so very different from the man he himself was becoming.

Douglass's first extant comment on Washington came in his speech on "American Prejudice against Color," delivered in Cork,

Ireland, on October 23, 1845. Challenging white conceptions of black inferiority, Douglass displays his own intelligence, oratorical resources, and will to freedom by offering one of the more dramatic descriptions (as discussed in Chapter 2) of his heroic efforts to speak about slavery on board the *Cambria*. From the account of his defiance of the racists on the *Cambria*, he makes a sudden and surprising shift to Washington's rebellion on the *Creole*. So in his first public comments on Washington, Douglass presents two heroic blacks on board ships who evince a "love of freedom." Douglass refuses the metaphorical chains that would have kept him silent on the *Cambria;* Washington escapes from the chains of slavery. And Washington does so not as a black "savage" (the white stereotype of the black rebel), but as a pragmatic revolutionary who kills only when necessary for freedom. Douglass describes the scene as he imagines it on the *Creole:* "As he [Washington] came to the resolution he darted out of the hatchway, seized a handspike, felled the Captain—and found himself with his companions masters of the ship. He saved a sufficient number of the lives of those who governed the ship to reach the British Islands; there they were emancipated." The mention of the British Islands suggests another parallel between Douglass and Washington: they both took refuge in the British empire. At the conclusion of his speech, Douglass remarks that "our Congress was thrown into an uproar that *Maddison Washington* had in imitation of *George Washington* gained liberty. They branded him as being a thief, robber and murderer; they insisted on the British Government giving him back. The British Lion refused to send the bondsmen back."[18] The British Lion likewise stood by the heroic slave of the *Cambria* during his nearly two years in Britain.

Douglass's other lectures on Washington during his British tour offered a similar mix of autobiography and biography, while continuing to focus on contrasts between American and British responses to rebellious slaves. In a lecture delivered in Paisley, Scotland, on April 6, 1846, Douglass depicts Washington in Nassau as something like himself in Scotland, "basking under the free sun . . . of a free monarchical country." One month later, while in Edinburgh, Douglass spoke on "American and Scottish Prejudice against the Slave," remarking on connections between the "moral or intellectual" abilities of blacks and Washington's use of a measured strategic violence to gain his freedom. Turning to the diplomatic issues of the *Creole* case, which were relevant to Douglass's own status as a fugitive slave, he directs his ire at Daniel Webster. Douglass describes the diplomatic situation: "But this [the *Creole* rebellion] was not relished by brother Jonathan— he considered it as a grievous outrage—a national insult; and in- structed Mr. Webster, who was then Secretary of State, to de- mand compensation from the British Government for the injury done; and characterised the noble Maddison Washington as being a murderer, a tyrant, and a mutineer. And all this for the punish- ment of an act, which, according to all the doctrines 'professed' by Americans, ought to have been honoured and rewarded."[19] Linking Washington to the American revolutionary tradition that he (and Garrison) invoked in the 1845 *Narrative,* Douglass un- derscores the irony that it is the British, not Americans, who are most willing to honor black patriots.

Douglass delivered his fourth and final extant British lecture referring to Madison Washington on the occasion of the March 30, 1847, banquet in London honoring Douglass for his nearly two- year antislavery tour of Great Britain. In "Farewell to the British

People," Douglass again highlights parallels between his and Washington's situations, making it clear that he, just like Washington, had become a free man with the help of the British. Washington's freedom was ultimately enabled by the British justice system and government officials who refused to be intimidated by U.S. leaders; Douglass's freedom was enabled by the British supporters who purchased him out of slavery. Douglass depicts Daniel Webster as the enemy that he and Washington have in common, referring to how "this proud statesman [Webster] tells you, that if you do not send this noble negro back to chains and slavery, he will go to war with you." The British in Nassau resisted Webster, and Washington became a free man; the British in England, Ireland, and Scotland similarly offered Douglass refuge, and he was now "a free man" on the verge of returning to the United States to begin a new phase of his antislavery career.[20]

As described in Chapter 2, soon after his return Douglass infuriated Garrison, in effect ending their friendship, by establishing his own antislavery newspaper, the *North Star,* with the help of funds from his British supporters. Five days after the publication of the first issue on December 3, 1847, Douglass received a letter from the New York State philanthropist and reformer Gerrit Smith, the leader of the Liberty Party, welcoming him to his new home in Rochester. Accompanying the letter, which Smith signed "With great regard, Your friend and brother," was a five-dollar money order for a two-year subscription to the *North Star,* along with a deed to a parcel of land in upstate New York.[21]

Smith reached out to Douglass at a propitious time for both men. Increasingly at odds with Garrison on a wide range of issues, Douglass welcomed the support of a white antislavery leader who valued all forms of resistance to slavery, including physical resistance, a position Douglass himself began emphasizing in his speeches on Madison Washington. Smith and Douglass met in 1848, and as their friendship developed over the years leading to the Civil War, Douglass also valued an alliance with a white antislavery leader who worked in tandem with him while never expressing even a hint of racial condescension. Smith, who remained critical of Garrisonian abolition after breaking with the group in 1840, must have taken great pleasure in his burgeoning friendship with a famous black abolitionist leader who was once in the Garrisonian fold. As opposed to Garrison, Smith believed that the Constitution was an antislavery document (a position Douglass would publicly espouse by 1851). Thus Smith rejected one of the primary tenets of Garrisonian abolitionism: that participation in the political system was a mark of corruption. Central to Smith's political abolitionism was the belief that whites and blacks alike should be participating in the political process, and to that end, to return to Smith's letter to Douglass of December 1847, during the 1840s he gave away 140,000 acres to approximately 3,000 black settlers, with the goal of helping blacks meet New York State's $250 property requirement for voting.[22] In the context of Douglass's establishment of a newspaper that challenged the hegemony of Garrison's moral-suasionist *Liberator*, his more militant language, and his new friendship with a white political abolitionist, we need to consider the important place of Madison Washington in two of Douglass's speeches of the late 1840s, particularly the speech that has come to be known as "Slavery, the Slumbering Volcano," which he delivered in New York City on April 23, 1849, to approximately 1,200 black New Yorkers.

Douglass anticipated the tenor of that speech in "The Slave's Right to Revolt," delivered in Boston on May 30, 1848. Sounding like the black militant David Walker of the 1829 *Appeal to the Coloured Citizens of the World,* Douglass declares to the black men in his audience: "we are MEN! (Cheers.) You may pile up statutes against us and our manhood as high as heaven, and still we are not changed thereby. WE ARE MEN. (Immense cheering.)" In the course of the speech he celebrates Madison Washington, whose revolt resulted in the death of a white slave trader, in relation to Nat Turner, whose Southampton, Virginia, revolt resulted in the deaths of over sixty whites. "There are many Madison Washingtons and Nathaniel Turners in the South," Douglass proclaims, "who would assert their right to liberty, if you would take your feet from their necks, and your sympathy and aid from their oppressors." As he maintains one year later in "Slavery, the Slumbering Volcano," the slave masters, by their very practice of slavery, are in "a *state of war*" against blacks, and blacks should consider responding in kind with their own war of rebellion. Embracing the possibility of violence in the manner of a Madison Washington, Douglass says about the slaveholders:

> I want them to know that at least one coloured man in the Union, peace man though he is, would greet with joy the glad news should it come here to-morrow, that an insurrection had broken out in the Southern States. (Great applause.) I want them to know that a *black man* cherishes that sentiment. . . . Sir, I want to alarm the slaveholders, and not to alarm them by mere declamation or by mere bold assertions, but to show them that there is really danger in persisting in the crime of

continuing Slavery in this land. I want them to know that there are some Madison Washingtons in this country."[23]

Douglass imaginatively identifies himself as one of those Washingtons, and it is from this oddly personal and impassioned perspective that he retells the story of the *Creole*.

As in his earlier speeches, Douglass in "Slavery, the Slumbering Volcano" recounts how the fugitive slave Washington, after making his way to Canada, decides "in the true spirit of a noble-minded and noble-hearted man" to return for his wife in Virginia. Rejecting the advice of the man Douglass terms "my friend Gurney" (the white British abolitionist Joseph John Gurney, whom Washington may have met in Canada), and the black Philadelphian abolitionist Robert Purvis, Washington persists in his rescue attempt, even at the risk of being captured and reenslaved. Douglass then makes a chronological leap in the speech (which he would replicate in *The Heroic Slave*), for after mentioning Gurney and Purvis, Douglass says that "we see nothing more of Madison Washington, until we see him at the head of a gang of one hundred slaves [in Richmond, Virginia] destined for the Southern market."[24]

Something new about Douglass's perspective on Washington can be discerned in this lecture: there is an even greater degree of sympathetic identification. Imagining himself on board the *Creole*, Douglass seems to be directing his own gaze at the white slave trader who would be killed in the revolt, as if that man were his personal enemy: "I sometimes think I see him—walking the deck of that ship freighted with human misery, quietly smoking his segar, calmly and coolly calculating the value of human flesh beneath the hatchway." Washington watches that man, too, and on his eighth day at sea manages to remove his irons (in fact, Washington, who served as a cook, was probably not in irons), free eighteen others, and for a while work with the group to pretend that they are still under the power of their masters. Douglass describes the subsequent rebellion:

> About twilight on the ninth day, Madison, it seems, reached his head above the hatchway, looked out on the swelling billows of the Atlantic, and feeling the breeze that coursed over its surface, was inspired with the spirit of freedom. He leapt from beneath the hatchway, gave a cry like an eagle to his comrades beneath, saying, *we must go through.* (Great applause.) Suiting the action to the word, in an instant his guilty master was prostrate on the deck, and in a very few minutes Madison Washington, a black man, with woolly head, high cheek bones, protruding lip, distended nostril, and retreating forehead, had the mastery of that ship, and under his direction, that brig was brought safely into the port of Nassau, New Providence.

In this dramatic scene, Douglass himself seems to be feeling the breeze infused with "the spirit of freedom." There is also a clear racial identification between the black man telling the story and the black hero who acted on the *Creole*. With his reference to Washington's "woolly head" and other exaggerated features, Douglass mocks the minstrel stereotypes and racial exaggerations of the time. Speaking to his primarily black audience in New York City, and still as if somewhat "inside" Washington's head, Douglass takes note of reporters on the scene and uses their presence to address the South from the perspective of a black revolutionary who, in the way he had been viewing the cigar-smoking slave trader, has the region's slaveholders in his sights: "There are more Madison Washingtons in the South, and the time may not be distant when the whole South will present again a scene something similar to the deck of the Creole."[25]

Issuing a threat from his imagined place on the deck of the *Creole*, Douglass implicitly tells an autobiographical story, as mediated through Washington, of his increasing attraction to the black revolutionary tradition that had been so powerfully invoked in Garnet's 1843 "Address to the Slaves." In doing so, he tells the related autobiographical story of his impending public break with the moral-suasionist Garrison, the man whose views had influenced Douglass's decision to vote against Garnet's "Address," and of his firming alliance with the political activist Smith, one of the men who would eventually help to fund John Brown's attack on Harpers Ferry. Imagining himself at sea on the *Creole*, he also taps into the culture's increasingly pervasive ship of state imagery that conceived of the nation, in the midst of the debates that would culminate in the Compromise of 1850, as facing storms, mutinies, and other possible disturbances threatening to bring about a national shipwreck. Douglass would continue to work with such imagery in the early 1850s, and at a key moment of his famous lecture of 1852, "What to the Slave Is the Fourth of July?," he offers a prophesy: "From the round top of your ship of state, dark and threatening clouds may be seen. Heavy billows, like mountains in the distance, disclose to the leeward huge forms of flinty rocks! That *bolt* drawn, that *chain* broken, and all is lost." Douglass wrote these words just a few months after he received a letter from the black abolitionist William C. Nell, who reported that "Nassau is the home of the heroes of the

Creole. Madison Washington himself is there." Nell's letter would have brought Washington back to the forefront of Douglass's mind at a time when he was at odds with Garrison and had joined with Smith in calling for violent resistance to the Compromise of 1850's Fugitive Slave Law. In 1852, after three years of not commenting on Washington, Douglass returned to the heroic black man who had broken from the chains of slavery, writing a novella that he viewed in personal terms, as he confided in a June 1852 letter to Henry Wadsworth Longfellow, as "my *'fugitive Slave Ship.'*"[26]

THEIR HEROIC CHIEF AND DELIVERER

Douglass initially published *The Heroic Slave* in the 1853 *Autographs for Freedom,* a fundraising miscellany of stories, poems, and essays by black and white abolitionists, edited by Douglass's British supporter and friend Julia Griffiths. The purpose of the volume was to raise money for Douglass's financially struggling newspaper, now titled *Frederick Douglass' Paper,* which Griffiths, who (somewhat scandalously) had been living with the Douglasses since 1849, helped to manage. Each selection was followed by a reproduction of the signature, or autograph, of the contributing author, thereby marking the selections as highly personal contributions to what the volume suggested were the interrelated causes of freedom and Douglass's newspaper. For many of the contributors, Garrisonian moral suasion was no longer an option in the wake of the newly firmed-up Fugitive Slave Law. *The Heroic Slave*, for instance, appeared between essays celebrating the Hungarian revolutionary Louis Kossuth and the Cuban revolutionary Plácido, with the suggestion that both men could be viewed as models for revolutionary leadership in the United States. But even as Douglass increasingly advocated violent resistance to slavery, he held onto ideals of interracial cooperation and never relinquished his belief that writing itself, as a mode of moral suasion, could help to bring about social change. In that regard, Harriet Beecher Stowe's participation in *Autographs* was significant, for the 1853 volume, to which she contributed a poem and short story, appeared less than a year after the book publication of *Uncle Tom's Cabin* (1852). Going against the grain of Martin Delany and other black abolitionists distressed by what they perceived as the novel's racialism, paternalism, and colonizationism, Douglass argued that *Uncle Tom's Cabin* could serve the pragmatic ends of galvanizing white support for antislavery. Thus he championed the novel in his newspaper while attempting to develop a friendship with Stowe that he hoped would lead her to fund a black mechanics institute in Rochester. Although there are aspects of *The Heroic Slave* that revise Stowe's racialism—unlike Stowe, Douglass depicts a dark-skinned man who is willing to use violence to achieve black freedom—the novella, which focuses on a white man responding sympathetically to the plight of a black man, is very much of the *Uncle Tom's Cabin* moment.[27]

But *The Heroic Slave* is also very much of Douglass's Gerrit Smith moment. Partly in response to Griffiths's aggressive fundraising, Smith in 1851 promoted the merger of Douglass's *North Star* with Smith's own *Liberty Party Paper* to create *Frederick Douglass' Paper*, offering Douglass a subsidy of $100 a month for two years. In practical terms, the merger was not really a merger, for Douglass remained the sole editor, though an editor who shared Smith's beliefs about the value of interracial cooperation *and* the need for activist interventions in the political arena. Douglass viewed Smith's participation in the successful October

1851 plot to free the fugitive slave William "Jerry" McHenry in Syracuse, New York, as exemplary of Smith's willingness to take interracial cooperation to the next level—what Douglass and Smith called "the Jerry level"—in using violence to resist the slave power. Douglass was therefore thrilled when Smith was elected to Congress in November 1852. "The cup of my joy is full," he wrote Smith upon hearing the news of the election. "You will go to Congress with the 'Jerry Level' in your hand— regarding slavery as *'naked piracy.'*" If slavery is regarded as a form of "naked piracy," or what Douglass in an earlier letter to Smith called *"Lawless Violence,"* then violent resistance really was heroic, which is precisely the point of Douglass's novella about a black revolt at sea that he completed right around the time he sent Smith his letter on piracy.[28]

In *The Heroic Slave*, Douglass tells the story of Madison Washington in four distinct parts, or chapters, drawing on the oral and printed history, including his own speeches, central to the cultural conversation on the *Creole* during the 1840s. Dialogue, soliloquies, and other forms of talk predominate in each of the four parts, which at times read more like acts in a play than chapters in a novella. As is true of many U.S. plays of the 1850s, such as theatrical versions of *Uncle Tom's Cabin*, melodrama and coincidence have a central place in *The Heroic Slave*; coincidence itself works as an artful shorthand that allows Douglass to move forward in history from 1835, the historical setting of Part I, to 1841, the historical setting of Parts III and IV. In all four parts, Douglass provides Washington with the opportunity to tell his story through oratorical set pieces reminiscent of Douglass's oratorical style. For good reason, the novella sometimes has the feel of a play starring Frederick Douglass.

But *The Heroic Slave* is much more than Douglass's "fantasy of his own heroism," as McFeely somewhat patronizingly terms the novella.[29] It is a historiographical meditation on the challenge of writing a black life in a white racist culture—the very challenge that Douglass takes up in his own life writings. Thus Douglass begins *The Heroic Slave* not with a scene between the two main characters—the Virginia slave Washington and the sympathetic white Listwell of Ohio—but with a philosophical discussion of the historiographical issues critical to black (auto)biography. Why is it the case, Douglass asks at the opening of the novella, that there are biographies, autobiographies, and histories of white Virginian "statesmen and heroes," but none of black Virginian heroes? One answer, he says, is obvious: that white culture tells stories about itself and simply is incapable of perceiving the existence of a black hero, even one with the wonderfully resonant name of Madison Washington. But there's a larger issue, too, which helps to explain why white Virginians of "ordinary parts" get more attention than one of the "bravest of her children," and that has to do with the archives. Unlike the typical white, the slave Washington holds "no higher place in the records of that grand old Commonwealth than is held by a horse and ox." Accordingly, Douglass states at the outset that the best he will be able to offer readers of his historical fiction are "Glimpses of this great character" drawn from "marks, traces, possibles, and probabilities."[30] With respect to such marks and traces, there is absolutely no evidence suggesting that Washington was spied on by a white man and then, five years later, was aided by the same white man on his way to Canada (Parts I and II of the novella), and there is no evidence of a white man giving Washington files that would enable his escape from the *Creole* (Part III). The novella stays closest to the "possibles, and probabilities" in the concluding Part IV, when Douglass provides a white officer's version of the rebellion that draws on the actual depositions of the *Creole*'s white officers. Overall, *The Heroic Slave* is a compelling mix of fact and fiction that self-consciously addresses the challenge of knowing and representing the life of a black hero. If that black hero at times seems a blend of Washington and Douglass, so much the better for the light the novella casts on Douglass's conception of himself as an autobiographer, biographer, and black freedom fighter in the early 1850s.

Such a blending of the two black heroes is crucial to the novella's opening scene, in which Washington in 1835, six years before the *Creole* rebellion, delivers a soliloquy in a pine woods in Virginia that has oratorical similarities to Douglass's apostrophe to the Chesapeake in the 1845 *Narrative*. The enslaved Washington regards the birds of the woods, as Douglass regards the boats on the Chesapeake, as the very incarnation of the freedom he desires: "They *live free*. . . . They fly where they list by day, and retire in freedom at night." Like Douglass's famous apostrophe, Washington's soliloquy is meant to be overheard, which is to say that both speech acts are highly performative. Overheard by Listwell, who remains in hiding when he notes that the speaker is a black man with "a brow as dark and as glossy as the raven's wing," the visiting Ohioan finds himself stimulated by a black speaker who (like Douglass) knows how to elicit sympathetic responses from whites anxious about black bodies. According to the narrator, Listwell had "long desired to sound the mysterious depths of the thoughts and feelings of a slave," and while listening to Washington's artfully crafted words, he happily believes that he has accomplished that goal. For good reason, then, the critic Carrie Hyde describes Listwell's extended spying on the eloquent black speaker as a form of "eroticized surveillance." But as it turns out, the pleasure that Listwell experiences in Washington's oratory is more than simply erotic. Stirred by Washington's declaration of his love of freedom and his devotion to his family, Listwell has been thoroughly transformed. He proclaims to the forest after listening to Washington: "From this hour I am an abolitionist." Given his cross-racial responsiveness to Washington's rhetoric, Listwell, who indeed does listen well, can be taken as an imaginative surrogate of Douglass's ideal white auditor or reader. In short, the opening scene provides a master class in Douglass's rhetorical genius.[31]

This is a pivotal early moment in the novella, worth keeping in mind when Douglass later appears to present Washington as overly dependent on the friendship of a somewhat limited white man. Much that happens in *The Heroic Slave* is the result of coincidence or even the happenstances of the weather,[32] but in this first section something critical to the overall novella occurs through human agency: black oratory, in an autobiographical mode similar to Douglass's own oratory, creates a white abolitionist. Though we don't see anything in the novella about what Listwell's newfound abolitionism means for his day-to-day life, there is a clear sense that the assistance he will later offer Washington is the result of what Washington's words have earlier done to him. It is equally clear that the interracial friendship that develops between the two men has been forged and shaped by Washington.[33]

With Listwell's announcement of his conversion to abolitionism at the end of Part I, we could imagine the dropping of a curtain and the ensuing audience applause. With Part II, which seems like Act 2, the metaphorical curtain rises and the scene jumps forward five years to the winter of 1840, as "Mr. and Mrs. Listwell sat together by the fireside of their own happy home, in the State of Ohio." In a scene modeled on the Senator and Mrs. Bird chapter in *Uncle Tom's Cabin*, Douglass describes the arrival at a white home in Ohio not of a light-complected fugitive slave woman with her son, but of the black-skinned fugitive slave Madison Washington. In Stowe, matriarchy rules; in *The Heroic Slave*, Listwell is clearly the patriarch of the household, and he asserts a certain power over Washington by revealing his earlier spying: "I have seen your face, and heard your voice before. I am glad to see you. *I know all.*"[34] Initially unsettled by Listwell's revelations, Washington quickly realizes the powerful effect his words have had on his secret white auditor, so he chooses to tell a story that is calculated to enlist the Listwells in his effort to make his way to Canada.

The strands of Washington's dramatic story—his escape from slavery, his decision to live in the swamps so he could visit with his wife and two children, and his eventual journey north—work together to create sympathy and political common cause. In a significant "autobiographical" moment that evokes Douglass's current common cause with Gerrit Smith, Washington tells how he felt justified in stealing food in order to avoid starvation while making his way to Canada. Listwell, who can seem a bit timid, nonetheless condones Washington's "illegal" actions and then rather startlingly, and anachronistically for a scene set in 1840, tells Washington that his own views on stealing and other forms of resistance have been influenced by his conversations with Gerrit Smith (Douglass's new friend of the late 1840s). Applauding Washington's act of theft, Listwell remarks, "And just there you were right, . . . I once had doubts on this point myself, but a conversation with Gerrit Smith, (a man, by the way, that I wish you could see, for he is a devoted friend of your race, and I know he would receive you gladly,) put an end to all my doubts on this point." There are additional autobiographical resonances in this section. After Listwell brings the fugitive slave Washington to a ship with "liberty-loving passengers" at Lake Erie, Part II concludes with Washington's December 1840 letter of thanks from Windsor, Canada. In the letter, which Washington signs "your profoundly grateful friend," Washington tells his "dear Friend" Listwell that "I nestle in the mane of the British lion, protected by his mighty paw from the talons and the beak of the American eagle."[35] The language anticipates the protection Washington will receive from the "British lion" after the *Creole* rebellion, and speaks as well to Douglass's situation in Britain circa 1845–1847.

The opening sections of *The Heroic Slave* provide the "possibles" to the prehistory of the *Creole* rebellion. In Part III, Douglass moves the action forward to 1841, the year of the actual rebellion. The setting is a tavern near Richmond, and coincidence is again central to the novella's theatrical form: Listwell arrives at the tavern the day before Washington is to be shipped to New Orleans on the *Creole* with 130 other slaves. As a historian, Douglass presents the tavern as a metaphor or synecdoche for the decline of Virginia from the glory days of 1776, even as the drunken Virginians cling to the idea (which Douglass demolishes in the novella's prefatory paragraphs) of Virginia's illustrious historical tradition. The connections between the novella's opening historiographical remarks and Part III are underscored by a new self-consciousness in Douglass's storytelling, for Douglass now presents the narrator as a historian who has actually spoken to Listwell as part of his effort to construct Washington's history. Again and again the narrator shares with the reader what "Mr. Listwell says" (presumably to the narrator) about his encounters with Washington. For instance, when Listwell ventures outside and views a slave coffle "for the first time in his life," with "mothers, fathers, daughters, brother, sisters" who are "to be sold and separated from home, and from each other *forever*," the Ohioan abolitionist, who is now called "our informant," "said he almost doubted the existence of a God of justice!"[36]

It is from the "informant," then, that the narrator reports on Washington speaking from within a slave coffle to the man he calls "a friend of mine." As with his earlier stories, Washington's autobiographical account is shaped to have an impact on Listwell (and readers of *Autographs for Freedom*). Washington tells the story, which Douglass would have gleaned from the 1842 *Liberator* article "Madison Washington: Another Chapter in His History," about how he began to miss his wife, Susan, after he escaped to Canada. So he made his way back to Virginia, where (in a scene Douglass invents) his failed attempt at a rescue leads to the death of his wife and his reenslavement. Listening and sympathizing as a friend, Listwell can't resist criticizing Washington for his "madness" in returning to a slave state and taking such risks. Uncertain about how he can help his black friend, Listwell feebly offers Washington $10 while urging him to "trust in God."[37] Quickly aware of the limits of his initial response, however, he returns to the coffle just before the *Creole* disembarks for New Orleans and manages to smuggle to Washington "three strong *files*."[38] That crucial act, which will allow Washington and his compatriots to use violence to gain their freedom, is the end result of Washington's rhetorically strategic autobiographical storytelling. Through his words, the black man transforms the white man into an abolitionist who in 1841 comes close to rising to what Douglass and Smith in the late 1840s and 1850s called the "Jerry Level."[39]

But then Douglass abruptly and rather audaciously drops List-well from the novella's concluding Part IV, which is set at a marine coffeehouse in Richmond two months after the slave revolt on the *Creole*. Continuing to work with dramatic form, Douglass presents a conversation between Jack Williams, a blustery sailor who believes the revolt "was the result of ignorance of the real character of *darkies* in general," and Tom Grant, the first mate on the *Creole*, who believes that whites like Williams "underrate the courage as well as the skill of these negroes." The revolt itself is described retrospectively by Grant, with the help of speechifying remarks from Washington that Grant incorporates into his story. More than the other sections of the novella, Part IV is grounded in historical fact, drawing on documents from the *Creole*'s post-revolt history. It is also grounded in Douglass's political history. Ten years before publishing *The Heroic Slave*, we recall, Douglass as a loyal Garrisonian had voted against Garnet's "Address to the Slaves" at the black convention in Buffalo. That speech had urged the slaves to adopt violent resistance in the spirit of Madison Washington, and had adduced Byron's revolutionary call in *Childe Harold*. Indicative of Douglass's rejection of moral suasionism and of his post-*Narrative* embrace of a tradition of black freedom fighting, one of the two epigraphs to Part IV of *The Heroic Slave* is a version of the injunction from Byron/Garnet: "Know yet not / Who would be free, *themselves* must strike the blow."[40]

Choosing to tell the story of those who struck the blow on the *Creole* through a conversation between two proslavery whites, Douglass ingeniously foregrounds the historiographical problem addressed in the novella's prefatory paragraphs about whites' inability to acknowledge black heroism. Among Douglass's striking choices in this final section is to have Williams's representative racism refuted, not by the narrator, but by the proslavery white southerner Grant, who defends his white manhood by making the case for Washington's intelligence, bravery, and humanity. Arguably, it is his apprehension of that humanity that leads Grant to declare "that this whole slave-trading business is a disgrace and scandal to Old Virginia." And yet he is unable to renounce southern slave culture. Thus when Williams asserts that Grant is "as good an abolitionist as Garrison himself," Grant angrily responds: *"That man does not live who shall offer me an insult with impunity."*[41] Grant remains a proslavery southerner by virtue of his hatred for Garrison. Douglass may have broken with Garrison, and their relationship would become even worse after the publication of *The Heroic Slave*, but in this exchange he pays tribute to the Massachusetts antislavery leader by deploying him as the figure of the South's most infamous abolitionist.

Prompted by Williams's continued insinuations of his cowardice and abolitionist sympathies, Grant finally describes the *Creole* rebellion itself. Much of what he tells Williams follows the known facts, while providing a perspective, similar to what Douglass would have read in the 1841 "Protest," about what the rebellion must have looked like to the surprised white sailors. As Grant recalls, "the very deck seemed covered with fiends from the pit." Confronting those "fiends," Grant is knocked unconscious, and when he regains consciousness, Washington stands nearby. And so Grant engages Washington in a conversation, which means that during Grant's extended recounting of the *Creole* rebellion he is often ventriloquizing the words of a black rebel who sounds very much like Douglass. For example, when Grant accuses Washington of being "a *black murderer*," Washington, in the mode of Douglass's 1852 "What to the Slave Is the

Fourth of July?," declares to Grant, who now speaks Washington's words to Williams and the other white racists in the Virginia coffeehouse: "God is my witness that LIBERTY, not *malice* is the motive for this night's work. I have done no more to those dead men yonder, than they would have done to me in like circumstances. We have struck for our freedom. . . . We have done that which you applaud your fathers for doing, and if we were murderers, *so were they.*" Like Listwell, Grant comes under the sway of the Douglass-like black speaker. But he refuses to help Washington until the "murderer" saves him from a black rebel about to club him with a handspike (this is a scene that draws on Douglass's reading of the historical Washington's rescue of the white officer named Zephaniah C. Gifford as described by Gifford himself in the 1841 "Protest" and the January 19, 1842, Senate Documents of the 27th Congress). Grant subsequently agrees to sail the ship to Nassau, not because he recognizes Washington's humanity (which is how Douglass and other antislavery writers had understood Washington's act of saving the white officer and keeping the killing on board the *Creole* to a minimum), but because he assumes he will be helped by "the American consul at that port" and that the "murderers" will be brought "to trial."[42]

Significantly, the diplomatic issues that were so central to Douglass's earlier lectures—the role of Daniel Webster and the sympathetic British officials—do not have a place in *The Heroic Slave*. In a bold revisionary move, Douglass chooses to blacken Nassau, presenting his black American hero in a larger diasporic context. Despite his name, Madison Washington by the end of the novella seems less a James Madison or George Washington than a Toussaint L'Ouverture. The concluding paragraph of the novella, which is told from Grant's perspective, describes the

Creole's arrival in Nassau. There are no whites to be seen. Instead, Grant reports, "a company of *black* soldiers came on board, for the purpose, as they said, of protecting the property." The novella ends not with the appearance of white British authorities or the white U.S. consul, but with the former slaves parading down the gangway behind the black leader who has helped to liberate them. The appalled Grant describes his last vision of Washington and his fellow rebels: "uttering the wildest shouts of exultation, they marched, amidst the deafening cheers of a multitude of sympathizing spectators, under the triumphant leadership of their heroic chief and deliverer, MADISON WASHINGTON."[43]

The final words of the novella are "MADISON WASHINGTON," and directly beneath those two words is the signature "Frederick Douglass" (Figure 6). With the juxtaposition of the two names on the closing page of the first printing of the novella in the 1853 *Autographs for Freedom*, it is difficult not to read the ending of the novella as something like this: "the triumphant leadership of their heroic chief and deliverer, MADISON WASHINGTON/Frederick Douglass." The critic Ivy Wilson writes that here and throughout the novella "it is as if the author is inserting himself into the protagonist, as if Douglass is attempting to make himself Washington."[44] McFeely and others have ridiculed Douglass for the way that fantasy or wish fulfillment can seem to inform his characterization of Washington, especially in this final section. But rather than scoff at Douglass, we might take his strong identification with Washington as similar to Flaubert's identification with the heroine of his most famous novel when he reputedly declared: *"Madame Bovary, c'est moi."* In his lecture "Slavery, the Slumbering Volcano," and in *The Heroic Slave* in particular, Douglass, precisely because of his

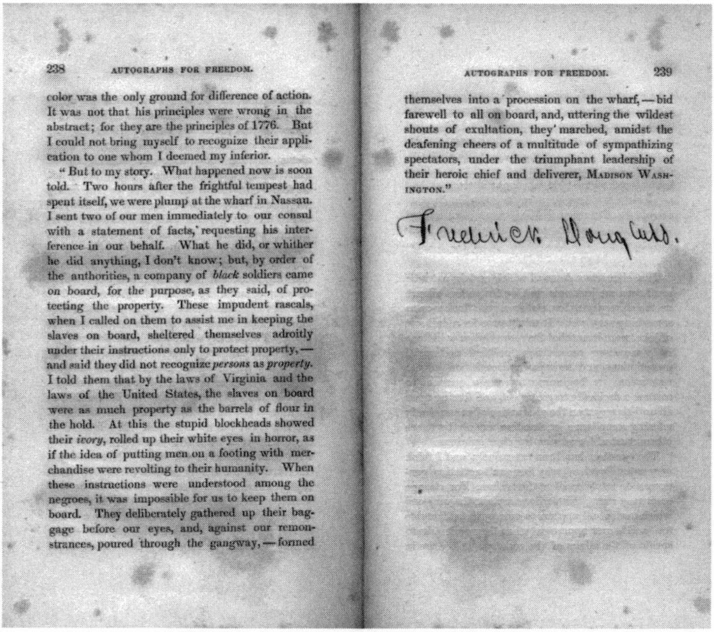

238 AUTOGRAPHS FOR FREEDOM.

color was the only ground for difference of action. It was not that his principles were wrong in the abstract; for they are the principles of 1776. But I could not bring myself to recognize their application to one whom I deemed my inferior.

"But to my story. What happened now is soon told. Two hours after the frightful tempest had spent itself, we were plump at the wharf in Nassau. I sent two of our men immediately to our consul with a statement of facts, requesting his interference in our behalf. What he did, or whither he did anything, I don't know; but, by order of the authorities, a company of *black* soldiers came on board, for the purpose, as they said, of protecting the property. These impudent rascals, when I called on them to assist me in keeping the slaves on board, sheltered themselves adroitly under their instructions only to protect property,—and said they did not recognize *persons* as *property*. I told them that by the laws of Virginia and the laws of the United States, the slaves on board were as much property as the barrels of flour in the hold. At this the stupid blockheads showed their *ivory*, rolled up their white eyes in horror, as if the idea of putting men on a footing with merchandise were revolting to their humanity. When these instructions were understood among the negroes, it was impossible for us to keep them on board. They deliberately gathered up their baggage before our eyes, and, against our remonstrances, poured through the gangway,—formed

AUTOGRAPHS FOR FREEDOM. 239

themselves into a procession on the wharf,—bid farewell to all on board, and, uttering the wildest shouts of exultation, they marched, amidst the deafening cheers of a multitude of sympathizing spectators, under the triumphant leadership of their heroic chief and deliverer, MADISON WASHINGTON."

Frederick Douglass.

FIGURE 6. *Autographs for Freedom* (Boston: John P. Jewett, 1853). Collection of John Stauffer.

imaginative investment in the heroic slave—*c'est moi*—is able to tell his story so well.

That imaginative investment, I have been suggesting, also helps Douglass tell his own autobiographical story about his turn to a militant antislavery politics grounded in black solidarity and community. In the 1845 *Narrative*, Douglass can often seem at a distance from the slaves, such as when he reports on his mock envy of those who lacked his political consciousness: "I envied my fellow-slaves for their stupidity." Early on in *The Heroic Slave*, in Part II, Washington shares similar sentiments with Listwell about his observations of the slaves while hiding out in the swamps: "Peeping through the rents of the quarters, I saw my fellow-slaves seated by a warm fire, merrily passing away the time, as though their hearts knew no sorrow. Although I envied their seeming contentment, all wretched as I was I despised the cowardly acquiescence in their own degradation which it implied." Washington is also disturbed when he looks down at black lumber workers from a treetop and takes note of their "uncontrolled laughter." By Part III, however, Washington is chained with his fellow slaves, and those chains, which Washington instructs the slaves are a reminder that "ours is common lot," work to connect him to the black men who, as a group, engineer their freedom in the spirit of Garnet's call for slave resistance.[45] In the *Narrative,* by contrast, Douglass seems mostly on his own. Washington's transformation in *The Heroic Slave* from an isolated black rebel to a black revolutionary freedom fighter who works in tandem with his fellow slaves speaks to Douglass's sense of his own transformation over the years that he was telling his stories about Washington. His embrace of that new identity is one of the stories that he tells about himself in *My Bondage and My Freedom.*

THE BLACK MAN AND THE BROTHERHOOD

Shortly after publishing *The Heroic Slave* in *Autographs for Freedom,* and two months before he would serialize it over the four March 1853 issues of *Frederick Douglass' Paper,* Douglass wrote Gerrit Smith about changing the name of his paper to one of four possibilities: "'The Black man,' 'The agitator,' 'The Jerry Level,' or 'The Brotherhood.'" Though he kept the name unchanged, Douglass during the early to mid-1850s began more emphatically to talk about himself as a black man. Thus *My Bondage and My Freedom*, Douglass's second autobiography, does not build toward a telos of Douglass joining a white-led antislavery organization; instead, it offers a more open-ended conclusion in which Douglass, in the spirit of the ending of *The Heroic Slave*, links himself with the cause of black freedom fighters. To circle back to the opening of the chapter, *Bondage and Freedom*'s paratexts signal the important differences between the first two autobiographies. James McCune Smith's introduction may present Douglass as a representative American, but it also places him in a larger black diasporic context by discussing him in relation to three black artists: the French writer Alexandre Dumas, the Anglo-American actor Ira Aldridge, and the American singer Eliza Greenfield, who was wildly popular in Europe. In his 1854 "The Claims of the Negro Ethnologically Understood," Douglass pridefully states that it is a "physiological fact" that mixed-race blacks' "intellect is uniformly derived from the maternal side"; and in his introduction McCune Smith follows Douglass in asserting that it was from his black grandmother and mother that Douglass got the intelligence and "strong self-hood" that "led him to measure strength with Mr. Covey, and to wrench himself from the embrace of the Garrisonians." As the comparison between Covey and the Garrisonians suggests, McCune Smith is unsparing toward the latter, claiming that they "did not delve into the mind of a colored man for capacities which the pride of race led them to believe to be restricted to their own Saxon blood."[46] Douglass makes similar claims about the Garrisonians in *Bondage and Freedom*. Douglass may have been of mixed blood, but in his second autobiography he presents himself much more self-consciously and aggressively as a black man who, like his black-skinned hero Washington, forges interracial friendships on his own terms and is prepared to fight for his compatriots.[47]

Approximately three times the length of the *Narrative*, *Bondage and Freedom* draws on the *Narrative*, and even quotes from it on occasion, while for the most part reconceiving key scenes, adding new scenes, and taking the life of Douglass in new directions. Like *The Heroic Slave*, *Bondage and Freedom* is marked by a complex and searching historicism. As Sundquist observes, Douglass in his second autobiography "now stands outside his former self as it appeared in the first narration so as to reflect on the process of construction."[48] In his first autobiography, Douglass rarely pauses to consider the historiographical issues that he later addresses in the opening paragraphs of *The Heroic Slave* about archives, historical recovery, and black heroism. Those issues are central to *Bondage and Freedom*, in which Douglass regularly remarks on the role played by oral history and memory in his reconceived life history as a heroic slave and freeman.

Historiographical matters have an especially important place in the opening chapters of *Bondage and Freedom*'s long first part, "Life as a Slave," for the good reason that Douglass remains uncertain about his historical past (such as his birthdate and the identity of his father). He conveys some of that uncertainty in the *Narrative*, but in his second autobiography he is much more the historian. "Genealogical trees do not flourish among slaves," he writes early on, calling attention to the lack of archives for historical reconstruction. Thus he needs to rely on oral history and often vague memories to develop what becomes a racially self-conscious story about his indebtedness to his black matrilineal line. When he introduces his grandmother, for instance, he acknowledges the limits of his memory: "The first experience of life with me that I now remember—and I remember it but hazily—began in the family of my grandmother." Douglass's account of the pain that he felt at being separated from his grandmother when he was moved to the house of his master, and even his tales about her continued efforts to serve as his guardian and protector, derive from memories that he concedes never fully come into focus. The same is true for his account of his mother, whom, as he relates in the *Narrative,* he barely knew and thus found it difficult as a young child to mourn when he heard news of her death. But because he now wants to tell more about the woman to whom he feels indebted for his intelligence, he draws on oral history, from his grandmother and other sources, to remark on her literacy. Extolling "the native genius of my sable, unprotected, and uncultivated *mother,*" and even comparing her to an Egyptian prince depicted in James Cowles Prichard's *Natural History of Man* (1843), he suggests the difficulty of learning about his mother when he describes her resting place (which is not mentioned in the *Narrative*): "Her grave is, as the grave of the dead at sea, unmarked, and without stone or stake."[49]

Working with "marks, traces, possibles, and probabilities," Douglass in his second autobiography presents himself as a historian of slavery on the Eastern Shore and of his younger self. Douglass states about his historical interest in slavery while still a slave at Colonel Lloyd's: "I could not have been more than seven or eight years old, when I began to make this subject my study." The boy historian was especially dependent on oral history in order to develop his knowledge of slavery beyond his immediate locale. For instance, when he describes the overseer Gore's brutal murder of Denby, which is also described in the *Narrative,* he makes clear that he was not actually there to view the horrible scene, and that his story has been constructed from accounts of black witnesses: "It is said that Gore gave Denby three calls, telling him that if he did not obey the last call [to get out of a creek], he would shoot him." Much of the other information that he recounts in the opening chapters of "Life as a Slave" have their sources in black oral history. He reports about Colonel Lloyd's favored black coachman, for instance: "It was whispered, and pretty generally admitted as a fact, that William Wilks was a son of Col. Lloyd, by a highly favored slave-woman." Of course there are similar whisperings about Douglass's connection to his white owner, Aaron Anthony, and thus to Thomas Auld's first wife, who is Anthony's daughter, but he remains forever uncertain about his patrilineal line and thus about key aspects of his personal history. Still, compared to the *Narrative*, it is with a larger historical vision and a fuller cast of characters that Douglass sets up his personal story, which doesn't move to center stage until chapter 9, "Personal Treatment of the Author." As in the *Narrative*, Douglass writes about his good fortune in being sent to Baltimore to live with Hugh and Sophia Auld, his efforts to teach himself to read and write while in Baltimore, his eventual return to the Eastern Shore to live with the "cruel" Thomas Auld and his new wife, and his increasing rebelliousness in response to Auld's cruelty.[50] (On Douglass's representations of his relations with the Auld family in all of the autobiographies, see Chapter 5.)

Douglass's depiction of his rebelliousness is considerably different from the moral-suasionist *Narrative*. Angered by Auld's miserly rationing of food, Douglass chooses to satisfy his hunger by stealing from him, which he justifies in this way: "Considering that my labor and person were the property of Master Thomas and that I was by him deprived of the necessaries of life—

necessaries obtained by my own labor—it was easy to deduce the right to supply myself with what was my own." In the guise of his teenaged self, Douglass then sets forth the position that he would regularly set forth *after* he had broken from Garrison and aligned himself with Gerrit Smith's Liberty Party: "I hold that the slave is fully justified in helping himself to the *gold and silver, and the best apparel of his master, or that of any other slaveholder; and that such taking is not stealing in any just sense of that word*." The language resembles Madison Washington's when he explains to Listwell how he could justify stealing food while making his way north. (Listwell responds that Gerrit Smith would approve.) Though Douglass certainly didn't use this sort of language to Auld, it is precisely because Auld senses that Douglass has become rebellious that he sends him to "Covey, the Negro Breaker."[51]

It is at this point in the new autobiography that we see the important influence of *The Heroic Slave* on Douglass's reconception of himself as a Washington-like black rebel. Somewhat strangely, we could say about Douglass in *Bondage and Freedom* something like what Ivy Wilson says about him in *The Heroic Slave*: It is as if the author is inserting himself into the protagonist, as if Douglass is attempting to make himself Douglass. To put this another way, in the 1845 *Narrative* Douglass chose to work with the script of the slave narrative that served the ends of Garrison and his antislavery society. In the 1855 *Bondage and Freedom*, he presents himself on his own terms, and one of the selves he chooses to present is that of a black freedom fighter who has joined hands with his black compatriots.

Arguably the most famous scene in the *Narrative* is Douglass's rebellion against the slave breaker Covey. In his first autobiography, Douglass emphasizes the significance of the rebellion at both its beginning—"You have seen how a man was made a slave; you shall see how a slave was made a man"—and con-clusion—"It was a glorious resurrection, from the tomb of slavery, to the heaven of freedom." The framing and presenta-tion of the rebellion make it a red-letter moment in the *Narra-tive*, the event that in many ways helped to create the man who would become the Garrisonian abolitionist of its final pages. But because Douglass now wants to present himself as a group leader, he chooses to downplay his heroic individualism in this second telling of his rebellion against Covey, showing how the other slaves on Covey's farm were critical to his success. Though Douglass retains some of the language from the Covey section in the *Narrative*, such as his apostrophe to the Chesapeake, he drops the language about heroic manhood and Christlike resur-rection. In physically resisting Covey, Douglass does indeed come to feel like "a freeman in *fact*, while I remained a slave in *form*," as he puts it in *Bondage and Freedom*.[52] But the more cru-cial development from the rebellion is his newfound sense of soli-darity with his fellow slaves.

At Covey's, Douglass is regularly beaten; that remains a con-stant between the two autobiographies. But in *Bondage and Freedom*, Douglass presents himself as part of a larger commu-nity that includes Covey's cousin William Hughes, Caroline the black cook, a hired black man named Bill Smith (who is forced to breed slave children with Caroline), a slave named Eli, the slave Sandy Jenkins, and several others. As in the *Narrative*, after Doug-lass is viciously beaten by Covey, and Thomas Auld refuses to shelter him, Sandy offers him the root of an herb that, according to African traditions, should protect him (yet fails to). But in *Bondage and Freedom*, after Auld sends Douglass back to Covey, Sandy also invites him to dinner with his wife, a free black who is not mentioned in *Narrative*. Recalling that dinner years later,

Douglass writes that "though I have feasted since, with honorables, lord mayors and alderman, over the sea, my supper on ash cake and cold water, with Sandy, was the meal, of all my life, most sweet to my taste, and now most vivid in my memory." The solidarity that he experiences at this healing dinner carries over into his account of the rebellion against Covey, which is successful (as Douglass presents it in *Bondage and Freedom*) precisely because of his solidarity with blacks. "We were all in open rebellion, that morning," Douglass writes. It is the slaves' refusal to assist the master that allows Douglass successfully to resist Covey; and it is Douglass's recognition of the important role of black community that keeps him from making the scene into a celebration of a single heroic slave. Douglass concludes the chapter with "Hereditary bondmen, know ye not / Who would be free, themselves must strike the blow"—the very words from Byron quoted by Garnet in his 1843 "Address to the Slaves of the United States," the speech at the Buffalo convention which had extolled Madison Washington, and which Douglass at that time had voted against from his moral-suasionist perspective; and of course very close to the words that the post-Garrisonian Douglass used as an epigraph to Part IV of *The Heroic Slave*.[53] As in the novella, Douglass's invocation of these lines at the end of the Covey section tells a larger autobiographical story about his changed perspective on black revolutionism in the years following the Buffalo convention.

That story of Douglass's evolving perspective on black revolutionism is given its fullest figuration in a subsequent chapter of *Bondage and Freedom* called "The Run-Away Plot," which focuses on Douglass's relationship with the slaves at William Freeland's plantation. In the *Narrative*, Douglass makes clear that he developed friendships at Freeland's and that the runaway plot was a group venture. But in *Bondage and Freedom,* those friendships are given much more emphasis; we even learn the names of most of his coconspirators. He also gives the runaway plot many more pages than he did in the *Narrative.* In fact, the chapter titled "The Run-Away Plot" is twenty-six pages in the 1855 printing of *Bondage and Freedom,* which makes it more than twice the length of "The Last Flogging," which describes the rebellion against Covey. As his use of the Byron quote suggests, in his retelling of the runaway plot in his second autobiography Douglass presents it as an insurrectionary plot in the tradition of the *Creole* and other black uprisings.

In passages that are new to *Bondage and Freedom,* Douglass depicts the rebellious slaves at Freeland's as a black revolutionary "unit" that rejects the idea that "dark color [is] God's mark of displeasure." Meeting secretly at Douglass's Sabbath school, the slaves share "thoughts and sentiments . . . which might be called very incendiary, by oppressors and tyrants." Accordingly, Douglass describes the slaves as planning more than simply an escape. He writes: "These meetings must have resembled, on a small scale, the meetings of revolutionary conspirators, in their primary condition. We were plotting against our (so called) lawful rulers." In the *Narrative,* the runaway plot is conceived almost entirely in relation to the American revolutionary tradition; and indeed Douglass retains from his first autobiography the analogy he developed between the ideology of the rebellious black plotters and that of the Patrick Henry who declares, "GIVE ME LIBERTY OR GIVE ME DEATH." But when he writes in *Bondage and Freedom* that "incomparably more sublime, is the same sentiment, when *practically* asserted by men accustomed to the lash and chain," he decouples the sentiment from the specifics of the

American Revolution, making it more in accord with the revolutionary spirit he depicts at the end of *The Heroic Slave*. And he adds something new from the 1845 rendering, asserting that he and his black compatriots "fully intended to *fight* as well as *run*, if necessity should occur for that extremity."[54]

Though the plot at Freeland's collapses when Freeland and his associates take Douglass and his fellow slaves into custody (Douglass cannot change that essential fact), the fighting spirit of the plot lives on in the blacks' consciousnesses and subsequent actions. The coconspirator slave Henry chooses to fight back, and his resistance distracts the whites long enough for Douglass to burn the passes the had written up for his fellow conspirators. Douglass remarks about his compatriots' refusal to divulge details of the plot or to implicate one another: "We were a band of brothers, and never dearer to each other than now." He even loves Sandy, to the point that he refuses to say absolutely that he had been their betrayer. As a result of their solidarity, the blacks are eventually returned to Freeland's farm, with the exception of Douglass, who is sent back to Hugh and Sophia Auld in Baltimore by his owner, Thomas Auld. There, Douglass becomes involved with the free blacks of the East Baltimore Improvement Society, who possibly help with his eventual escape. As he extolled the blacks on Freeland's farm, he now extolls the free blacks of Baltimore: "I owe much to the society of these young men."[55] Significantly, after making his escape from slavery (the details of which he continues to keep secret), Douglass records his indebtedness to a host of people who help to make him feel at home in New Bedford, including the unnamed blacks of New Bedford's African Methodist Episcopal Zion Church, who are described as so tightly committed to each other's welfare, and so resistant to the practice of slavery, that they are prepared to kill one of their members for threatening to betray a fugitive slave. Douglass doesn't dissent. Having reconceived of himself as a black revolutionary leader in the first part of *Bondage and Freedom,* he now turns in the second (and concluding) part to another large theme that he had addressed in *The Heroic Slave*: interracial friendship.

❧

There is a wealth of new material about Douglass's life in the short concluding section, "Life as a Freeman." Nevertheless, the two most recent editors of *Bondage and Freedom* are in agreement about the limits of this second part. John Stauffer remarks that "representing himself as a free man seemed to induce in Douglass a crisis of language and aesthetics," while David W. Blight asserts that "in the second part, . . . Douglass's voice seems at times to fall flatter."[56] Perhaps the problem is that the final section, with its focus on Douglass's several years in New Bedford, his initial association with Garrison, his triumphal British tour, and his break with Garrison, doesn't seem quite as universal as the archetypal story of Douglass's rise from slavery to freedom. But this section, which is hardly flat, helps us to better understand why Douglass has written a second autobiography just ten years after his first: he wants to address the political transformation that led to his break with Garrison. To be sure, Douglass to some extent "took back" the *Narrative* with his Dublin editions of 1845 and 1846, but even those revised autobiographies remained true to the Garrisonian storyline of the rise of an extraordinary slave to a position within the Massachusetts Anti-Slavery Society. In light of his public break from Garrison, Douglass sought to retell his life story, and as I have been arguing throughout this chapter, his evolving thinking about black revolutionism (with its focus on Madison Washington) had become crucial to his increasing differences with Garrison. To some extent Douglass writes that political and personal history into *The Heroic Slave*; and he foregrounds that history in the "Life as a Freeman" section of *Bondage and Freedom*. Though the account of Garrison in this section mainly addresses the 1845–1847 period, it is motivated by Douglass's reconception of himself as a black leader in the late 1840s and early 1850s, and in particular by his disputes with Garrison in the immediate wake of the publication of *The Heroic Slave*.

In 1853 and 1854, following the publication of a novella that implicitly and explicitly honored Gerrit Smith, Garrison went on the offensive, printing numerous articles in the *Liberator* on Douglass's bad politics, and even accusing him of having an affair with Julia Griffiths. Responding to the sharp criticism from Garrison, as well as from William C. Nell and other black Garrisonians, Douglass confessed in an article printed in the December 9, 1853, *Frederick Douglass' Paper:* "Their assaults are now unbearable." Particularly embarrassed by the charge of adultery, he had his wife, Anna, send Garrison a letter, probably authored by Douglass, declaring that theirs was a happy household: "SIR—It is not true, that the presence of a certain person in the office of Frederick Douglass causes unhappiness in his family. Please insert this in your next paper." Garrison printed the letter in the December 16, 1853, *Liberator.* In a subsequent raging attack precipitated by Douglass's various efforts to defend himself, Garrison pronounced on his former associate: "Mr. DOUGLASS now stands self-unmasked, his features flushed with passion, his air scornful and defiant, his language bitter as wormwood, his pen dripped in poison; as thoroughly changed in his spirit as was ever 'arch-angel ruined,' as artful and unscrupulous a schismatic as has yet appeared in the abolition ranks."[57] Douglass offered an extended response to Garrison in a March 1855 lecture in which he argued that while Garrison may have helped to revive antislavery activity in the United States, he "neither discovered its principles, originated its ideas, nor framed its arguments."[58] Several months after delivering this lecture, Douglass published *Bondage and Freedom*, whose opening paratexts trumpet the autobiography as a work that has been reconceived in light of his break with Garrison, his friendship with Gerrit Smith, and his alliance with the Liberty Party. In a striking full-page dedication to Smith, Douglass praises "HIS GENIUS AND BENEVOLENCE," and records his "GRATITUDE FOR HIS FRIENDSHIP," signing himself Smith's "FAITHFUL AND FULLY ATTACHED FRIEND" (Figure 7). That dedication could be read as a slap in the face to Garrison. But the real slap comes in *Bondage and Freedom*'s "Life as a Freeman" section. In sharp contrast to the Listwell-Washington relationship in *The Heroic Slave*, Douglass presents his relationship with Garrison as a glaring instance of a bad interracial friendship.

Douglass begins his account of Garrison on an upbeat note, remarking on how he discovered the *Liberator* shortly after arriving in New Bedford: "I not only liked—I *loved* this paper, and its editor." But as the "loved" suggests, this is all in the past, and Douglass emphasizes the pastness of the past at the very moment that he introduces Garrison into his narrative: "Seventeen years ago, few men possessed a more heavenly countenance than William Lloyd Garrison, and few men evinced a more genuine or a more exalted piety." As in the *Narrative*, Douglass describes his

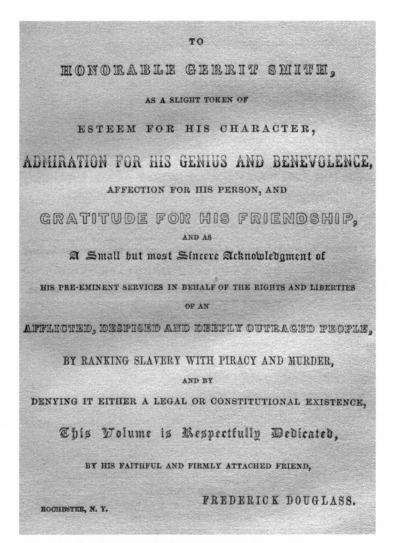

TO

HONORABLE GERRIT SMITH,

AS A SLIGHT TOKEN OF

ESTEEM FOR HIS CHARACTER,

ADMIRATION FOR HIS GENIUS AND BENEVOLENCE,

AFFECTION FOR HIS PERSON, AND

GRATITUDE FOR HIS FRIENDSHIP,

AND AS

A Small but most Sincere Acknowledgment of

HIS PRE-EMINENT SERVICES IN BEHALF OF THE RIGHTS AND LIBERTIES

OF AN

AFFLICTED, DESPISED AND DEEPLY OUTRAGED PEOPLE,

BY RANKING SLAVERY WITH PIRACY AND MURDER,

AND BY

DENYING IT EITHER A LEGAL OR CONSTITUTIONAL EXISTENCE,

This Volume is Respectfully Dedicated,

BY HIS FAITHFUL AND FIRMLY ATTACHED FRIEND,

FREDERICK DOUGLASS.

ROCHESTER, N. Y.

FIGURE 7. *My Bondage and My Freedom* (New York: Miller, Orton and Mulligan, 1855), dedication page. Image reproduction courtesy of the Williams College Archives and Special Collections, Williamstown, Massachusetts.

first short speech before Garrison's society and his subsequent recruitment as a lecturer. Working with the conventions of the seduction novel, Douglass depicts himself as an innocent: "Young, ardent, and hopeful, I entered upon this new life in the full gush of unsuspecting enthusiasm." What he hadn't anticipated, he now says from his disillusioned perspective in 1855, is that he would be regarded as an inferior—a black subordinate—in a hierarchically based white antislavery organization who was expected to play the role of the escaped black slave. (As I argue in Chapter 1, Douglass may be overstating or inventing here as a result of his anger at Garrison.) In an oft-quoted passage near the end of *Bondage and Freedom*, Douglass insists that Garrison mainly wanted him to speak about his history as a slave: " 'Tell your story, Frederick,' would whisper my then revered friend, William Lloyd Garrison, as I stepped upon the platform." Douglass confides to his readers: "I could not always obey, for I was now reading and thinking."[59] In a subsequent chapter on his "Twenty-One Months in Great Britain," Douglass highlights his growing independence as an antislavery speaker and thinker, while making clear that he has been developing new interracial friendships, such as with the white British abolitionists who purchased him out of slavery.

Near the end of *Bondage and Freedom*, the reading and thinking Douglass returns to the story of his relationship with Garrison. Unlike the final pages of the *Narrative*, the concluding chapter is almost completely lacking in triumphalism; instead, it builds to a statement of mission. Douglass's main contention is that Garrison and his associates are bad friends because they are racists. Douglass moves the reader to this dispiriting insight by telling the story of the *North Star*. Instead of encouraging Douglass to establish a vital black newspaper, the Garrisonians angrily insist that he continue to lecture for their organization. Douglass attempts to gain the goodwill of his paternalistic "Boston friends" by moving to "Rochester, Western New York, among strangers, where the circulation of my paper could not interfere with the local circulation of the Liberator," but his relationship with Garrison continues to deteriorate, especially after he publicly announces his break from Garrisonian abolitionism in 1851. Douglass summarizes the next few years of his interactions with Garrison by stating that "the common punishment of apostates was mine." But he is no mere "apostate"; he is a black apostate. In the closing pages of *Bondage and Freedom,* Douglass discusses Garrison in the larger context of "American prejudice against color, and its varied illustrations in my own experience," commenting on Jim Crow cars and other manifestations of racism, and then on the Garrisonians. "When I first went among the abolitionists of New England, and began to travel," Douglass writes, "I found this prejudice very strong and very annoying. The abolitionists themselves were not entirely free from it."[60] In *The Heroic Slave*, Listwell is hardly race-blind; he gazes obsessively at Washington's black body when he first eavesdrops on him. But when they announce themselves as friends, race seems secondary to their shared commitment to human freedom. In his wry comments on Garrison at the end of *Bondage and Freedom,* Douglass suggests that Garrison, for all the wrong reasons, never stopped seeing him as a black man.

And so it is as a prideful black leader that Douglass concludes his second autobiography. He states that precisely because he decided in 1847 to edit a black newspaper, "I have had my mind more directed to the condition and circumstances of the free colored people than when I was the agent of an abolition society." In ways that parallel the ending of *The Heroic Slave*, he situates himself in relation to blacks both within and beyond the United States by quoting the prophecy of Psalms 68.31: "Ethiopia shall yet reach forth her hand unto God." In the autobiography's final sentence prior to the appendix, Douglass states that he will be working "to advocate the great and primary work of the universal and unconditional emancipation of my entire race."[61] At various moments in his career Douglass affirms his connection to the human race, but here, at the end of his 1855 autobiography, the heroic slave and freeman conceives of himself in relation to black people. Taken together, *The Heroic Slave* and *Bondage and Freedom* can be read as a composite autobiography, as mediated by his thinking about Madison Washington, of Douglass's development of a racial consciousness that links him with a larger black diaspora. Crucial to the story that he tells in both works is an enhanced commitment to traditions of black revolutionism and an ongoing concern about the risks of interracial friendship.

THE TILLMAN ARGUMENT

Douglass's relationship with Garrison hit its nadir following the publication of *My Bondage and My Freedom*. Angered by the positive review that the autobiography got in the December 15, 1855, London *Empire*, Garrison decided to review the book, and unsurprisingly, he offered particularly harsh words about the depiction of himself and his associates. Almost as if wanting to reinforce Douglass's charge of paternalism, he remarks that the final section, "Life as a Freeman," "reek[s] with the virus of personal malignity towards WENDELL PHILLIPS, myself, and the old organizations generally, and [is] full of ingratitude and baseness towards as true and disinterested friends as any man ever yet had on earth, to give him aid and encouragement." Garrison also as-

serts that "the preface by J. MCCUNE SMITH is, in its innuen-
does, a very base production." In response to the review, Douglass wrote Garrison on January 13, 1856, asking him "(if not
incompatible with your chosen mode of dealing with me) to point
out in the pages of My Bondage and my freedom [*sic*], the offensive portions of the Book to which you refer" so that people "may
read and judge for themselves, the justice of your denunciations."[62]
Following this exchange, the two great antislavery leaders toned
down their adversarial rhetoric, and by the time of the Civil War
they had become much more respectful towards one another, if
not downright friendly.

As it turned out, the dispute between Garrison and Douglass
may have been good for sales of *Bondage and Freedom*. The
controversy had been featured in both the *Liberator* and *Frederick
Douglass' Paper*, and when the book was published in August
1855, Douglass displayed his skills in marketing. In late 1855,
Douglass ran a slew of in-house reviews and advertisements
for *Bondage and Freedom*. "5,000 COPIES SOLD IN TWO
DAYS!," the first ad proclaimed on August 24, 1855, celebrating
the autobiography's "Truth and Power!" A subsequent ad in the
September 7, 1855, *Frederick Douglass' Paper* used bold-face
type to feature quotes from glowing reviews, such as "A SELF-
MADE MAN," "WORTH A HUNDRED VOLUMES OF
ROMANCE," and "THE EVILS OF SLAVERY CALMLY
UNFOLDED." Douglass also ran an in-house review that
was probably written by Julia Griffiths, or Douglass himself.
Attempting to tap into the market for antislavery novels, the
reviewer proclaims: "We have read nothing since Uncle Tom's
Cabin, which so thrilled every fibre of the soul and awoke such
intense sympathy for the slave as this touching autobiography."
Thanks to Douglass's marketing efforts, *Bondage and Freedom*

sold well, going into several editions and selling upwards of 20,000 copies by 1860. As Douglass wrote Gerrit Smith on May 23, 1856: "My Bondage and my freedom—will Sell, as long as I can lecture—so that I regard myself well provided for—for the present."[63]

In "the present," Douglass was consolidating his position that slavery was a state of war that required a violent response. Just a few months before the publication of *Bondage and Freedom*, Douglass attended the inaugural convention of the Radical Abolition Party, which he helped to form with Smith. Among those attending the convention were James McCune Smith and John Brown, whom he had met in 1848. Garrison denounced the Radical Abolitionists as "madmen," but with its mix of black and white abolitionists who shared a belief in the need for aggressive political action against the slave power, this group lifted the "Jerry Level" up a notch and offered a more compelling model of interracial cooperation than Douglass depicts in the 1853 *The Heroic Slave*.[64] The increasingly bloody battles between proslavery and antislavery forces in the Kansas Territory, which ensued from the passage of the Kansas-Nebraska Act in 1854, only strengthened Douglass's conviction that the forces of slavery were waging a war against freedom that had to be met head on. Accordingly, like Gerrit Smith, he supported John Brown's guerrilla tactics in Kansas, and stood by him after Brown and his fighters hacked to death five men in the 1856 massacre at Pottawatomie Creek.

Even as Douglass worked interracially with the Radical Abolitionists, he continued to find inspiration in Madison Washington and the heroic tradition of black revolutionism. Four months after the Supreme Court's 1857 Dred Scott ruling that blacks had no rights to U.S. citizenship, Douglass spoke on West Indies emancipation to a predominately black audience of over 1,000 people at Canandaigua, New York. West Indies emancipation speeches typically praised British leaders for the August 1, 1834, British emancipation of West Indian slaves, but in this speech Douglass credits the blacks of the West Indies for bringing about their own emancipation. "What Wilberforce was endeavoring to win from the British Senate by his magic eloquence," Douglass declares, "the Slaves themselves were endeavoring to gain by outbreaks and violence." There is much in the speech in the spirit of Henry Highland Garnet's 1843 "Address to the Slaves," and Douglass pays tribute to that great black leader by calling him "my loved, and honored and much respected friend." Like Garnet in 1843, Douglass celebrates a diasporic tradition of black rebels that includes Nat Turner, Cinqué, and Washington. In that context, when he asserts that "Madison Washington who struck down his oppressor on the deck of the *Creole*, is more worthy to be remembered than the colored man who shot [the British officer] Pitcaren at Bunker Hill," he suggests the limits of viewing Washington simply as a U.S. revolutionary. Washington belongs to the larger pantheon of black freedom fighters in the Americas.[65]

Three months after the outbreak of the Civil War, Douglass reveled in another inspirational black freedom fighter, the twenty-seven-year-old free black William Tillman, who almost single-handedly led an uprising on a Long Island-based ship seized by Confederate privateers, killing several of the seamen and returning the schooner to New York Harbor, where he was greeted as a hero. In "A Black Hero," published in the August 1861 issue of *Douglass' Monthly*, Douglass rejoices in Tillman's "fearful work" of killing three of the southerners with a hatchet, knowing "that if he failed, an excruciating death would be the consequence." At a time when Douglass was angry that Abraham Lincoln and other northern leaders refused to view the Civil War as a war of emancipation, and thus were unwilling to recruit black soldiers, Douglass portrays Tillman as in the heroic tradition of black revolutionaries who, like Washington, have fought for their own freedom in the American hemisphere. Douglass proclaims: "Love of liberty alone inspired him and supported him, as it had inspired Denmark Vesey, Nathaniel Turner, Madison Washington, Toussaint L'Ouverture, Shields Green, Copeland, and other Negro heroes before him." He concludes the essay by asking his readers: "When will this nation cease to disparage the negro race? When will they become sensible of the force of this irresistible TILLMAN argument?"[66]

The Tillman argument is the Madison Washington argument is the Douglass argument as he waged it through the late 1840s, the 1850s, and then into the Civil War, often in response to what he regarded as the temporizing of Abraham Lincoln. That temporizing, very different from John Brown's more aggressive efforts to overthrow slavery, would become an important subject of Douglass's Civil War and post–Civil War autobiographical depictions of his complicated, and often very frustrating, interracial friendship with President Lincoln.

⟫ 4 ⟪

TALES OF ABRAHAM LINCOLN
(AND JOHN BROWN)

F IVE YEARS AFTER the publication of his third autobiography, *Life and Times of Frederick Douglass, Written by Himself* (1881), Douglass was invited by Allen Thorndike Rice, editor
of the *North American Review*, to contribute to Rice's edited
volume *Reminiscences of Abraham Lincoln, by Distinguished Men
of the Time*. Among the contributors were General Ulysses S.
Grant, General Benjamin F. Butler, Henry Ward Beecher, and
Walt Whitman. In his chapter, Douglass draws from the 1881 *Life
and Times* to describe his three meetings with Lincoln during the
Civil War. Those meetings, which Douglass had spoken about on
numerous occasions before the publication of *Life and Times*, had
helped to make Douglass's reputation as the African American
who had become Lincoln's friend and political ally. But Douglass
adds something new about the admiration that he felt for Lincoln. He confides to readers of Rice's collection: "I felt in his
presence I was in the presence of a very great man, as great as the
greatest. I felt as though I could go and put my hand on his if I
wanted to, to put my hand on his shoulder. Of course I did not do

it, but I felt that I could. I felt as though I was in the presence of a big brother, and that there was safety in the atmosphere." In this Whitmanian outpouring, Douglass conveys his sense of the two leaders' interdependency and intimacy. Douglass imagines himself placing a hand on Lincoln's shoulder, perhaps with the hope he could have saved him from John Wilkes Booth's bullet, while Lincoln is depicted as the older brother Douglass never had who offers a similarly protective guidance. This 1886 reminiscence of President Lincoln is a far cry from Douglass's in-the-moment critique of September 1862, when he stated in his newspaper: "Mr. Lincoln is quite a genuine representative of American prejudice and negro hatred."[1]

As is clear from these 1862 and 1886 descriptions, Douglass over the years wavered in his views of the president; and because he actually met with Lincoln in 1863, and then met with him twice more in 1864 and 1865, his tales of their encounters have autobiographical implications with respect to what I am calling the lives of Frederick Douglass. They have particular implications for the way Douglass sought to represent himself, at different times and to different audiences, in relation to the Civil War and the legacy of the martyred president. I will be discussing a wide range of Douglass's writings about Lincoln, but it should be said right from the start that nowhere is Douglass more compelling as a storyteller about Lincoln than in his 1881 *Life and Times,* the principal source for his chapter in *Reminiscences of Abraham Lincoln* and (years later) for our historical understanding of his relationship with the president.

Douglass wrote the 1881 *Life and Times* at the historical moment when Lincoln had become apotheosized in American culture and when Douglass himself had become a controversial figure in the Republican Party, attacked for his oversight of the

Freedman's Bank and for his criticism of the Southern blacks—
known as Exodusters—who chose to move north shortly after
the Compromise of 1877. Douglass used the 1881 autobiography,
as he used some of his post–Civil War speeches, to link his star
with Lincoln's. Thus he writes in *Life and Times* about how he
campaigned for Lincoln and contributed to the "triumphant election" of "a man who in the order of events was destined to do a
greater service to his country and to mankind than any man who
had gone before him in the presidential office." He hoped and
expected that President Lincoln would share his view that the war
was not simply about preserving the Union but also about putting
a permanent end to slavery, and in *Life and Times* he portrays Lincoln as committed precisely to those goals almost from the time
of his election. Though Douglass asserts that Lincoln immediately understood that the Civil War offered "the opportunity to
destroy slavery," he concedes that there were occasions when his
faith in Lincoln was "shaken," such as in late 1862, "when even
Mr. Lincoln could tell the poor Negro that 'he was the cause of
the war.'" But overall Douglass presents Lincoln in *Life and Times*
as a man who, from the moment he was elected to the presidency,
sought nothing less than the "ultimate extinction" of slavery.[2]

What Douglass chooses not to discuss in his 1881 autobiography are the many doubts and criticisms he had expressed
about Lincoln throughout the Civil War. He does not mention
that he supported the Radical Abolitionist candidate Gerrit
Smith, not Lincoln, for the presidency in 1860, and that in 1864 he
would have preferred John C. Frémont as the Republicans' presidential candidate. Especially in the opening years of the war,
Douglass was one of Lincoln's toughest critics, in large part because of his frustration at Lincoln's reluctance to use the full force
of the military to bring about the end of slavery. Douglass's

editorials and speeches about Lincoln during this period typically depict the president as a temporizer who sought to appease
the southern slave power. Following the Emancipation Proclamation, Douglass became warmer toward Lincoln, but he would
continue to speak critically of the president's policies, and of the
man himself, in speeches and essays of 1863 and 1864. It was not
until after Lincoln's assassination that Douglass came to celebrate what Walt Whitman called "the first great Martyr Chief."[3]

Douglass's editorials and speeches of 1861 and 1862 reveal that
his faith in Lincoln was much more tentative than he conveys in
Life and Times. Did his sense of Lincoln dramatically change in
1863, the year of the Emancipation Proclamation and of Lincoln's
introduction of black troops into the Union Army? And did his
first meeting with Lincoln later that year inaugurate a friendship? In his influential and often quite wonderful study of Douglass and Lincoln, historian James Oakes suggests that these two
great leaders developed a significant interracial friendship that
had consequences for the ways in which both men approached
the war. According to Oakes, Douglass, under the tutelage of
Lincoln, became more pragmatically political, while Lincoln,
under the tutelage of Douglass, became more politically radical.[4]
Several other recent studies of the relationship between the two
men tell fairly similar stories about what has come to be celebrated as one of the great interracial friendships in American
history.[5]

But caution and skepticism (and a close attention to Douglass's
complex autobiographical writings) are in order. After all, over
the course of the war Douglass met with Lincoln just three times,
twice privately, for a total of probably sixty to ninety minutes. As
short as these meetings were, they have become central to what I
regard as the mythologization of the Douglass-Lincoln friend-

ship, the belief that these two great leaders in effect helped to bring the war to its successful outcome of preserving the Union and ending slavery. This is a myth that was created in large part by Douglass in his autobiographical writings *after* the death of Lincoln. Douglass is such a rhetorically persuasive writer that his accounts of his meetings and exchanges with Lincoln, especially as presented in *Life and Times,* have generally been accepted as reliable. (Lincoln never wrote about Douglass, so we don't have contravening accounts.) But there is evidence that those meetings, which I discuss in greater detail below, did not go exactly as Douglass described them in 1881, and one cannot but wonder at the presumptuousness of Douglass's "big brother" presentation in 1886. This is not to say that the meetings didn't have an impact on the two men and that there wasn't some sort of friendship (in the way that political leaders can call themselves friends). But we can develop a more nuanced understanding of that friendship, and of Douglass as an autobiographer, by paying close attention to the different occasions and historical moments in which Douglass writes and speaks about Lincoln. Douglass's tales of Lincoln are testaments to his rhetorical skills as an autobiographer; they also offer insights into the president while revealing much about Douglass himself.

Douglass's rhetorical skills are on full display as well in his various accounts of his friendship with "that noble old John Brown," as Douglass referred to him in 1863, the militant who in life and in death had modeled what Douglass called "the John Brown way" of violent opposition to slavery.[6] Central to Douglass's disillusionment with Lincoln during much of the Civil War, I argue in this chapter, was his conviction that Lincoln simply was no John Brown. Douglass knew Brown, wrote about him autobiographically, and developed a much richer friendship with the rebel than he ever did with Lincoln. Over the twelve years of their acquaintance, they had moments when they lived together and planned together. There was a personal dimension to Douglass's Brown-inflected distrust of Lincoln that would not change until he actually met with Lincoln, and even then Douglass had hesitations about whether Lincoln was committed to black freedom and equality in the way of Brown. In his study of Douglass and Lincoln, Oakes criticizes Douglass for regarding Brown "in implausibly grandiose terms," claiming that when Douglass defended Brown's terroristic tactics he "shelved his faith in the U.S. Constitution and replaced it with cynical clichés of a disillusioned Romantic."[7] What Oakes's critical remarks fail to capture is Douglass's admiration for the passion of Brown's anti-slavery convictions and for his almost unprecedented ability as a white man to treat blacks as his equals. Oakes also fails to engage the full force of Douglass's post-Garrisonian belief, expressed in *The Heroic Slave* and elsewhere, that violence was a sometimes necessary response to the violence of slavery. Lincoln, in Oakes's story, ultimately teaches Douglass important lessons on Constitutionalism and pragmatism, while Brown falls by the wayside.

Removing Brown from his story of Douglass and Lincoln, Oakes does what just about every historian does when writing about Douglass and Lincoln: he writes *only* about Douglass and Lincoln. In his overall study, it can seem that during the Civil War Douglass thought exclusively about Lincoln when considering white political leaders and that Lincoln thought exclusively about Douglass when considering black political leaders. But Lincoln actually met with a number of black leaders during the Civil War, and he may have had his most satisfying encounter with Douglass's rival and former coeditor, the black nationalist Martin Delany, who is not discussed in any of the recent work on Douglass and Lincoln. Delany, like Douglass, was friends and coconspirators with Brown, and in his 1864 meeting with Lincoln, which led to his appointment as the first black major in the Union Army, he drew on what he had learned from Brown about insurrectionism to impress the president with his promise as a military tactician. Though Brown was executed in 1859, he remained alive in the imaginations of Delany and Douglass.

Douglass, for instance, published a letter on Brown in the April 1881 *New York Times* shortly after the appearance of *Life and Times*, which included several chapters on Brown. The letter spoke to their personal acquaintance and to Douglass's continuing wonder at Brown's uncompromising idealism. Douglass writes: "I never had under my roof at any time such an incarnation of justice and the true martyr spirit as when John Brown lived with me. He was a constant thorn in my side. I could not help feeling that this man's zeal in the cause of my enslaved people was holier and higher than mine. I could speak for my race—he could fight for my race. I could live for my race—John Brown could die for my race."[8] Compared to his "big brother" remembrance of Lincoln, this letter, with its image of a thorn, is pricklier. Nathaniel Hawthorne once remarked that Thoreau made him feel guilty for buying new clothes; here we have a man who makes Douglass feel guilty about his lack of commitment to African Americans and the cause of antislavery.[9] The prickliness aside, the letter suggests that Douglass had the sort of friendship with Brown that he never achieved with Lincoln. And it suggests the high moral standard that Brown set for Douglass. As a man who was absolutely committed to ending slavery, and who was willing to sacrifice his life to bring about that goal, Brown in Douglass's imagination was a sort of shadow figure to Lincoln. Implicitly and explicitly, Douglass measured Lincoln against Brown and for a long while saw Lincoln falling short. Any discussion of Douglass and Lincoln needs to take account of Brown.

Because so much of the analysis in this chapter draws on Douglass's third and final autobiography, it would be useful to say a few words about the current critical status of *Life and Times*. Compared to the first two autobiographies, the 1881 *Life and Times*, which Douglass revised and expanded in 1892, has generally been regarded as something of an embarrassment, a self-indulgent work of over 600 pages that need be read only by Douglass specialists. Even the editors of the 2012 scholarly edition of *Life and Times*, published in Yale University Press's Frederick Douglass Papers Series, adopt a critical tone about the autobiography, declaring that "this tome, of all his autobiographical writings, is in form the most overwrought, replete with temporal digressions, frequent lengthy lists of persons and objects, and extracts from speeches and correspondence." The editors' critical evaluation echoes what has become the consensus: that *Life and Times* is "without much force," "tired," "self-indulgent," "tedious," and "complacent."[10] The problem with this consensus is that it can discourage fresh reading. To be sure, in sections of *Life and Times*, Douglass sounds defensive (such as when he describes his tenure as president of the Freedman's Bank) or a bit too much like a Republican stump speaker. But *Life and Times* is the only autobiography in which Douglass discusses John Brown, Abraham Lincoln, the Civil War, Reconstruction, his return to Maryland's Eastern Shore, his second marriage, and his vexed role as U.S. minister and consul to Haiti, to name just some of the highlights of the volume. The editors of the Frederick Douglass Papers edition refer to *Life and Times'* "enduring unpopularity"; and yet despite its humdrum sales in the 1880s and 1890s, it remained the only Douglass autobiography that was widely available in the twentieth century until the *Narrative* was republished in 1960. In 1939 J. Saunders Redding declared that, of the three Douglass autobiographies, *"Life and Times* is his best book." The notable Harlem Renaissance critic Alain Locke similarly proclaimed in his foreword to the 1941 Pathway Press reissue that Douglass's *"Life and Times,* now for the first time reprinted, [is] the classic of American Negro biography."[11]

In his underrated classic, *Life and Times,* Douglass for the most part tells a compelling story about his unfolding life history over the large canvas of the nineteenth century, and he does so in ways that are highly rhetorical, performative, and not completely to be trusted. After all, Douglass was a serial autobiographer whose life writings, as Celeste-Marie Bernier nicely puts it, work with "an aesthetics of obfuscation as much as revelation."[12] As I hope this and the next chapter will demonstrate, *Life and Times* is both a revelatory resource for Douglass studies and a great read in the art of obfuscation.

A NOBLE, HEROIC, AND CHRISTIAN MARTYR

To begin with John Brown, who will then move into the shadows: Douglass himself provides the warrant, in his 1881 *Life and Times,* for thinking about Brown and Lincoln together. In the chapter "Increasing Demands of the Slave Power," Douglass introduces Lincoln in relation to Brown by showing how closely the two were linked in terms of the politics of the 1850s. The chapter begins with the hanging of Brown on December 2, 1859, and then moves back in time to tell the story of the crisis precipitated by the Kansas-Nebraska Act of 1854. Brown and his supporters became involved in the violent battles in the Kansas territory between proslavery and antislavery forces, while the debates on the Kansas-Nebraska Act and "popular sovereignty," Douglass notes, "brought Abraham Lincoln into prominence." But the main focus of the chapter is on Douglass's personal encounters with Brown. Unlike with Lincoln, Douglass over the years provided a fairly consistent portrait of Brown as a man who, as he puts it in *Life and Times*, "never lost sight of what he called his greater work—the liberation of all the slaves in the United States."[13] Whether writing in the early 1860s or in 1881 (and beyond), Douglass portrayed Brown as a hero and friend who used violence in calculated and justifiable ways to contest the violence of slavery. To be sure, there may have been some hero worship in Douglass's response to Brown, as Oakes suggests, but there was also a clear-eyed political judgment that in the wake of the Compromise of 1850, the Kansas-Nebraska Act, and the Supreme Court's 1857 ruling on the Dred Scott case, which declared that blacks could never become U.S. citizens, a significant rethinking of antislavery action was in order. In both the 1881 *Life and Times* and his 1860 lectures on Brown, Douglass presents himself as doing that rethinking in tandem with the man who attacked Harpers Ferry.

Douglass first met Brown in Springfield, Massachusetts, in late 1847 or early 1848. At that meeting Douglass heard about Brown's plan to use the Allegheny Mountains as a staging ground, or what Brown called a subterranean pass way, for armed men who would infiltrate southern lines and liberate the slaves. Though Douglass still professed to be a moral-suasionist Garrisonian, he published a short article in the February 11, 1848, *North Star* suggestive of his support for Brown. In that article, Douglass gives initial expression to what he would emphasize about Brown for decades to come: his passion for antislavery and his ability to treat blacks as his equals. As Douglass writes, Brown is "a white gentleman,

[who] is in sympathy a black man, and is as deeply interested in our cause, as though his own soul had been pierced with the iron of slavery."[14] It was precisely Brown's outrage at the pain and suffering that slavery inflicted on blacks that led him to Kansas in 1855. When Brown and his men, including four of his sons, brutally killed five proslavery settlers at Pottawatomie Creek, Kansas, on May 24, 1856, three days after proslavery forces pillaged the antislavery stronghold of Lawrence, Douglass, who probably knew that Brown was involved, remained quiet on that incident, even as he continued to argue for antislavery violence. Brown made an extended visit to Douglass's Rochester home in January 1858, and while there wrote a "Provisional Constitution and Ordinances for the People of the United States," which he presumably wanted to put into effect after a successful attack on the federal arsenal at Harpers Ferry. Brown didn't share his Harpers Ferry plan with Douglass in 1858, but he did in 1859, just weeks before the attack. Though Douglass decided against joining the raiders, he affirmed his solidarity with Brown by choosing not to reveal the plot to federal authorities.[15] On October 16, John Brown and twenty of his supporters, including two of his sons and five African Americans, stormed the arsenal and for a short while had it under their control. Over the next two days, a force of U.S. marines led by Colonel Robert E. Lee battled with Brown's forces. Ten of Brown's raiders, including his two sons, were killed in the combat. Taken prisoner, the wounded Brown was tried and convicted in a widely publicized trial. He was hanged on December 2, 1859.

Aware that he, too, could be tried and executed as a coconspirator, Douglass made his way to Canada almost immediately after the attack, and on November 12, 1859, took a steamer to England. Shortly after arriving in England, he hailed "that noble hero and martyr, John Brown," the man who in 1855–1856, with limited resources and manpower, managed "to put to flight a body of four hundred men from Missouri." In his first major speech on Brown, "John Brown and the Slaveholders' Insurrection," which he delivered in Edinburgh on January 30, 1860, nearly two months after Brown's execution, Douglass more extensively told the autobiographical tale of his friendship with Brown, while bringing Lincoln into the speech as well. According to a reporter for the Edinburgh *Witness,* Douglass stated that, in part because of "the recent outbreak at Harper's Ferry," it was increasingly likely "that before the end of the present year they should have an antislavery President." That president, it is clear from the speech, would be measured against "that brave, heroic, and Christian man, John Brown. . . . a noble, heroic, and Christian martyr." In this and other speeches of 1860, Douglass said little about his interactions with Brown in the weeks before the attack on Harpers Ferry; he would save that story for *Life and Times.* Still, even as he avowed in letters and lectures that he had nothing to do with the attack, he hinted at greater knowledge. As reported in the *Witness:* "It was not for him [Douglass] to say whether he was justly implicated in the matter or not just there—(laughter and cheers)—as they might in that event, perhaps, look upon him in the light of a man exculpating himself from a grievous charge in what he was about to say." Instead of choosing self-exculpation, Douglass described himself in a number of his speeches as buoyed by the positive response to Brown in the North, and he took it upon himself to justify and explain Brown's actions for those who were troubled by his turn to violence. He pointedly told the crowd in Edinburgh: "John Brown did not invade a peaceful neighborhood or community. What was slavery? A standing insurrection from beginning to end." Keeping his own relation to the Harpers Ferry attack shrouded in secrecy, Douglass was willing to reveal that he and Brown were close personal friends who had resided together for days and even weeks at a time. The reporter paraphrased Douglass's revelation of this aspect of his friendship with Brown: "John Brown had lived under his roof in Rochester for seven weeks when he had many opportunities of conversing with him, and he had at all times found him, what he had indeed amply shown at his last moments,—an honest, truthful, earnest, God-fearing man."[16]

When Douglass learned that his daughter Annie had died in Rochester on March 13, 1860, he abruptly returned to the United States to be with his family. But rather than hide away, he continued to celebrate Brown, now in relation to the upcoming presidential election. In a speech delivered in Geneva, New York, on August 1, 1860, Douglass referred to Brown as "a splendid meteor" and "the hero of Harper's Ferry," extolling him as the white man against whom all white leaders would have to be measured: "Brave and glorious old man! Yours was the life of a true friend of humanity, and the triumphant death of a hero. The friends of freedom shall be nerved to the glorious struggle with slavery by your example." Douglass further displayed his commitment to Brown during a riot that took place in Boston's Tremont Temple on December 3, 1860, shortly after Lincoln's election. Douglass was the featured speaker of the "John Brown Anniversary Committee," sponsored by James Redpath and other antislavery leaders, and when he attempted to speak on Brown's behalf, proslavery sympathizers rushed the stage and Douglass had to fight off his attackers. That night the antislavery group reassembled at Boston's Joy Street Baptist Church, and Douglass gave one of his most impassioned speeches on Brown. In the aggressive manner of David Walker, Douglass declared: "we must . . . reach the slaveholder's conscience through his fear of personal danger. We must make him feel that there is death in the air about him, that there is death in the pot before him, that there is death all around him." Then he turned his attention to the newly elected president Lincoln: "My opinion is that if we only had an anti-slavery President, if we only had an abolition President to hold these men in the Union, and execute the declared provisions of the Constitution. . . . I should be for the continuance of the Union." Failing to see such a president, despite what he would later write in *Life and Times,* Douglass considered the possibility of emigrating to Haiti, a plan that he abruptly dropped following the Confederacy's attack on Fort Sumter.[17]

In short, at considerable risk to himself and his reputation, Douglass remained true to Brown in the aftermath of Harpers Ferry. He shared his continued admiration in a letter to Brown's friend Redpath published in the July 27, 1860, *Liberator:* "To have been acquainted with John Brown, shared his counsels, enjoyed his confidence, and sympathized with the great objects of his life and death, I esteem as among the highest privileges of my life."[18] He remained true to him years later in his 1881 *Life and Times,* providing an autobiographical account of his long-standing friendship and political affiliation with Brown. At some risk to his reputation as a Republican political appointee in Reconstruction America, he offered his support in that work for what many still regarded as the brutally murderous violence that Brown had deployed as "Ossawatomie Brown." Recalling how Brown on his way to Kansas would pass through Rochester, "spending hours and days with me," he concedes that the "horrors wrought by his iron hand cannot be contemplated without a shudder." And yet, he defends Brown's violence, as he had in the 1850s and early 1860s, by saying that it was "the logical result of slave-

holding persecutions." Though the chapters in *Life and Times* recounting his association with Brown begin with a mention of
Lincoln, Douglass nonetheless portrays Brown as acting in a sort
of vacuum. As he remarks on the increasingly polarized debates
on slavery in the late 1850s: "From 1856 to 1860 the whole land
rocked with this great controversy . . . and when all hope of compromise had nearly vanished, as if to banish even the last glimmer
of hope and peace between the sections John Brown came upon
the scene."[19] At no time was he more dramatically on the scene
than when he attacked Harpers Ferry.

In the chapter in *Life and Times* titled "The Beginning of the
End," Douglass works in a confessional mode, at long last ready
to divulge the full details of his knowledge of Harpers Ferry:
"What was my connection with John Brown, and what I knew of
his scheme for the capture of Harper's Ferry, I may now proceed
to state." It is an odd chapter, for while Douglass's declared intent is to show that he chose not to participate in the attack, he as
much as confesses to being a coconspirator by virtue of the fact
that he knew about the "scheme" just weeks before it was set to
happen—and did nothing to stop it. In one of the most dramatic
scenes in *Life and Times*, Douglass recalls how he received a letter
from Brown requesting that he meet him at "an old stone-quarry
near Chambersburg, Penn." On his way there with Shields Green,
a fugitive slave from South Carolina, Douglass solicits contributions for Brown, who no doubt used the funds for some of his last-
minute preparations and purchases. Douglass then adopts a
Gothic mode in his novelistic rendering of the meeting. Initially,
he has trouble locating the quarry and has to ask for directions
without revealing why he is there. When he finally reaches the
quarry, he finds Brown disguised as a fisherman and accompanied by his black supporter and friend Kagi. The four men

subsequently "talked over the enterprise which was about to be undertaken," and Douglass presents his opposition to the plan in terms similar to what he had maintained in his speeches of 1860—that Brown "was going into a perfect steel-trap, and that once in he would never get out alive." Douglass also reports that he objected to the plan because "it would be an attack upon the federal government." Here, Douglass may be inventing dialogue appropriate to a man who, in the years after the Civil War, had been serving the government through the Republican Party. But the description of the meeting ends not with Douglass affirming his loyalty to the federal government but with a confession of his "cowardice." Douglass's friend Green decides that he will "go wid de ole man," so of the four at the meeting, only Douglass declines to participate. As he tells the story, following the attack Douglass flees to Canada and then to England because he knows that Virginia authorities could prove the following: "that I was in correspondence and conspiracy with Brown against slavery . . . that I brought Shields Green, one of the bravest of his soldiers, all the way from Rochester to him at Chambersburg . . . [and] that I brought money to aid him."[20] And of course they could prove that his silence enabled the attack that followed.

As it turned out, by choosing not to join Brown, Douglass missed a chance at immediate posthumous glory. According to his account in *Life and Times,* Douglass had predicted to Brown that the attack "would array the whole country against us." But he quickly realized that Brown had engaged the sympathies of many northerners, especially following his execution, where he was a model of bravery and integrity. Douglass describes the surprising impact of the white martyr on the cause of antislavery: "All over the North men were singing the John Brown song. His body was in the dust, but his soul was marching on. . . . What he had lost by the sword he had more than gained by the truth." After Brown's hanging, Douglass remarks, "the nation found it necessary to gird on the sword for the salvation of the country and the destruction of slavery."[21] And Douglass frames that salvation and destruction in *Life and Times* in relation to the presidential election of 1860, portraying himself as Lincoln's great supporter.

But does Lincoln take up that sword and commit himself to the destruction of slavery? And does he ever imagine African Americans as actual citizens of a redeemed United States? Given Brown's clear commitment to the cause, these are the questions that Douglass would ask about Lincoln over the course of the war (and beyond). In *Life and Times*, the answers to these questions would seem to be a resounding yes, but Douglass told more equivocal and critical tales about Lincoln during the Civil War.

EVIL BY CHOICE, RIGHT FROM NECESSITY

Douglass first met Lincoln in 1863, and shortly thereafter he offered his initial autobiographical account of the two together. But their lives intersected well before that meeting. During the mid-to-late 1850s, Douglass had a role in the formation of the Republican Party in Illinois. He toured the state and gave speeches promoting Republican candidates in 1854, 1857, and 1859. But 1858 was the year the two men became acutely aware of each other. On June 16 of that year, Lincoln emerged from the Illinois Republican State convention as the party's candidate for the U.S. senate, and at the close of the convention he gave his famous "House Divided" speech in which he proclaimed (drawing from the Gospel of Mark): " 'A house divided against itself cannot stand.' I believe this government cannot endure, permanently half *slave* and half *free*." Douglass read a transcript of the speech, and in a lecture of August 2, 1858, delivered in Poughkeepsie, New York, he referred to "the great speech of Mr. Lincoln," and went on to characterize Lincoln's remarks as "well and wisely said. . . . Liberty or Slavery must become the law of the land." Decades later, in a chapter in *Life and Times* that mostly focused on John Brown, Douglass once again praised Lincoln's 1858 "House Divided" speech, describing it as "the calm, cool, deliberate utterance of a statesman, comprehensive enough to take in the welfare of the whole country. . . . In a few simple words he had embodied the thought of the loyal nation, and indicated the character fit to lead and guide the country amid perils present and to come."[22] At that moment in the autobiography, Douglass initiated his account of a Lincoln who was well on his way toward issuing the Emancipation Proclamation and achieving his martyrdom as the Great Emancipator. But in 1858 Douglass had not yet completely grasped Lincoln, though he remained hopeful that Lincoln would emerge as an influential antislavery leader.

A few weeks after Douglass gave his lecture in Poughkeepsie, the famous Lincoln-Stephen Douglas debates got underway. The Illinois senatorial candidates had six joint debates, and at five of them Douglas exploited the issue of race by associating Lincoln with Frederick Douglass. If Lincoln had limited knowledge of Douglass prior to those debates, he would have quickly become acquainted with the man as a cultural figure, for his opponent took every opportunity to associate Lincoln with so-called black Republicanism through Douglass. At their first debate on August 21, 1858, Douglas asserted that Lincoln supported "the Abolition-Black Republican platform," and "could receive baptism from . . . Fred. Douglass on Abolitionism." At the second debate, on August 27, 1858, Douglas reported that he saw Frederick Douglass accompanied by white women in a carriage driven by a white man, and "that one of Fred. Douglass's kinsmen, another rich black negro, is now traveling this part of the State making speeches for his friend Mr. Lincoln, who is the champion of the black man's party." (During this time Douglass was in New York; earlier in the year he had visited Ohio and Indiana, but not Illinois.) Douglas followed up on these accusations in the third debate on September 15, 1858, reporting (falsely) that Douglass was seen at Freeport, Illinois, "in a carriage with a white lady and her daughter in the carriage sitting by his side." Claiming that Douglass made a special visit to Illinois to campaign against him, Douglas in the fourth debate, on September 18, 1858, cunningly reversed the terms of the Fugitive Slave Law by asserting that Douglass was "hunting me down."[23] He briefly mentioned Douglass at the sixth and final debate as part of his overall racist strategy of raising questions about the policies Lincoln would pursue as a senator.

Lincoln of course lost the senate election, but the debates positioned him for the presidential election of 1860. In *Life and Times*, Douglass expressed his excitement about the Republicans' nomination of Lincoln, while failing to report that he attended the Radical Abolition Party convention in Syracuse, which nominated Douglass's friend and benefactor (and fellow John Brown supporter) Gerrit Smith for the presidency and named Douglass himself as one of Smith's New York State electors.[24] He also chose not to reveal in *Life and Times* that, after the election of Lincoln, he was almost immediately disillusioned by what he regarded as the new president's commitment to Union over emancipation. His frustration with the president in the early years of the Civil War was on clear display in the pages of his newspaper,

Douglass' Monthly. In response to Lincoln's First Inaugural Address, delivered shortly after southern secession, Douglass wrote that the president "announc[ed] his complete loyalty to slavery in the slave States . . . prostrating himself before the foul and withering curse of slavery." He asserted in another editorial that "from present appearances, nothing is contemplated but the restoration of the country to the same condition in which rebellion and bloodshed found it," and that "unless a new turn is given to the conflict, and that without delay, we might as well remove Mr. LINCOLN out of the President's chair, and respectfully invite JEFFERSON DAVIS or some other slaveholding rebel to take his place." When General John C. Frémont issued a proclamation on August 30, 1861, confiscating the property and liberating the slaves of those in Missouri helping the Confederates, Douglass commended the move as in keeping with his own emancipatory aims, declaring that this "celebrated Proclamation is by far the most important and salutary measure which has thus far emanated from any General during the whole tedious progress of the war." In response to Lincoln's subsequent overruling of Frémont's policy as hostile to a border state, Douglass wrote that "the lawyer had prevailed over the warrior," and that the "weakness, imbecility and absurdity of this policy are sufficiently manifest without a single word of comment." Increasingly angered by what he perceived as Lincoln's reluctance to make the war into a war of emancipation, Douglass stated in 1862 that "the friends of freedom, the Union, and the Constitution, have been most basely betrayed, deceived and swindled, and the sooner they reach a firm conviction of this fact, the better." Later that year Douglass wrote that "the President of the United States seems to possess an ever increasing passion for making himself appear silly and ridiculous," and that his politics have "been calculated . . .

to shield and protect slavery from the very blows which its horrible crimes have loudly and persistently invited." Convinced that the Union Army needed the help of black soldiers, Douglass in speeches and editorials of 1862 maintained that Lincoln's unwillingness to allow blacks to fight for the Union was just one more instance of the temporizing and appeasement that was unnecessarily extending the war. The Union Army, Douglass lamented, was "striking the guilty rebels with our soft white hand, when we should be striking with the iron hand of the black man."[25]

During 1862 in particular, Lincoln, who hated slavery but (unlike John Brown) seemed not to care about black people, worked on impractical and arguably racist schemes to colonize African Americans to Central America, convinced that the United States would work best as a nation without slavery and without blacks. Douglass, on the other hand, argued that the very blacks Lincoln wished to remove from the country should be deployed as soldiers in the Union Army. On August 14, 1862, Lincoln met with a delegation of African Americans, not including Douglass, and lectured the black leaders about the advantages of black colonization while appearing to blame the blacks themselves for the Civil War. According to a report of the meeting in the August 15, 1862, *New-York Tribune*, Lincoln told the group that "but for your race among us there could not be a war," and he concluded that it would be "better for us both [whites and blacks], therefore, to be separated."[26]

After reading about the meeting, Douglass was furious at Lincoln and lambasted him in several lectures. Some historians believe the meeting was staged, and that Douglass was naïve in not understanding that Lincoln was making an effort to keep the border states in the Union fold by appearing to be unsympathetic to blacks, even as he was moving toward the Emancipation

Proclamation. But such an interpretation underestimates the strength of Lincoln's conviction about the value of colonization, while assuming long after the fact that Lincoln was unequivocally committed to emancipation. For Douglass in August and September 1862, nothing could be taken for granted, and in September that year he published one of his harshest attacks on Lincoln, rebuking him for the racist underpinnings of colonizationism and warning of its possibly dire consequences for the free blacks. Douglass elaborates for his readers: "Mr. Lincoln takes care in urging his colonization scheme to furnish a weapon to all the ignorant and base, who need only the countenance of men in authority to commit all kinds of violence and outrage upon the colored people of the country." As for Lincoln's declaration that blacks had caused the war, Douglass remarks that anyone "who has an ounce of brain in his head—no matter to which party he may belong, and even Mr. Lincoln himself must know quite well that the mere presence of the colored race never could have provoked this horrid and desolating rebellion." Douglass concludes his editorial by stating that Lincoln's meeting with the black delegation "confirms the painful conviction that though elected as an anti-slavery man by Republican and Abolition voters, Mr. Lincoln is quite a genuine representative of American prejudice and Negro hatred and far more concerned for the preservation of slavery, and the favor of the Border Slave States, than for any sentiment of magnanimity or principle of justice and humanity."[27]

In *Life and Times,* Douglass celebrates Lincoln as an emancipator, and thus moves quickly from Lincoln's August 1862 meeting with the black delegation, which he presents as an aberration, to the Emancipation Proclamation and Lincoln's willingness to deploy black troops in the Union Army. In his writings of late 1862, however, Douglass continued to wonder if Lincoln would actually follow through on his proposed emancipation plan. He complains in October 1862 about Lincoln's "slothful deliberation," warning that emancipation, which did not affect the border states, would not occur if the Confederate States decided to make peace with the Union. In an editorial printed in the January 1863 *Douglass' Monthly*, but written before Lincoln formally issued the proclamation, Douglass conveys his concerns about Lincoln changing his mind, and he asks what would happen "if the President fails in this trial hour" and "now listens to the demon slavery—and rejects the entreaties of the Angel of Liberty?" Even if Lincoln were to go ahead with the proclamation, Douglass writes, he is not exactly a Moses-like liberator; he is simply doing what history has made inevitable. "Powerful as Mr. Lincoln is," Douglass reminds his readers, "he is but the hands of the clock."[28]

Douglass makes a similar observation about Lincoln in his initial celebration of the Emancipation Proclamation, emphasizing the role of abolitionists (and history) in bringing about what was still only a partial emancipation of the slaves. (Border state slaves remained under the jurisdiction of the border states.) But Douglass gives Lincoln his due in a February 1863 speech delivered in New York City on the need to introduce blacks into the Union Army. "There are certain great national acts, which by their relation to universal principles, properly belong to the whole human family," Douglass declares, "and Abraham Lincoln's Proclamation of the 1st of January, 1863, is one of these acts." Terming the emancipation "the greatest event of our nation's history" and the harbinger of "the doom of Slavery in all the States," Douglass then does a remarkable thing: he brings John Brown into the speech. In Douglass's celebratory formulation, Brown now seems like both a prophet and centrist (and one of the principal agents in bringing forth the proclamation): "Good old John

Brown (loud applause) was a madman at Harper's Ferry. Two years pass away, and the nation is as mad as he." Having hailed the militant Brown, the man who fought against slavery side by side with black men who were willing to die at Harpers Ferry, Douglass then evokes the Byron/Garnet epigraph that he previously used in *The Heroic Slave* and *My Bondage and My Freedom*, and concludes with a call to Lincoln to follow the example of Brown in allowing blacks to join with whites in the Union Army: "The colored man only waits for the honorable admission into the service of the country. They know that who would be free, themselves must strike the blow, and they long for the opportunity to strike that blow."[29]

The Emancipation Proclamation in fact had a provision allowing black soldiers to fight in the Union Army, which Lincoln soon made his official policy. By spring 1863 Douglass had become a recruiting agent for the 54th Massachusetts Volunteer Infantry Regiment, one of the first black units, and in his memorable broadside, "Men of Color, To Arms!," he appealed for black volunteers who would fight in the heroic tradition of Nat Turner. Douglass's sons Charles and Lewis enlisted in the 54th and the soldiers as a group quickly distinguished themselves in a major assault on Fort Wagner in South Carolina. Convinced that the black troops were just as brave and effective as white troops, Douglass became concerned about two matters: unequal pay for black soldiers and the Confederates' practice of treating blacks as insurrectionists who could be killed upon capture. In August 1863, Douglass decided that he needed to share his concerns with President Lincoln.

This background sets the scene for the first of Douglass's three meetings with Lincoln at the White House between 1863 and 1865, all of which are described in dramatic detail in the 1881 *Life and Times*. Because we do not have any accounts of the meetings from Lincoln's perspective, we must depend upon Douglass's renderings, which no doubt capture the broad outlines with some accuracy. But all of the accounts are informed by Douglass's effort to convey the subjectivities of both himself and Lincoln, which perforce make them suspect, too. As Douglass would have it, Lincoln's point of view invariably is that he is honored to meet with the great African American leader of the time, from whom he invariably learns a good deal. Additionally, in the 1881 *Life and Times* Douglass chooses to say nothing about the continued suspicion and anger he felt toward the president. The post–Civil War autobiographical accounts can thus seem almost as sanitized as a children's book, even as they convey Douglass's great excitement about his meetings with the president. By portraying Lincoln in all his glory, Douglass becomes part of that glory. His narratives of their meetings are highly effective rhetorical moments that aim, at least in part, to create what I have called the myth of the Douglass-Lincoln relationship, a myth that came to serve both men well.

Douglass's and Lincoln's political friendship, or association, was initiated by their first meeting, on August 10, 1863, when Douglass arrived at the White House to make his case for equal treatment of the black soldiers in the Union Army. It was a very different world back then: presidents spent a good part of their day meeting with people who visited the White House. Accompanied by Senator Samuel C. Pomeroy of Kansas, who had been a supporter of Lincoln's black colonization plan, Douglass, after a relatively brief wait (which suggests that he was taken seriously by White House leaders), managed to meet privately with Edwin

M. Stanton, Lincoln's secretary of war, and then with Lincoln himself. In what was probably a short but gracious meeting, Lincoln and Douglass addressed the issue of equal pay for black soldiers; they may have also discussed policies of retaliation. The evidence suggests that Stanton and Lincoln talked about making Douglass an officer in the Union Army, and that Stanton informed Douglass about a probable appointment.

These are the accepted facts of the meeting. Working with the facts, Douglass in the 1881 *Life and Times* offers a vivid account of his first meeting with Lincoln that puts on display the best attributes of both men. From beginning to end, Douglass emphasizes Lincoln's willingness to deal with Douglass as an equal (in that sense, Douglass presents Lincoln as at least partly cut from the mold of John Brown). "I shall never forget my first interview with this great man," Douglass writes in *Life and Times*. "Happily for me, there was no vain pomp and ceremony about him. I was never more quickly or more completely put at ease in the presence of a great man than in that of Abraham Lincoln." He recalls that "long lines of care were already deeply written on Mr. Lincoln's brow, and his strong face, full of earnestness, lighted up as soon as my name was mentioned." Lincoln may have been pleased to see Douglass, but Douglass is reverential as he looks into the careworn face of the president. When Douglass begins to identify himself, Lincoln interrupts him to say, "I know who you are Mr. Douglass; Mr. Seward has told me all about you. Sit down, I am glad to see you." As mentioned, Douglass's main purpose in meeting with Lincoln was to argue for equal pay for the black troops and for retaliation when black prisoners were summarily executed by the Confederate Army. Douglass reports that "Mr. Lincoln listened with patience and silence to all I had to say."

After mulling over Douglass's arguments, Lincoln explains that he has to move slowly because there are popular prejudices against blacks, but that the pay for black and white soldiers will one day be equal. On the matter of retaliation, in the 1881 account Douglass presents Lincoln as saying that killing southern soldiers in an eye-for-eye way would be "a terrible remedy" that could lead to the deaths of innocent people. Douglass's response is to display a surprising sympathy for Lincoln's position: "In all this I saw the tender heart of the man rather than the stern warrior and commander-in-chief of the American army and navy, and while I could not agree with him, I could but respect his humane spirit." As described in *Life and Times*, the meeting ends with Lincoln promising that "he would sign any commission to colored soldiers whom his Secretary of War should commend to him," and with Stanton himself saying that a military commission for Douglass is in the works.[30] Douglass acknowledges in the 1881 autobiography that he expected to get the commission in two weeks' time, but it never came through. Despite this disappointment, Lincoln in this retrospective account of their first meeting emerges as a great man, not a racist, a huge admirer of Douglass, and, as befitting the 1881 context of reunion and reconciliation, deeply concerned about North and South alike.

In lectures of late 1863, Douglass described the first meeting somewhat differently, but before turning to one such instance, it is worth noting that in the same month that Douglass met with the Lincoln he presents so reverentially in 1881 as the man he "could love, honor, and trust without reserve or doubt," he had some unsparing words for the president in his newspaper. Responding to the murder of scores of blacks during the July 1863 New York City draft riots and to the unequal treatment of black soldiers, Douglass in the August 1863 *Douglass' Monthly* accused Lincoln of "indifference and contempt for the lives of colored men." "What has Mr. Lincoln to say about this slavery and murder? What has he said?" he asks his readers. And he responds: "Not one word." He then insists that Lincoln should adopt a policy of retaliation for any black soldier killed in cold blood by Confederate troops: "For our Government to do less than this, is to deserve the indignation and execration of mankind." Interestingly, by the time of their meeting later in the month, Lincoln *had* issued an Order of Retaliation, and according to a letter that Douglass wrote privately to his friend George L. Stearns two days after he met with Lincoln, he thanked Lincoln in person for issuing that order.[31] But in his public statements he presented Lincoln as reluctant to sign a retaliation order into law—in 1881 because he wanted to present Lincoln as a national leader who refused to be vindictive toward the South, and in 1863 because he suspected that Lincoln didn't care about blacks in light of his failure to comment on the horrors of the draft riots.

Precisely because of those suspicions, in his lectures of late 1863, eighteen years before the first edition of *Life and Times*, Douglass presents himself as not particularly deferential to the president during their August meeting, especially when compared to the version of the same meeting that he writes up for the 1881 autobiography. That lack of deference is apparent, for example, in a reporter's transcript of Douglass's speech of December 4, 1863, to the American Anti-Slavery Society. In the 1881 *Life and Times*, Douglass is guided to Lincoln by Senator Pomeroy; in the speech of December 4, 1863, Douglass describes a more chaotic scene that is lacking in the dignity he would convey in the autobiography but which adds to the comic effect of a visit that has not yet been mythologized. Sounding a bit like a western humorist, Douglass recounts his successful effort to gain access to Lincoln (the reporter on the scene also records the crowd's response):

> I have been to Washington to see the President; and as you were not there, perhaps you may like to know how the President of the United States received a black man at the White House. I will tell you how he received me—just as you have seen one gentleman receive another! (great applause). . . . I tell you I felt big there. (Laughter.) Let me tell you how I got to him; because every body can't get to him. . . . The stairway was crowded with applicants. . . . They were white, and as I was the only dark spot among them, I expect[ed] to have to wait at least half a day; I have heard of men waiting a week; but in two minutes after I sent in my card, the messenger came out, and respectfully invited "Mr. Douglass" in. I could hear, in the eager multitude outside, as they saw me pressing and elbowing my way through, the remark, "Yes, damn it, I knew they would let the nigger through," in a kind of despairing voice—a Peace Democrat, I suppose. (Laughter.) When I went in, the President was sitting in his usual position, I was told, with his feet in different parts of the room, taking it easy. (Laughter.) Don't put this down, Mr. Reporter, I pray you; for I am going down there again to-morrow. (Laughter.) As I came in and approached him, the President began to rise, and he continued to rise until he stood over me (laughter); and he reached out his

hand and said, "Mr. Douglass, I know you; I have read
about you, and Mr. Seward has told me about you;"
putting me quite at ease at once.[32]

Overall, the playfulness of Douglass's account demonumental-
izes the visit. Douglass says nothing about the fact that Senator
Pomeroy had arranged the meeting; and Lincoln initially comes
across as a sort of Midwestern country bumpkin who, even in the
midst of war, is "taking it easy."

Douglass then describes the meeting itself. In his December
1863 speech, Douglass suggests that he did most of the talking,
and he certainly has good things to say about the president as "an
honest man" who is forthright in conceding that he moves slowly
and pragmatically in making decisions about such matters as
equal pay for black soldiers. Douglass tells his audience that he
found Lincoln's explanations to be "reasonable," and that he has
new admiration for the man: "I came to the conclusion that while
Abraham Lincoln will not go down to posterity as Abraham the
Great, or as Abraham the Wise, or as Abraham the Eloquent, although he is all three, wise, great, and eloquent, he will go down
to posterity, if the country is saved, as Honest Abraham (applause)." And yet even as he celebrates the president, Douglass
makes clear that forces larger than Lincoln have put the nation on
the path toward emancipation: "But we are not to be saved by the
captain this time, but by the crew. We are not to be saved by
Abraham Lincoln, but by that power behind the throne, greater
than the throne itself. You and I and all of us have this matter in
hand." Speaking at a meeting organized by Garrison, Douglass
insists that white and black abolitionists, working in tandem
with God, have made the true difference. And these sentiments
lead him to conclude his speech, not with Lincoln, but with John

Brown. Abolitionists, he states, "had come to think that the little finger of dear old John Brown was worth more to the world than all the slaveholders in Virginia put together. (Applause.) What business, then, have we to fight for the old Union? We are not fighting for it. We are fighting for something incomparably better than the old Union. We are fighting for unity: unity of object, unity of institutions, in which there shall be no North, no South, no East, no West, no black, no white, but a solidarity of the nation, making every slave free, and every free man a voter. (Great applause.)"[33] Lincoln may have vanished from the close of the speech, but he is there in absentia, for Douglass continues to fear that Lincoln would be willing to preserve the Union at the cost of black freedom. In this moving peroration, Douglass revises the very meaning of Union, making it into a unity of interests and institutions, by which he means a union without sectional conflict, without slavery, and without arbitrary distinctions between men (whatever their color). This is the union imagined by John Brown. So in a speech that starts out by praising Lincoln, Douglass warns against celebrating him unthinkingly, for the president has not yet achieved the vision of Brown. Four years after his death, Brown continues to shadow Lincoln in Douglass's imagination.

Arguably it is precisely because of that shadowing that Douglass turned on Lincoln yet again during much of 1864. In his famous January 1864 speech "The Mission of the War," Douglass felt compelled to remind both Lincoln and the nation: "no war but an Abolition war; no peace but an Abolition peace." And because he continued to believe that Lincoln was willing to negotiate peace terms with the southern slave states that would preserve the Union and slavery, Douglass initially chose not to support Lincoln for reelection.[34]

Probably aware of Douglass's criticisms, and certainly cognizant by this point of Douglass's important leadership role among African Americans and abolitionists, Lincoln requested a second meeting with Douglass, and on August 25, 1864, more than a year after they first met, they reunited at the White House to discuss a large question on Lincoln's mind: how to mobilize the southern slaves of the Confederate states so that they could contribute to the war effort. During their meeting, Douglass set forth a plan to organize groups of northern blacks to infiltrate southern lines and spread the news of the slaves' emancipation. Though Lincoln never adopted the plan, the result of the meeting, at least as Douglass presents it in the 1881 *Life and Times,* is that Douglass came to feel even more warmly toward Lincoln. He asserts in *Life and Times* that Lincoln was "not only a great president, but a GREAT MAN," whose reelection promised to bring about "the total destruction of slavery."[35] Douglass's 1881 account thus begs the question of why Douglass in 1864 initially chose to support John C. Frémont for the presidency.

This question once again takes us to the critical nub of how to read Douglass's representations of his meetings with Lincoln in his 1881 autobiography. James Oakes argues (sentimentally) that the "second meeting changed forever the way Frederick Douglass viewed Abraham Lincoln." Oakes's evidence for such a judgment is mainly Douglass's retrospective account in *Life and Times,* which, he says, "must be read as the memory of a conversation that took place more than fifteen years earlier."[36] But why not read it as an autobiographical performance calculated to enhance Douglass's reputation in 1881? In his recounting of his second meeting with Lincoln, Douglass tells the remarkable story of how Lincoln refuses to abruptly end their conversation when Governor William A. Buckingham of Connecticut arrives for his appointment. As Douglass recalls the scene, Lincoln tells his secretary that "I want to have a long talk with my friend Frederick Douglass," and that Buckingham will have to wait his turn. Douglass writes in 1881: "This was probably the first time in the history of this Republic when its chief magistrate found occasion or disposition to exercise such an act of impartiality between persons so widely different in their positions and supposed claims upon his attention." Douglass, who concedes that he may be "bragging of the kind consideration which I have reason to believe that Mr. Lincoln entertained towards me," then remarks on how he turned down Lincoln's invitation to have tea with him later in the month at the Soldiers' Home in the District, where Lincoln often slept. (Douglass chose to keep to his speaking schedule.) My point isn't that Douglass made up this material—he may well be remembering accurately—but that his 1881 rendition mainly emphasizes the admiration that Lincoln felt toward him. According to this account, Lincoln especially admires Douglass for his representative leadership (which Douglass was as intent on shoring up in 1881 as he was in 1864). Douglass pointedly remarks in the 1881 *Life and Times:* "I am quite sure that the main thing which gave me consideration with him was my well-known relation to the colored people of the Republic, and especially the help which that relation enabled me to give to the work of suppressing the rebellion and of placing the Union on a firmer basis than it ever had or could have sustained in the days of slavery."[37]

It is Douglass who shines in the 1864 meeting as presented in his 1881 autobiography. And when the meeting turns to the main reason that Lincoln summoned him to the White House, a familiar third party shadows the conversation. For when Douglass talks about "organizing a band of scouts, composed of colored men," who would travel into the South, "beyond the lines of our armies, and carry the news of emancipation, and urge the slaves to come within our boundaries," he says that the idea was "somewhat after the original plan of John Brown" to use the Alleghenies as a pass way for runaway slaves.[38] As I discuss below, another African American leader, Martin Delany, met with Abraham Lincoln around this same time to propose a plan that was much more in keeping with the radical spirit of Brown's plottings in the Alleghenies and at Harpers Ferry, and *that* was the plan that most appealed to Lincoln. For now, it should be noted that however adulatory Douglass was in the 1881 *Life and Times,* he remained hesitant about Lincoln in 1864, and his 1881 reference to Brown may well point to the problem. In 1864, Douglass continued to think that Lincoln wasn't fully committed to blacks' rights to citizenship in the United States, that Lincoln simply couldn't regard blacks as social and political equals in the way of Brown.[39] Thus Douglass continued to offer critical remarks on Lincoln in his speeches and writings, and during the presidential election of 1864 he mostly stayed on the sidelines.

Douglass's harshest criticisms during this time were expressed to English correspondents. Initially refusing to support Lincoln for the presidency, Douglass laid out his brief against Lincoln in a letter written during the summer of 1864 (before their second meeting), which was nonetheless published in Garrison's *Liberator* (after the meeting) in a column titled "Frederick Douglass on President Lincoln." Garrison, who sought to embarrass Douglass, claimed in a prefatory headnote that the letter was met with "exultation" by "the secessionist newspapers in Great Britain." So there's a mean-spirited politics involved in printing the letter. Still, the criticisms voiced in it are consistent with Douglass's earlier criticisms of Lincoln and his criticisms to come. In the letter, Douglass says that he would have preferred the "possibility of securing the nomination and election of a man to the Presidency of more decided anti-slavery convictions and a firmer faith in the immediate necessity and practicability of justice and equality for all men, than have been exhibited in the policy of the present administration." From this disillusioned perspective, Douglass acerbically writes: "The President has virtually laid down this as the rule of his statesmen: *Do evil by choice, right from necessity.*"[40] Here, the deliberation and pragmatism that Douglass would later celebrate in his account of Lincoln in *Life and Times* seem less wise than contemptible.

Even after Douglass had come to terms with the reality that the 1864 presidential election was between Lincoln and General George McClellan, he states in a letter of September 1, 1864, written shortly after his second meeting with Lincoln and subsequently published in British periodicals, that he's mainly intent on defeating McClellan, whom he terms a "bitterly pro-slavery man." He informs his unnamed British correspondent that Lincoln "is not my first or even second choice for the Presidency during the next four years," but that he will do "all I can—it is not much—to promote the election of Mr. Lincoln." After offering this half-hearted endorsement, he discloses (somewhat self-promotingly) that he had recently visited the White House: "While at Washington, a few days ago, President Lincoln invited me to see him, and gave me a lengthy interview." Asserting that he is glad he made the visit, for he could see that the president was more committed to blacks' rights than he had believed, he nevertheless spends a considerable portion of the letter rehearsing his familiar charges against Lincoln, such as "his culpable failure to pay and protect his colored soldiers, and his refusal to permit colored men to vote in the States reconstructed under his auspices." He also complains about "what amounted to a re-enslavement of the colored people" of Louisiana by one of Lincoln's generals, Nathaniel P. Banks, who had issued an order regulating black labor according to a peonage system.[41] It was not until October of that year that Douglass fully committed himself to Lincoln, but he affirmed that commitment in a private letter to Theodore Tilton, which reveals another reason he chose not to campaign for Lincoln: he didn't want to expose Republicans "to the charge of being the 'N—r' party." As for Lincoln, he states to Tilton: "When there was a shadow of a hope that a man of a more decided anti-slavery conviction and policy could be elected, I was not for Mr. Lincoln. But as soon as the Chicago convention, my mind was made up, and it is made still."[42]

A late supporter of Lincoln's reelection, Douglass attended the second inauguration on March 4, 1865, and on this third and final occasion met with him at the inaugural reception. In the 1881 *Life and Times,* Douglass presents his attendance at the inaugural speech and reception as something like a sacred moment involving two great men: Lincoln and Douglass. Douglass is viscerally moved by Lincoln's Second Inaugural Address, almost as if it were a private utterance intended mainly for him. The key scene between Lincoln and Douglass then follows. Barred from the inaugural reception by two White House policemen, who were under orders "to admit no persons of color," Douglass insists that they consult with Lincoln, whom he refuses to believe would issue such an order. He is eventually allowed to enter the White House after someone (perhaps authorized by Lincoln) gives him clearance. As he writes in 1881, he spots Lincoln in the crowd and makes his way toward him. What ensues is fairly magical:

> Like a mountain pine high above all others, Mr. Lincoln stood, in his grand simplicity, and *home-like*

beauty. Recognizing me, even before I reached him,
he exclaimed, so that all around could hear him, "Here
comes my friend Douglass." Taking me by the hand,
he said, "I am glad to see you. I saw you in the crowd
to-day, listening to my inaugural address; how did
you like it?" I said, "Mr. Lincoln, I must not detain
you with my poor opinion, when there are thousands waiting to shake hands with you." "No, no,"
he said, "you must stop a little, Douglass; there is no
man in the country whose opinion I value more than
yours. I want to know what you think of it?" I replied, "Mr. Lincoln, that was a sacred effort." "I am
glad you liked it!" he said; and I passed on feeling
that any man, however distinguished, might well regard himself honored by such expressions, from such
a man.[43]

Douglass may have presented the conversation as he remembered
it, and as it actually took place, though it should be acknowledged
that remembering the facts in this way did good things for
Douglass's reputation in 1881. Whatever one thinks of this narrative in terms of historical veracity, it has to be admired for its
rhetorical effectiveness. Coming at the end of the Civil War, the
brief conversation at the White House has the feel of a hallowed
interracial moment that bodes well for the future of the nation.

But just one month later Lincoln was struck down by John
Wilkes Booth. As a result, Andrew Johnson, whom Douglass
describes in *Life and Times* as "no friend of our race" and "like
one just from a drunken debauch," assumed the presidency.
Douglass delivered a eulogy for Lincoln at Rochester, New
York, on April 15, 1865, the day of the assassination, which he

termed "a personal as well as national calamity." In the eulogy Douglass mentions his final meeting with Lincoln, recalling that it was "only a few weeks ago that I shook his brave, honest hand, and looked into his gentle eye and heard his kindly voice." The mythologization of the Douglass-Lincoln friendship begins with this speech, which anticipates Douglass's future writings on Lincoln. As if ratifying Douglass's vision of their friendship, Mary Todd Lincoln several months later sent him a gift: Lincoln's favorite walking stick.[44]

The evidence suggests that by the end of the Civil War, Douglass and Lincoln thought of themselves as political friends, useful to one another. A deeper connection may well have developed during the sixty to ninety minutes that they spent together over their three years of personal acquaintance. But a question remains: If Lincoln admired Douglass in the way that Douglass suggests in his descriptions of their three meetings in *Life and Times,* and if Lincoln was so taken with Douglass's 1864 plan to have black units spreading the news of emancipation in the southern slave slates, why didn't he name Douglass one of the first black officers in the Union Army? That is one of many probably unanswerable questions about their relationship, but I am going to attempt to answer it. John Brown shadows this story as well.

LINCOLN'S TALE OF DOUGLASS

In his account in the 1881 *Life and Times* of his first meeting with Lincoln in August 1863, Douglass concludes by saying that Stanton and Lincoln promised to name him "assistant adjutant to General Thomson, who was then recruiting and organizing troops in the Mississippi Valley." Douglass assumed he would get this or some other military commission in short order, but he never heard back from Stanton. After his second meeting with Lincoln a year later, Douglass followed up with a letter of August 29, 1864, in which he gave Lincoln additional details about his plan to spread the word of emancipation to "the Slaves in the Rebel States." In the letter, he suggests that Lincoln should send groups of twenty-five to fifty free blacks into the Confederate states to alert the slaves to their freedom, and that these groups should report to a "general agent" and "to the Generals." With this letter, Douglass implicitly makes the case that he should be one of the officers or general agents overseeing the operation; the letter can be read as one last effort to revive what he thought was a promised commission from Lincoln. In *Life and Times*, Douglass offers a terse, wry comment on his disappointment at the failure to get such a commission: "For some reason, however, my commission never came. The government, I fear, was still clinging to the idea that positions of honor in the service should be occupied by white men."[45]

It was certainly true that most positions of honor went to white men. But as historian Benjamin Quarles observes in his classic *The Negro in the Civil War*, by the end of the war there were over a hundred commissioned African American officers. Given Douglass's failure to get a commission, we could ask about the reliability of his account of his August 1863 meeting with Lincoln and Stanton, and even of the August 1864 meeting with Lincoln. Were these meetings as warm and mutually admiring as Douglass suggests? We'll never know because we only have Douglass's (evolving) accounts of the meetings. But let us assume for the moment that Douglass's retrospective narratives are reasonably accurate. Then his disappointment is real, which may help to explain why he initially supported Frémont for the presidency in

1864. In the 1881 autobiography, there is only one other moment in which Douglass acknowledges the sort of disappointment that he expresses when he fails to get a military commission, and that is when Harriet Beecher Stowe fails to follow through on what he believed was her promise to help him fund a black mechanics institute during the 1850s.[46] That first disappointment with Stowe may help to cast light on his second disappointment with Lincoln. In both cases, the black nationalist Martin Delany played a significant role.

Delany was a well-known black leader in the nineteenth century, but if you want to learn more about him, don't look to Douglass's 1881 *Life and Times* because Douglass never mentions him. This is surprising because Delany was the coeditor of Douglass's first newspaper, the *North Star,* and the person Douglass regularly debated about critical issues in the culture, including their responses to the 1852 *Uncle Tom's Cabin.* From Delany's point of view, as he argued in three public letters to Douglass, Stowe was a racist and colonizationist, and Douglass was a fool not to see that. But even as Delany attacked Stowe for being a colonizationist (someone who wanted to ship U.S. blacks to Africa), he was developing plans for blacks to emigrate on their own to Central America or Africa. Responding to Delany's criticisms of Stowe, Douglass asserted that Delany's black emigrationism worked against African Americans' efforts to gain their rights of citizenship in the United States and wasn't all that different from Stowe's alleged colonizationism. In response to Douglass's charges, Delany in 1854, at a black convention in Cleveland, offered his most powerful defense of black emigrationism, "Political Destiny of the Colored Race on the American Continent," in which he argued that blacks could gain the rights of citizenship and become part of the ruling classes by emigrating to Central America.[47] Ten years after Delany delivered his black emigrationist manifesto, Lincoln in 1864, as Douglass does not mention in his 1881 *Life and Times,* appointed Delany the first black major in the Union Army. Why should this have been so?

One possible answer to this question is that Lincoln found Delany to be more impressive than Douglass. Though Douglass presents himself as the only African American meeting with Lincoln during the Civil War, Lincoln actually met with a number of other black leaders, including Delany. Shortly after meeting with Douglass in August 1864, when he asked him how the southern slaves could be deployed to bring about the end of the war, Lincoln met with Delany to ask him the same question. Delany described that meeting in an "as told to" biography published in 1868. In significant ways, Delany's story about his meeting with Lincoln resembles (and thus possibly served as a model for) the story that Douglass would tell years later in *Life and Times* about his similar meeting with Lincoln. In Frances Rollin's *Life and Public Services of Martin R. Delany,* Delany says that the main reason he got the commission is because it was he (Delany) who proposed the most compelling plan to Lincoln for encouraging black insurrection among the Southern slaves. Delany claims that he said to Lincoln (and who knows what he actually said, for there are no other reports of this conversation, either): "I propose, sir, an army of blacks, commanded entirely by black officers, . . . this army to penetrate through the heart of the South, and make conquests, with the banner of Emancipation unfurled, proclaiming freedom as they go, sustaining and protecting it by arming the emancipated, taking them as fresh troops, and leaving a few veterans among the new freedmen, when occasion requires, keeping this banner unfurled until every slave in the south is free, according to your proclamation." In the Rollin biography, Lincoln exultantly responds: "This . . . is the very thing I have been looking and hoping for; but nobody offered it. I have thought it over and over again. I have talked about it; I hoped and prayed for it." And he asks: "Will you take command?" In a letter to Secretary of War Edwin M. Stanton included in the 1868 biography, Lincoln refers to Delany as "this most extraordinary and intelligent black man."[48] And it is Delany, not Douglass, who receives the commission as major.

Perhaps Delany got the commission because Lincoln was more willing to deploy a terroristic sort of violence than Douglass would have imagined. In this respect, it was Delany, not Douglass, who presented a plan in the spirit of John Brown. Delany had his own encounter with Brown in May 1858, when he met with him in Chatham, Canada, along with forty-five others, to discuss how to overthrow the U.S. government. At that meeting, Brown presented the mixed-race group with his "Provisional Constitution and Ordinances for the People of the United States," a blueprint for establishing an interim government for a nation without slavery. Delany, who had moved to Chatham in February 1856, assumed a leadership role at the convention, and he voted to approve the new constitution.[49] Though Douglass did not attend the convention, Brown (as mentioned) had stayed with him in Rochester for three weeks early in 1858, and it was at Douglass's house that he had drafted the "Provisional Constitution." He probably shared it with Douglass, and perhaps Douglass helped him to write it. In the end, Delany and Douglass both chose not to participate in the raid on Harpers Ferry (Delany was in the Niger region of Africa working on a plan for African American emigration), but Delany, who authored *Blake* (1859, 1861–1862), a serialized novel about black insurrectionism in the Americas, may have been even more responsive to Brown's militancy than Douglass.[50] And that militancy seems to have appealed to Lincoln in late 1864.

But another possible answer to the question of why Lincoln chose Delany over Douglass as the first black major is that when Lincoln in 1862 was most intent on developing his plan for black colonization to Central America, he, or one of his advisors, somehow stumbled across the transcript of Delany's 1854 "Political Destiny of the Colored Race on the American Continent." Lincoln or someone on his staff was so impressed by the speech that it was reprinted in the House of Representatives' *Report of the Select Committee on Emancipation and Colonization* (Washington, DC, 1862), which was prepared by Republican supporters of Lincoln's colonization plan. Ironically, then, Lincoln may have chosen Delany over Douglass because he regarded him as something of a fellow traveler in colonizationism (even though Delany supported selective black emigration and not a coercive colonizationism). That said, Lincoln and Delany went back and forth on colonizationism and emigrationism during the Civil War. Lincoln probably abandoned his plan by 1864, though there is evidence that he was rethinking black colonization just before the assassination.[51] Meanwhile, the celebrated Major Delany sustained his belief in U.S. nationalism into the late 1870s, only to begin mapping out new plans for black emigration with the apparent end of Reconstruction.

But to return to Douglass's failure to get any sort of military commission, which I think still remains a mystery: Given that, as Quarles shows, Lincoln appointed many other blacks to such commissions, the president may have decided against offering Douglass a commission because of their political differences on colonization. In addition, Douglass's other sharp criticisms of Lincoln during the 1861–1864 period may have convinced the president that Douglass was someone whom he would not be able to control in a position of leadership. In his 1895 eulogy for Douglass, the lawyer-novelist Albion W. Tourgée implied that Lincoln thought precisely along those lines, and in the course of the eulogy he shared a fascinating story from an anonymous informant who claimed to have asked Lincoln in 1864 or 1865 this very question: "Why do you not give FRED DOUGLASS a commission?" According to Tourgée's informant, Lincoln said the following: "If Mr. DOUGLASS had a military training and we could find colored men capable to serve as field, line, and staff for such a command, it would be different. But you must remember that even then the problem would not be solved. *Mr. Douglass is not a citizen of the United States!* Would I be justified in appointing him to a responsible command? The truth is, he is too big for a small place. He is the representative of his people, and it would not be to their interest that he should hold a subordinate position."[52] Recounting this story in 1895, Tourgée meant to flatter Douglass, and to include Lincoln in that flattery, by suggesting that Lincoln knew that Douglass was indeed "too big" for a subordinate position. But with the odd allusion to the Dred Scott case, which would have made all African Americans ineligible for military commissions, Lincoln ultimately comes off as a racist who was reluctant to put a black man in a position of authority.

Intriguing as it is, Tourgée's story is retrospective, second-hand, and not to be fully trusted. I would propose a different explanation as a way of thinking more skeptically about the Douglass-Lincoln relationship during the Civil War period: Douglass's failure to get a military commission can be taken as a metaphor for the missing side of the storytelling that has become the main source of our understanding of the Douglass-Lincoln relationship. Although we don't have Lincoln's reports of his meetings with Douglass, we could regard Lincoln's decision not to appoint Douglass as, in effect, his "tale" of Douglass. Maybe Lincoln hadn't taken to Douglass as much as Douglass thought, and maybe Lincoln was simply being strategic in meeting with the best known African American leader of the time. What we do know is that the Douglass-Lincoln relationship was a bit more troubled and much less of a hermetic binary than Douglass lets on, and at least one important facet of the relationship was that each person knew how to make use of the other. All of which is to say that if we take this tale of Lincoln seriously, we can think more realistically about the limits of the Douglass-Lincoln relationship during the Civil War. After the Civil War, with Lincoln silenced, it was an entirely different story.

THE WHITE MAN'S PRESIDENT

In the wake of the assassination, Lincoln quickly emerged as the sacred figure who had preserved the Union, and Douglass found it useful to present himself as one of Lincoln's great friends.[53] John Brown, too, had achieved a sacred status in some circles in the North, but he was hardly regarded as warmly by the wide constituency that admired Lincoln. Moreover, Douglass's friendship with Lincoln, much more than with Brown, served Douglass well when he began to seek a more significant role in the Republican Party. But even as Douglass worked to develop the myth of his closeness with Lincoln, he remained loyal to the memory of Brown and often talked about the two men together. In his speech on "The Assassination and Its Lessons," delivered in

Washington, DC, on February 13, 1866, for instance, Douglass recalls how "loyal black troops had marched through the streets to the tune of 'Old John Brown.'" When he turns to the subject of Lincoln, he offers his highest praise by linking the dead president to the man whose cross-racial sympathies inspired the black troops: "when our great military chieftains are forgotten, and the war itself shall seem a mere speck in the distance, Abraham Lincoln, like dear old John Brown, will still find eloquent tongues to speak of his name."[54] In the post–Civil War period, Brown continued to shadow Lincoln in Douglass's mind, and in two of his greatest speeches of the post–Civil War era—his 1876 address on Lincoln in Washington, DC, and his 1881 address on Brown at Harpers Ferry—Douglass can seem to be thinking of both men together even when he focuses on just the one. He then conjoins the two figures most powerfully as part of his life, and as part of his lifelong autobiographical project, in his 1881 *Life and Times*.

Between the time of Lincoln's assassination and the publication of *Life and Times*, Douglass in his autobiographically inflected speeches on Lincoln would continue to raise questions about the president's handling of the war, focusing on his reluctance to use violence in the service of antislavery. And though he presents Lincoln in *Life and Times* as an emancipator, he was reluctant to give him that honor prior to the publication of his 1881 autobiography. In his August 3, 1869, British West Indian emancipation speech, for example, Douglass conveys his skepticism about crediting emancipation to a man who had moved so slowly on an issue that seemed secondary to his desire to preserve the Union. He asks his audience in Medina, New York: "Whence came the abolition of slavery? The theologian says, God. The politician says, Lincoln. The abolitionist says, Garrison.

The statesman says, the war. To me the result is no miracle. . . . The evil contained the seeds of its own destruction. . . . The world might have permitted slavery a good while longer, but for the pride and ambition of its votaries. Mr. Garrison would not abolish it. Mr. Lincoln did not wish to interfere with it."[55] In this formulation, Lincoln remains the politician who, as Douglass remarked during the Civil War, was at times willing to accommodate himself to evil.

But even as Douglass continued to express some skepticism about Lincoln, he had warmed to his memory, too. The presidency of Andrew Johnson made clear to Douglass and other African American leaders just how great the loss of Lincoln truly was for those who cared about the situation of blacks in a reconstructed United States. In a number of his post–Civil War speeches, Douglass began to present himself as Lincoln's friend and advisor in order to make the case that Lincoln's most important legacy to the nation was his commitment to full rights for African Americans. In his February 1866 speech on "The Assassination and Its Lessons," Douglass celebrated Lincoln's "moral courage" for inviting him to the White House and listening to what he had to say. In a speech delivered later that year, Douglass told his auditors in Philadelphia that "Mr. Lincoln was not ashamed to invite him [Douglass] to Washington, and to take tea with him."[56] But Douglass was not one to let friendship cut off political critique. Drawing on his sense of his personal friendship with Lincoln, and addressing both the strengths and limitations of the president, Douglass in his April 14, 1876, "Oration on the Occasion of the Freedmen's Monument in Memory of Abraham Lincoln" produced one of the subtlest historicist accounts extant of Lincoln's perspectives on slavery and race.[57] Not incidentally, the speech further helped to consolidate Douglass's celebrity status.

To set the scene: In 1876, the year of the nation's Centennial, Douglass was invited to be the main speaker honoring the unveiling of the sculptor Thomas Ball's "The Freedmen's Monument," a sculpture paid for by donations from the freed blacks. The sculpture depicted Lincoln as a benevolent Christ, Moses, or God figure offering his blessings over the body of a manacled black male slave, based on an actual fugitive slave from Missouri (Figure 8). The hierarchical image of the lordly Lincoln freeing the objectified, passive slave affirmed the idea of blacks' indebtedness to the Great Emancipator. Douglass, who at the end of the Civil War had opposed building a monument to Lincoln, hated the image of the manacled, kneeling slave, so he came to the lecture with some real animus against Ball's sculpture, along with a desire to tell the truth to the mixed-race audience assembled in Lincoln Park, Washington, DC. And what an audience it was! In attendance for the occasion were members of the president's cabinet, Supreme Court judges, numerous senators and congressmen, hundreds of ordinary citizens (many of whom were African American), and President Ulysses S. Grant, whom Douglass very much admired and had been working with on his ultimately failed plan to annex Santo Domingo. In his 1881 *Life and Times*, Douglass writes that "the part taken by me in the ceremonies of that grand occasion, takes rank among the most interesting incidents of my life." And though he doesn't actually discuss what he said in the speech, choosing to include an "Extract" in *Life and Times'* appendix, he points out that "occasions like this have done wonders in the removal of popular prejudice and lifting into consideration the colored race." Speaking in 1876, Douglass felt a special urgency about "lifting into consideration the colored race," for Reconstruction was failing, and it would come even closer to failing just one year later with the

FIGURE 8. Freedmen's Monument to Abraham Lincoln, Lincoln Park, Washington, DC. Photo by Carol M. Highsmith, The George F. Landegger Collection of District of Columbia Photographs in Carol M. Highsmith's America, Library of Congress, Prints and Photographs Division. Gift of George F. Landegger, 2010. Courtesy of the Library of Congress.

Compromise of 1877. Douglass's approach to removing popular prejudice rested in part on not genuflecting before Lincoln, not becoming the oratorical analogue to the image of the kneeling, shackled slave.[58]

So Douglass unshackled himself and spoke bravely and honestly, presenting Lincoln as indifferent to the plight of the black slaves and intent on appeasing border state racists. This is the temporizing Lincoln that Douglass criticized in his 1860s newspaper writings, and not the Lincoln he sanitizes in the 1881 *Life and Times*. Douglass states at the beginning of the speech: "truth compels me to admit even here in the presence of the monument we have erected in his memory, Abraham Lincoln was not, in the fullest sense of the word, either our man or our model. In his interests, in his associations, in his habits of thought, and in his prejudices, he was a white man. He was preeminently the white man's President, entirely devoted to the welfare of white men. He was ready and willing at any time during the last years of his administration to deny, postpone and sacrifice the rights of humanity in the colored people, to promote the welfare of the white people of his country." And he doesn't stop there. Lincoln, Douglass says to his distinguished audience, while reaching out to the many African Americans in the crowd, "strangely told us that we were the cause of the war; [and] more strangely told us to leave the land in which we were born"; and even "after accepting our services as colored soldiers, he refused to retaliate when we were murdered as colored prisoners." Additionally, Lincoln was willing "to pursue, recapture, and send back the fugitive slave to his master, and to suppress a slave rising for liberty, though his guilty masters were already in arms against the Government."[59] These are Douglass's familiar criticisms of Lincoln during the Civil War. The critique of Lincoln in 1876 as willing to appease the slave states by returning fugitive slaves was especially cutting given that the black man in the Freedmen's Statue was a fugitive slave, and not only that, was from the border state of Missouri. Ironically, Lincoln's Emancipation Proclamation did not free that particular slave; Missouri state legislation of 1865 did. In effect, Douglass was saying that Thomas Ball got things all wrong.

And yet even with Douglass's brave critique of Lincoln's hesitancy about fighting a war of emancipation, the speech remains one of the most profound and moving meditations that we have on Lincoln, in large part because Douglass's rhetorical tactics are so keenly and sympathetically historicist. The thrust of the first half of the speech is to situate Lincoln in his mid-nineteenth-century culture, in which most whites regarded blacks as not quite human and hardly their equals, and thus not worth dying for (which is precisely why Douglass found John Brown's willingness to die for blacks so extraordinary). Douglass presents these views as cultural givens, and then makes a remarkable turn in the second half of the lecture to underscore that Lincoln's greatness was about making bold and humane decisions that would "free his country from the great crime of slavery" from within a cultural mind-set that had made it next to impossible for most white American political leaders to imagine such a possibility. Though Douglass plays down his own influence on Lincoln in this particular speech, withholding his personal remarks until the very end, he presents himself as sharing in Lincoln's thoughts as he "save[d] his country from dismemberment and ruin . . . [and] free[d] his country from the great crime of slavery." Douglass is at his historicist best when he tells his auditors not to judge Lincoln on the basis of this or that action but to consider the big picture. "We saw him, measured him, and estimated him," Douglass remarks, "not by stray utterances to injudicious and tedious delegations who often tried his patience; not by isolated facts torn from their connection; not by any partial and imperfect glimpses, caught at inopportune moments; but by a broad survey, in the light of the stern logic of great events." From this perspective, Douglass insists, "it was enough for us that Abraham Lincoln was at the head of a great movement, and was in living and earnest sympathy with that movement; which, in the nature of things, must go on TILL SLAVERY SHOULD BE UTTERLY and forever abolished in the United States." Notably, before the president, his cabinet, members of the Supreme Court, and numerous congressmen and senators, Douglass suggests that forms of slavery still exist in the United States, and he enlists the spirit of the martyred Lincoln to help him continue the fight for racial equality. Douglass goes on to praise Lincoln for ending the slave trade in Washington, DC, for allowing 200,000 African Americans to fight for their liberty, and for being the first American president to recognize the black Republic of Haiti. It is only at the conclusion of the speech that Douglass lets the personal come to the fore. "No man who knew Abraham Lincoln," says Douglass, the man who regularly let the world know he knew Lincoln, "could hate him, but because of his fidelity to Union and liberty, he is doubly dear to us, and will be precious forever."[60]

Douglass told many tales of Lincoln, offering conflicting views on his management of the Civil War and various but generally complementary stories about their meetings. Here Douglass in his greatest speech about Lincoln offers judgment, and that judgment is good overall. Collectively, Douglass's writings about Lincoln evince anger, conflict, hope, and admiration, but what is most striking about his writings and speeches are Douglass's canny and often moving efforts to make use of his friendship or association with Lincoln to continue his fight for racial equality.

Douglass was no manacled slave looking up to a beneficent Lincoln in gratitude for the things he did and did not do. He was a rhetorically gifted political visionary who, as his 1876 speech shows, had a clear-eyed view of Lincoln and a keen understanding of the rhetorical uses he could make of his limited interactions with the president. But Lincoln's hesitance to use violence to fight the violence of slavery, and his suspect commitment to the practice of racial egalitarianism, were sticking points for Douglass, which is why Brown remained one of his great heroes in the post–Civil War years, the man against whom Douglass continued to measure other white antislavery leaders.

Near the end of the 1881 *Life and Times,* after his final mention of Lincoln, Douglass reports on his pilgrimage to Harpers Ferry, West Virginia, where he gave a lecture to honor the memory of Brown. Though five years separate his major lectures on Lincoln and Brown, Douglass in his 1881 autobiography discusses those talks in relative close proximity, conveying a sense of how intertwined these two great leaders continued to be in his political and autobiographical imagination. Joined at Storer College by Andrew J. Hunter, the Virginia state attorney who had prosecuted Brown, Douglass gave a memorial lecture that he describes in *Life and Times* as "not merely defending John Brown, but extolling him as a hero and martyr to the cause of liberty."[61] The cult of Lincoln may have offered the greatest hope for national reconciliation, but at a time when blacks were seeing a steady loss of their civil rights, Douglass in this 1881 speech made clear that Brown, too, spoke to the current moment.

Titled "John Brown" in the published version, and delivered at Harpers Ferry on March 30, 1881, Douglass honors Brown as "a great historical character, of our own time and country." Much more than in the 1876 Lincoln speech, Douglass uses autobiography to ground his claims about Brown's importance. Calling Brown "an old friend" who remains part of his "grateful memory," Douglass asserts that he can even speak to Brown's "inner life." As with the Lincoln speech, one of his large goals is to present Brown in his historical context. Douglass thus says about the attack on Harpers Ferry to his auditors at that very place, a number of whom would have been suspicious of such a celebration of Brown: "Viewed apart and alone, as a transaction separate and distinct from its antecedents and bearings, it takes rank with the most cold-blooded and atrocious wrongs ever perpetrated; but just here is the trouble—this raid on Harper's Ferry, no more than Sherman's march to the sea can consent to be thus viewed alone." Specifically, Douglass argues that the "bloody harvest of Harper's Ferry was ripened by the heat and moisture of merciless bondage of more than two hundred years." From that perspective, Brown, in the tradition of the nation's great revolutionary leaders, can be seen as a patriot committed to ideals of American liberty, for this is a man who "evinced a conception of the sacredness and value of liberty which transcended in sublimity that of her own Patrick Henry."[62]

Having made broad claims for Brown, Douglass spends much of his lecture rehearsing his own role in Brown's life as a friend and political ally. In both the speech and *Life and Times,* which appeared a few months later, Douglass insists that he did not have "an important agency in the John Brown raid," perhaps in order to maintain his profile as a black Republican leader committed to sectional reconciliation. However, Douglass acknowledges here and in his other writings, including his late 1859 and 1860 speeches on Harpers Ferry, that he knew about the planned raid, and therefore, implicitly, was a coconspirator. Douglass is even more forthright about his coconspiratorship in this 1881 address, presenting himself as someone with whom Brown regularly shared his plans. Brown may have adopted bloody military tactics in Kansas during the mid-1850s, but Douglass praises him for taking on the fight against the expansion of slavery, and admits openly: "During his four years' service in Kansas it was my good fortune to see him often." Douglass then tells the story of meeting Brown in Chambersburg, Pennsylvania, just two weeks before the planned raid on Harpers Ferry, and deciding against joining Brown's group because he felt the raid was doomed to failure. But Douglass now rhetorically (and aggressively) asks: "Did John Brown fail?" His answer in 1881 is very different from his pre-raid perspective in 1859: "No man fails, or can fail who so grandly gives himself and all he has to a righteous cause." In this context Douglass makes claims for Brown that he cannot make for Lincoln: "John Brown . . . began the war that ended American slavery and made this a free republic."[63]

In Douglass's speeches on Lincoln delivered after this John Brown address, Lincoln often falls short of the "hero and martyr" Brown, as Douglass terms him in a speech of 1884. Particularly in speeches that he gave to African American audiences, Douglass raised questions about Lincoln's iconic status as the Great Emancipator and continued to maintain that Lincoln's temporizing and racism extended the war. Addressing an African American audience at the First Congregational Church in Washington, DC, on the twenty-first anniversary of the emancipation of the slaves of the District of Columbia, Douglass celebrates the blacks themselves for having brought about their freedom: "Abraham Lincoln called upon the colored men of this country to reach out their iron arms and clutch with their steel fingers the faltering banner of the Republic, and they rallied, and they rallied, and they rallied." In 1890, in a speech that was also delivered to an African American audience, Douglass, as if still resentful, returned to the moment in 1862 when Lincoln met with the black delegation and blamed blacks (and not those who shelled Fort Sumter) for the outbreak of the Civil War. Douglass recalls the moment that so angered him in 1862: " 'The negroes were the cause of the war,' said Mr. Lincoln, and straightway the loyal soldiers of the Republic began to kick and beat the poor negroes on the banks of the Potomac, and the Irish began to hang, stab, and murder the negroes in New York."[64] In this way Douglass implies that lynchings and other forms of antiblack violence during the 1880s and early 1890s have their sources in the sort of scapegoating that Lincoln was guilty of in 1862.

At Republican gatherings, however, Douglass the Republican political appointee remained intent on developing the myth of his collaborative friendship with Lincoln. For example, in a speech delivered in February 1888 to the Republican National League, he avows that "I knew Abraham Lincoln personally. To have known him as I knew him, I regard as one of the grandest privileges experienced by me during a considerable lifetime." Praising Lincoln as "a great and good man" who, at their three meetings, "listened to what I had to say," the man who displayed slave chains to his crowds in Britain now has something new to display: the walking stick that was bestowed upon him by Mary Todd Lincoln. Exhibiting the cane to his audience, Douglass shares what he believes Mrs. Lincoln must have said to "her dressmaker, who was near by when she was gathering up her things to go away": " 'Here is Mr. Lincoln's favorite cane (this is the identical cane that I now hold in my hand), and I know of no man who will value it more than Frederick Douglass.' " Douglass concludes the speech by expressing his love of the fetishized object: "I am the owner of this cane, you may depend on that; and

I mean to hold it and keep [it] in sacred remembrance of Abraham Lincoln, who once leaned on it."[65]

Douglass gets even more personal in "Abraham Lincoln, the Great Man of Our Century," an autobiographical speech about Lincoln that he delivered in February 1893 at a banquet in Brooklyn on the occasion of the centenary anniversary of Lincoln's birth. Again, this was a heavily Republican Party affair, with over 300 prominent Republicans in attendance at Brooklyn's Union League Club. Douglass was the main speaker, and his charge was to respond to the topic of the toast: "Personal Recollections of Abraham Lincoln." Having recently been relieved of his position as consul to Haiti, Douglass had his own personal agenda of restoring his reputation, which he knew he could do through Lincoln. As in his 1888 lecture before the Republican National League, he drew on the stories he had already told in *Life and Times*. Confessing that "it is impossible for me and, perhaps, for anyone else, to say anything new about Abraham Lincoln," he asks for leeway to be "confidential and autobiographical" and shares what had become the familiar stories of his three meetings with Lincoln, though with even more reverence for what he calls Lincoln's "godlike nature." In this late speech, Douglass presents Lincoln during the Civil War as always on the side of "the unfortunate, defenceless, the oppressed and the enslaved"; and he omits any mention of tension between the two men. During the summer of 1863, Douglass was unrelenting in his criticisms of Lincoln's response to the New York City draft riots. Here, Lincoln is presented as resolute in his commitment to the blacks of New York: "The draft was being resisted. Loyal black men were being murdered in the streets of New York. . . . Out of this darkness and storm the soul of Lincoln shone with a light all the more clear, calm, and steady."[66]

Historical revisionism, in other words, is central to this last major autobiographical speech on Lincoln. Describing his initial interview with Lincoln, Douglass drops any disagreement from the account, saying that he put his full trust in Lincoln's promise to address issues of wages and promotion for African American soldiers at some future time (but without providing any evidence that Lincoln actually attended to the matter before his assassination). As for the issue of retaliation, he states that he was "silenced by [Lincoln's] over-mastering mercy and benevolence." In this final account of their first meeting, Douglass takes even greater pains to underscore their friendship. According to Douglass, Lincoln said in parting: "Douglass, never come to Washington without calling upon me." Douglass proclaims to his audience of Republican supporters: "And I never did." (In fact, Douglass subsequently went to Washington several times without seeing Lincoln.) Douglass is more to the point about his second visit. Though he once again reports on Lincoln's statement to Governor Buckingham that he would have to wait while "I am talking with my friend Douglass," he is honest about the fact that Lincoln did not adopt his plan to spread the news of emancipation to the southern blacks. In his account of his attendance at the Second Inaugural Address, Douglass takes advantage of his retrospective narration to maintain how concerned he had been about Lincoln's vulnerability: "I was oppressed with a dread foreboding as I followed his carriage. The fear was upon me that Mr. Lincoln might be shot down on his way to the Capitol." As in Douglass's 1886 reminiscence with which I began this chapter, he wishes he could have protected Lincoln from the assassination. He again tells the story about how he had to challenge White House security to gain admission to the inaugural reception, and he comments once more on how Lincoln greets him as "my friend,

Frederick Douglass!" Douglass's short description of the second inauguration reception and subsequent assassination is both haunting and moving, and, coming at the end of this late speech, can be taken as his last major effort to bequeath to posterity his vision of the Douglass-Lincoln friendship. Embellishing on the version in *Life and Times*, Douglass describes their final interaction:

> When I did succeed [in getting past White House security], and shook hands with him, he detained me and said, "Douglass I saw you in the crowd to-day, listening to my inaugural address. How did you like it?" I replied "Mr. Lincoln, I must not stop to talk now. Thousands are here, wishing to shake your hand." But he said, "You must stop. There is no man in the United States whose opinion I value more than yours. How did you like it?" (Applause.) I said, "Mr. Lincoln, it was a sacred effort," and passed on, amid some smiles, much astonishment, and some frowns. And this was the last time that I heard the voice and saw the face and form of honest Abraham Lincoln.
>
> A few weeks later he fell before the bullet of the assassin. His murder was the natural outcome of a war for slavery. He fell a martyr to the same barbarous and bloody spirit which now pursue, with outrage and vengeance, the people whom he emancipated and whose freedom he secured. Did his firm hand now hold the helm of state; did his brave spirit now animate the Nation; did his wisdom now shape and control the destiny of this otherwise great republic; did he now lead the once great republican party, we should

not, as now, hear from the Nation's capital the weak and helpless, the inconsistent humiliating confession that, while there are millions of money and ample power in the United States government to protect the lives and liberties of American citizens in the republics of Hayti and faroff Chili [*sic*], and in every other foreign country on the globe, there is no power under the United States Constitution to protect the lives and liberties of American citizens in any one of our own Southern states from barbarous, inhuman and lawless violence.[67]

Portraying Lincoln as the president who would have been willing to challenge racists in the North and South in order to protect the lives and rights of the nation's black citizens, Douglass poses a challenge to the nation's political leaders, Democrat and Republican alike, to live up to the legacy of Lincoln. It is good to think that Lincoln would have risen to the occasion as Douglass describes it, and in that regard Douglass attempts to do considerable cultural work at this Republican Party gathering by imagining the kind of president that the nation needs at the present hour. The speech also suggests that Douglass at long last regards Lincoln as worthy of entering the pantheon with his friend John Brown.

But one year later, in a speech on "The Blessings and Liberty and Education," which Douglass delivered to a mixed-race audience at the dedication of the Colored Industrial School at Manassas, Virginia, Douglass honors those white men who were not bounded by race in their thinking about human rights. Lincoln does not make his list. "Not for the race, not for color, but for man and manhood alone they labored, fought, and died," Douglass declares. "Neither Phillips, nor Sumner, nor Garrison, nor John Brown, nor Gerrit Smith was a black man. They were white men, and yet no black men were ever truer to the black man's cause." Douglass certainly came close to believing that Lincoln, like Brown and Smith (and the now dead and long forgiven Garrison), spoke for whites and blacks alike; and in a 1865 draft of a speech he never gave, Douglass referred to Lincoln as "the black man's president."[68] But precisely because of his friendship with Brown, he never fully came to believe that, try as he might over the next thirty years.

~5~

THOMAS AULD AND
THE REUNION NARRATIVE

NEAR THE END of the 1881 edition of *Life and Times of Frederick Douglass*, and also in the expanded 1892 edition, Douglass describes his return to Maryland's Eastern Shore, "the scene," he says, "of some of my saddest experiences of my slave life."[1] During this visit of June 1877, he meets with the dying Captain Thomas Auld, his former master, in a moment of reunion and seeming reconciliation. The men hold hands; they weep; they appear to find common ground. It is difficult not to be moved by this highly emotional autobiographical account, which indeed has had a major impact on Douglass's biography. Dickson Preston asserts in his 1980 *Young Frederick Douglass* that Douglass loved Thomas Auld, that he made this 1877 visit because he thought he owed Auld an apology, and that their meeting, though "brief," "had cleared the atmosphere of forty-one years of misunderstanding." Taking this argument even further, William McFeely proclaims in his 1991 biography that "Frederick loved Thomas, and that love was returned," and then he describes the reunion scene even more dramatically, or melodramatically, than Douglass himself, reporting that "Auld, shaken with palsy, wept; Douglass was so choked up that he could not speak." Though Douglass over the years had regularly depicted Auld as the embodiment of the mean-spirited slave owner, McFeely, like Preston, assures us that their relationship closed without "bitterness" and with "quiet satisfaction."[2]

But does the textual and biographical evidence support such readings, particularly in an autobiography published just a few years after the Compromise of 1877 and at a time when Douglass was disillusioned with cultural displays of reconciliation between white northerners and southerners?[3] My own view of the reunion scene comes closer to what Oscar Wilde reportedly said about the sad and touching death of Little Nell in Charles Dickens's *The Old Curiosity Shop:* "One must have a heart of stone to read the death of little Nell without laughing."[4] Now, while I wouldn't want to claim that the Douglass-Auld reunion scene in *Life and Times* is truly laughable, I am skeptical of readings that identify love at its core or that see Douglass as wanting to make amends to his former master. Such readings, which dovetail with Peter Walker's strangely influential claim that Douglass's visits to the Eastern Shore reveal his "hopeless secret desire to be white," have distorted Douglass's biography by linking him too closely to Auld and his extended family, thereby diminishing the importance of Douglass's continuing interactions with African Americans and his increasing attraction to Haiti.[5] I am concerned as well that such sentimental readings risk making Douglass into a kind of "boy" who has returned to a beloved father figure. Preston in his biography actually says that Douglass in 1877 had come "home."[6]

When Douglass decided to visit Baltimore in November 1864, thirty-six years after his escape, he mostly eschewed the language of homecoming. Instead, in a speech delivered in Rochester on November 13, 1864, and published in the Baltimore *American and Commercial Advertiser,* he marvels at the recent transformation of Maryland from a slave state to a free state, and declares that "I expect to have a good old-fashioned visit, for I have not been there for a long time." Then he brings Thomas Auld into the speech. As he regularly did during the 1840s and 1850s, he deploys Auld as the figure of the hypocritical slave owner, in this instance for comic effect: "I may meet my old master there, whom I have not seen for many years. I heard he was living only a short time ago, and he will be there, for he is on the right side. I made a convert of him years ago!" It would be far more accurate to say, as I discuss below, that he infuriated Auld years ago when he published his incendiary essay "To My Old Master, Thomas Auld" (1848) in the *North Star.* In the same speech Douglass states with more than a touch of irony that Auld "was a very good man, with a high sense of honor," and that as part of his goodness and honor he made sure that slaves and their masters "were all parts of one great social system, only we were at the bottom and they at the top!" Douglass's remarks on Auld's "goodness" ultimately serve his larger aim of demonstrating how slavery as an institution "shackles" the "ankles" of the slaves and the "necks" of the masters.[7]

Douglass's few private writings on Thomas Auld express sentiments that can seem more heartfelt. In a letter of June 10, 1859, to the Maryland physician and colonizationist James Hall, Douglass confides that he would like to hear about "all of the dear ones of my youth," and he even has good things to say about Thomas Auld, confessing that he "has shown himself far more benevolent and noble than I supposed him to be—and than I have given him credit for in my earlier speeches and publications."

The man whom he depicts in his first two autobiographies, and in "To My Old Master," as having sent his frail grandmother out to the woods to die, may have actually tried to help her. Still, Douglass does not express any desire to revise those earlier publications, and in the same letter he challenges the actions of a man who promised to emancipate Douglass and some of the other slaves by the time they reached their mid-twenties. As he remarks to Hall, "It seems to me that his Charity and justice would have appeared to far better advantage had he set an earlier age, as the one at which to emancipate his servants." Six years later, in 1865, Douglass wrote the reformer Lydia Maria Child about the potential difficulty of reuniting with Auld: "He would find it hard to approach me as Mr. Douglass and I should find it equally so to approach him as *Master* Thomas." Nevertheless, Douglass maintains that he "would be glad to see him" if they could find a meeting place somewhere between the Eastern Shore and Baltimore, for "I do not fancy making a journey to see a man who gave me so many reasons for wishing the greatest distance between us." On second thought, however, he declares that he would visit "Master Thomas" at his home if Auld "says he would be glad to see me" and requests the meeting "by letter."[8] Twelve years later, in 1877, Auld, according to Douglass, invited him to make just such a visit, and as Douglass anticipates in his letter to Child, the question of how they should address each other would become a point of controversy.

Douglass's feelings about Auld are complex and hard to pin down. But it's worth emphasizing that Douglass had virtually nothing to do with Auld from the time of his birth in 1818 until 1833 (when he was forced to move from Hugh and Sophia Auld's home in Baltimore to Thomas's in St. Michaels), and that he was not a blood relative. Douglass lived with Auld for only three years (March 1833–April 1836); and from the time of his escape in 1838 until their reunion in 1877 they had no personal encounters. Given the short amount of time that Douglass was directly under Auld's authority, it could be argued that Douglass's most intense relationship with him was not with the actual person but with the rhetorical figure of Auld that Douglass created for thousands of his readers and auditors. Working against the grain of those biographers who regard Auld as a beloved father figure in Douglass's life, I will be developing a reading of the reunion scene in *Life and Times* that emphasizes its performative (or staged) dimension, that sees Douglass as to some extent enjoying his power over Auld, and that considers the scene in the larger context of an autobiography that, even with its glorification of Lincoln, refuses to gloss over troubled personal histories. Resisting what David Blight terms the "pathos and sentiment" of North-South reconciliation narratives of the period, Douglass in his post–Civil War speeches called for "a full accounting for the past."[9] In 1877, he may not have made a direct demand for such accounting from the seriously ill Auld, but he is very clear in the 1881 *Life and Times* about who Auld is, what he represents, and why the two men will forever remain at a distance, tears and all.

Douglass does not let Auld off the hook in *Life and Times* or in any of his other writings of the pre– and post–Civil War period. Though my main focus will be on the reunion scene in *Life and Times*, I will be considering a range of other materials, beginning with Douglass's initial writings on Auld from the 1840s and including an anonymous reporter's newspaper article on the reunion itself. In Douglass's various accounts of Auld over an approximately forty-year period, I see no evidence of love between Douglass and Auld, and I wonder if critics who should have known better haven't fallen for the stereotype of the good master and the loyal slave and for the related stereotype of slavery as familial (one big happy family). This is not to say that no feeling was shared between these two men when they met in 1877; there surely was some warmth based on their personal and public history and on their mutual sense that old age and changing historical circumstances provided an occasion for some sort of reconciliation. And it's not to say that the emotional connections between these men were uncomplicated, going back to Douglass's years in the Eastern Shore. But as with Douglass's tales of Lincoln, ultimately we know nothing about Auld's perspective on the reunion beyond what we get from Douglass, and there is every indication that Douglass was keen to use the occasion of the reunion for his own rhetorical and political purposes.

When Douglass published the first edition of *Life and Times* in November 1881, the reunion helped him to make his case that blacks should continue to work toward full citizenship in the South, despite the concessions made to southern Democrats as part of the Compromise of 1877. After all, the 1875 Civil Rights Act remained on the books and the Republican Party continued to control the federal government. A still hopeful Douglass put his reputation on the line by opposing the Exoduster movement, which saw thousands of blacks moving from the Deep South to Kansas and other northern states. Supporters of the movement regarded Douglass's criticisms as naïve and elitist in discounting the extraordinarily difficult situation rural blacks were facing in the South, whether from the lawlessness of groups like the Ku Klux Klan or from the peonage system itself. While aware of these problems, Douglass continued to argue (as he had during the 1850s) against anything that seemed like black emigration, which he regarded as a form of surrender to the dominant white power.[10] When Douglass published the second edition of *Life and*

Times in 1892, at a time when he was disillusioned by the Supreme Court's 1883 overturning of the 1875 Civil Rights Act, the reunion scene, which he did not revise, spoke to his increasingly complicated thoughts about race following his marriage to the white Helen Pitts and his consulship work in Haiti. Given his disillusionment, the scene lost some of its political potency. I will discuss the reunion scene in the very different contexts of 1881 and 1892, but I turn first to Douglass's fairly consistent portrayal of Auld in his autobiographical writings from the early 1840s to the mid-1850s. Auld was the man Douglass loved to hate, in part because hating Auld made for some terrifically effective prose. But as we shall see, Douglass did seem to care for Auld's daughter.

A VERY MEAN MAN

As I have been arguing throughout this study, Douglass regarded his autobiographical writings as regularly subject to revision, and he saw the boundaries between his day-to-day life and these writings to be relatively porous. To make an obvious but important point: Characters in the 1845 *Narrative,* who in our reading of the hypercanonical text might seem like the sorts of characters found in novels—fixed in their traits and actions within the circumscribed text—were not so fixed for Douglass, not only because he revised accounts of his life history for different rhetorical purposes (or because he remembered differently at different moments), but also because in reality their stories continued to unfold beyond the frames of his previously published work, whether book-length autobiographies or speeches and essays. That is particularly true for the "character" who, over the years, most engaged Douglass's interest:

his second master, Thomas Auld, the husband of the daughter of his first master and probable biological father, Aaron Anthony. As a character, Thomas Auld has an important place in the *Narrative,* but in some respects he has an even more important place in Douglass's post-*Narrative* writings and lectures. We see Douglass addressing the Thomas Auld of both the *Narrative* and his post-*Narrative* life at a May 1846 meeting in London when an anonymous person in the crowd shouts out a question about Douglass: "Who is his legal owner?" As recorded in a pamphlet on the meeting, Douglass's response went as follows:

> I ran away from Thomas Auld, of St. Michael's, Talbot county, Maryland, who was my legal owner. Since I came to this country, I have, as our president has said, published a narrative of my experience, and I kindly sent a copy to my master. (Laughter, and cheers.) He has become so offended with me, that he says he will not own me any longer, and, in his boundless generosity, he has transferred his legal right in my body and soul to his brother, Hugh Auld (laughter), who now lives in Baltimore, and who declares that he will have me if ever I set my foot on American soil. (Hear, hear.)[11]

Hugh Auld had purchased Douglass from his brother Thomas for one hundred dollars in March 1846, and in December of that year he sold Douglass to his English benefactors for a little over seven hundred dollars, thus turning a healthy profit on Thomas's former slave. Douglass told the story of these two sales repeatedly during the 1846–1848 period, focusing mainly on Thomas Auld's initial sale to Hugh. He also told a number of other stories about Thomas Auld, culminating in his 1848 "To My Old Master."

Given how often and powerfully Douglass wrote and spoke about Thomas Auld during this period, it would be useful to review what Auld would have read about himself in the 1845 *Narrative* Douglass claims to have sent him in May 1846.[12] This is what can be stated fairly conclusively: Douglass conveys virtually no emotional connection to Auld anywhere in the *Narrative*. That said, Auld is one of the most compelling figures in Douglass's first autobiography and thus a figure Douglass would regularly return to, flesh out, and hold up to his readers and auditors as exemplary of some of the worst aspects of slavery.

Barely mentioned in the opening six chapters of the *Narrative*, Auld is initially identified as the husband of a woman whom Douglass very much likes, Lucretia Auld, the daughter of Aaron Anthony and the woman who protects him from the beatings of the black housekeeper Aunt Katy. As the husband of Anthony's daughter, Auld eventually inherits Douglass, but it was Anthony who, prior to his death, had sent the eight-year-old Douglass to Baltimore to live with Auld's brother, Hugh, and his wife, Sophia, where he was relatively happy. Thomas Auld honors that arrangement even after the deaths of Anthony, Lucretia Anthony Auld, and her drunken brother Master Andrew. Far less fortunate is Douglass's grandmother, Betsy Bailey, whom Douglass presents as "in the hands of strangers," as he terms "her present owners," who were "virtually turning her out to die!" In a bravura moment of compelling rhetorical force, Douglass imagines his grandmother's final moments sometime in the 1830s: "She stands—she sits—she staggers—she falls—she groans—she dies—and there are none of her children or grandchildren present, to wipe from her wrinkled brow the cold sweat of death, or to place beneath the sod her fallen remains. Will not a righteous God visit for these things?" That's how the long paragraph on her imminent death ends; the next paragraph begins: "In about two years after the death of Mrs. Lucretia, Master Thomas married his second wife."[13] Moving from sentimental abolitionist rhetoric to straightforward family history, Douglass implicates the blithely indifferent Thomas Auld in the sad fate of his grandmother. Though Douglass's account of the grandmother's death is "inaccurate"— in fact she lives a while longer and receives some assistance from Auld—Douglass is correct in depicting her as chattel dependent on the sympathy of white slave masters for her survival. I will return to the controversy about this moment in Douglass's family history when I take up "To My Old Master." But let us linger with Thomas Auld for a while longer as he emerges as one of the *Narrative*'s central characters.

Auld is decisively brought back into the *Narrative* when he takes his property (the fourteen-year-old Douglass) to the Eastern Shore town of St. Michaels after quarreling with his brother Hugh. Up to this time, Thomas Auld had been little more than a stranger to Douglass and hardly a father figure; now he becomes the autobiography's principal figure of cruelty. Douglass bluntly remarks of his former owner: "I do not know of one single noble act ever performed by him. The leading trait in his character was meanness." Hugh Auld had provided Douglass with plentiful food. True to character, Thomas Auld cuts back on food, and Douglass is unsparing in his criticism: "Not to give a slave enough to eat, is regarded as the most aggravated development of meanness even among slaveholders." Soon Auld will send Douglass off to Edward Covey—the "'nigger-breaker'" who is the *Narrative*'s very incarnation of cruelty—but before describing that moment of January 1833, Douglass does all he can to accentuate Auld's hypocrisy. Like Covey, Auld finds God at a Methodist camp meeting and then uses his religion to sanction his cruelty, invoking a scriptural injunction—"He that knoweth his master's will, and doeth it not, shall be beaten with many stripes"—in order to justify his bloody whippings of his slaves.[14] Auld's whippings of Douglass's cousin Henny are particularly reprehensible given that her hands had been burnt when she was a child, leaving her disabled and defenseless. Douglass is far less defenseless; and perhaps because Auld found him somewhat resistant, or perhaps because he wanted to make money from his human property, he hires out Douglass for a year to work on Covey's rented farm.

To rehearse what has become familiar: It is from this low point with Covey that Douglass achieves new heights. Auld, of course, plays a critical role in this transformation both by sending Douglass to Covey and then refusing to help his slave after Covey severely beats him. In a scene that Douglass includes in all three autobiographies, Douglass describes walking seven miles to St. Michaels in order to display his bloody body to Auld. The scene is worth quoting for a second time in this study: "I then presented an appearance enough to affect any but a heart of iron. From the crown of my head to my feet, I was covered with blood. My hair was all clotted with dust and blood; my shirt was stiff with blood. My legs and feet were torn in sundry places with briers and thorns, and were also covered with blood." True to his meanness, Auld, the man with "a heart of iron," ridicules the idea that Douglass suffers from physical abuse and sends him back to his fellow Methodist, insisting that Covey is "a good man."[15] Given that Douglass's triumphal act of resisting Covey's authority would not have happened had Auld succumbed to Douglass's pleas for protection, Auld can take some unintended credit for the emergence of Douglass's rebellious state of mind, which eventually leads to his escape.

After the scene with Covey, Auld makes only a few brief later appearances in the *Narrative,* including one that points to Auld's better qualities and his possibly warmer feelings about his chattel. When Douglass is jailed following his failed effort to lead the slaves of William Freeland's farm to freedom, Auld decides, "from some cause or other," to return Douglass to Hugh and Sophia Auld in Baltimore. As Douglass remarks, "My master sent me away [to Baltimore], because there existed against me a very great prejudice in the community, and he feared I might be killed."[16] Was Auld concerned about the loss of his income-producing property? Or did he have genuine concerns about Douglass as a human being? It's not clear, though Douglass's post-*Narrative* speeches suggest the former by highlighting the cruelty of Auld as a slave master.

In his account of his return to Baltimore, Douglass continues to represent Thomas Auld as considerably crueler than his brother Hugh. While Thomas had seemed unconcerned about Covey's physical assaults on Douglass, Hugh is angry about the beatings Douglass endures at the Fell's Point shipyard and considers pursuing legal redress. Pointedly comparing the brothers, Douglass states that Hugh's "conduct was heavenly, compared with that of his brother Thomas under similar circumstances." Douglass subsequently proposes to hire out his time so that he can make money on his own, but Thomas, his legal owner, "unhesitatingly refused my request."[17] That is the last we hear of Thomas Auld in the *Narrative.* Douglass then describes Hugh's willingness to negotiate what turns out to be a short-term agreement in which Douglass pays him six dollars a week for expenses but is allowed to keep the rest of his earnings. Hugh's relative kindness helps Douglass to broaden his acquaintances and initiate the plan that eventually leads to his escape.

Though Hugh is presented as the more positive figure in the *Narrative*, it should be remembered that he is the man who forbids his wife to teach Douglass how to read and write. Still, it is Thomas Auld, not Hugh, whom Douglass regularly discusses in his post-*Narrative* speeches and letters, perhaps because Thomas was Douglass's legal owner until March 1846, and perhaps because Douglass had stronger emotions about his former master (though not necessarily positive emotions). Or perhaps Douglass referred more often to Thomas because he recognized that this particular Auld was one of the great literary creations of the *Narrative*. Prior to the publication of the *Narrative*, Douglass would refer to Auld in passing as one of his masters. In the wake of the *Narrative*, where Auld has such a strong and distinctive presence, Douglass made him into something of a stock character in his autobiographical lectures, seemingly enjoying the fact that, once overseas, he could assume a sort of power over Auld through his oratorical command.

In his speeches during his 1845–1847 tour of the British Isles, Douglass regularly depicted Auld as evincing all of the hypocrisy and cruelty of the conventional slave master of abolitionist literature. At Cork, Ireland, in October 1845, for instance, Douglass asserts about the "religious" Thomas Auld: "My own master was a Methodist class leader . . . and he bared the neck of a young woman, in my presence, and he cut her with a cow skin." One month later in Limerick, Ireland, Douglass, drawing on his account in the *Narrative*, elaborates on Auld's cruelty toward his disabled cousin Henny. A reporter who was in attendance at the lecture describes Douglass's theatrical presentation: "Mr. Douglas[s] then went on to exhibit a horrid whip which was made of cow hide, and whose lashes were hard as horn. They were clotted with blood when he first got them. He saw his master tie up a young woman eighteen years of age, and beat her with that identical whip until the blood ran down her back." Douglass also drew on the *Narrative* to retell the story of Auld's cruelty to his grandmother. In a speech delivered in Ayr, Scotland, in March 1846, he presents his Scottish auditors with a "few facts" about his experience as a slave: "I was born a slave. My master's name is Thomas Auld. . . . I have a grandmother who has reared twelve children, all of whom have been driven to the Southern slave market and sold; and now she is left desolate and forlorn, groping her way in the dark, without one to give her a cup of water in her declining moments." Notably, Douglass here collapses his second legal master with Aaron Anthony, presenting Auld as Douglass's sole slave master. Much more explicitly than in the *Narrative*, Auld becomes directly linked not only to the plight of the grandmother but also to all other aspects of Douglass's slave life that he narrates in this speech. In lectures delivered over the next several months in London and Scotland, Douglass continued to describe Auld as "a very mean man."[18]

But this "mean man" did not remain silent; he became involved in the debate on A. C. C. Thompson's charges (discussed in Chapter 2) that the *Narrative* was a fraudulent text. For Auld, the issue wasn't Douglass's authorship of the *Narrative;* he was mainly concerned about what he regarded as Douglass's scurrilous presentation of the character in the *Narrative* called "Thomas Auld." Solicited by Thompson to refute the *Narrative*, Auld sent him a letter in which he denied having beaten Douglass: "I can put my hand upon the Bible, and with a clear conscience swear that I never struck him in my life, nor caused any person else to do it." Thompson included Auld's letter in his longer letter published in the December 31, 1845, *Albany Patriot* and subsequently reprinted in the February 20, 1846, *Liberator.* In a March 1846 speech in

THE LIVES OF FREDERICK DOUGLASS

London, Douglass scoffed at Auld's account, noting that the "very mean man . . . who has attempted a refutation of the truth of my narrative in a letter which he published in the United States, tried to show that he was an excellent man, and he has generously transferred his legal right in my body and soul to his brother. He has actually made his brother a present of the body and bones of Frederick Douglass." In short, whatever Thomas Auld may have to say for himself, he is at bottom a dealer in human flesh, and a liar besides. Douglass offered a fuller refutation in an April 1846 letter published in the June 26, 1846, *Liberator,* declaring that the duplicitous Auld wants "revenge" for having his crimes revealed to the public. This is the man, he says, who "can put his hand upon the Bible, and, with a clear conscience, swear he never struck me. . . . could put his hand into my pocket, and rob me of my hard earnings; and, with a clear conscience, swear he had a right not only to my earnings, but to my body, soul and spirit!"[19]

As Douglass suggests in this letter of April 1846, the sale of his "body, soul and spirit" had become an important issue among U.S. abolitionists. Despite the fact that Douglass's British friends had purchased his freedom from Hugh Auld, Douglass kept his focus on Thomas Auld whenever he discussed the sale. In a letter of December 22, 1846, to Garrisonian abolitionist Henry C. Wright, which was published in the January 29, 1847, *Liberator,* Douglass reviews the financial facts of the sale; and though he presents Hugh Auld as the person who sold his free papers to British abolitionists, Douglass says that Hugh served as little more than "the agent of Thomas Auld." Thomas Auld thus remains at the center of the transaction, and in Douglass's account can be regarded as the representative, and in some ways the agent, of the U.S. government. Douglass concludes his letter to Wright with both a concession and an accusation that together underscore

the continuing role that Auld had come to play in his accounts of
his life history:

> I agree with you, that the contest which I have to wage
> is against the government of the United States. But the
> representative of that government is the slaveholder,
> *Thomas Auld*. He is commander-in-chief of the army
> and navy. The whole civil and naval force of the na-
> tion are at his disposal. He may command all these to
> his assistance, and bring them all to bear upon me,
> until I am made entirely subject to his will, or submit
> to be robbed myself, allow my friends to be robbed, of
> seven hundred and fifty dollars. And rather than be
> subject to his will, I have submitted to be robbed, or
> allowed my friends to be robbed, of the seven hundred
> and fifty dollars.[20]

By depicting Auld as commander-in-chief of the U.S. Army
and Navy, Douglass conveys both the power that his master
once had over him and the power that slave interests continue to
wield over the U.S. government.

Even after obtaining his freedom, Douglass kept his sights
on Thomas Auld. In his March 30, 1847, "Farewell to the
British People," delivered at the celebratory dinner Douglass's
admirers held for him shortly before his return to the United
States, Douglass launched into yet another attack on Auld, the
figure his auditors and readers would have known from the *Narrative* and his recent speeches. But his treatment of Auld displays
a striking shift in emphasis from what we have seen in the *Narrative* and his initial post-*Narrative* letters and speeches. Referring
to the British abolitionists' recent purchase of himself from the
Aulds, Douglass states about Thomas in particular:

> I was given away (hear); I was given away by my
> father, or the man who was called my father, to his
> own brother. My master was a Methodist class-
> leader. (Hear.) When he found that I had made my
> escape, and was a good distance out of his reach, he
> felt a little spark of benevolence kindled up in his
> heart; and he cast his eyes upon a poor brother of
> his—a poor, wretched, out-at-elbows, hat-crown-
> knocked-in-brother (laughter)—a reckless brother,
> who had not been so fortunate as to possess such a
> number of slaves as he had done.[21]

Surprisingly, Douglass identifies Thomas Auld and not Aaron
Anthony as his father, and by extension Hugh Auld as his uncle,
even though there was no blood kinship in their actual relationship. The rhetorical point is that the legal master assumes paternal
status. By highlighting that status, Douglass calls attention to yet
another insidious aspect of slavery: the way it creates psycholog-
ical and other dependencies based on patriarchy.

Douglass makes one other surprising rhetorical move in this
July 1847 speech. As a free man, he imagines himself taking on
the role of master to the point that, by the end of the speech, he
can imagine Auld, however briefly, as his slave. In the dazzling
movement of the speech, Douglass transforms father (Thomas
Auld), uncle (Hugh Auld), and son and nephew (Douglass) to
master (Douglass) and slaves (the Aulds). When Douglass reaches
the point where he imagines the Aulds as slaves, he tries out a
darker assertion of mastery over Thomas Auld that will become
central to his 1848 "To My Old Master." Keeping the focus mainly
on Hugh, Douglass states to his auditors (and readers): "By and
by, though, I want to tell the audience one thing which I forgot,

and that is, that I have as much right to sell Hugh Auld as Hugh Auld had to sell me. If any of you are disposed to make a purchase of him, just say the word. (Laughter.) However, whatever Hugh and Thomas may have done, I will not traffic in human flesh."[22] In this formulation, Douglass is a master with a heart and ethical soul who is really no master at all.

Upon his return to the United States, Douglass continued referring to the Aulds, especially Thomas, in his speeches and essays. In light of Thomas Auld's open letter to Douglass of 1846, it is not surprising that Douglass, as the new editor of his own newspaper, responded with his own open letter, "To My Old Master," publishing it in the September 8, 1848, *North Star* (which he sent in its entirety to Auld). The open letter, or essay, is one of Douglass's boldest autobiographical works, displaying a considerable rethinking of the "humane," conciliatory, and understated narrative persona that Douglass deploys for most of the *Narrative*. On the occasion of the ten-year anniversary of his escape from slavery, Douglass evinces virtually no interest in using the letter to find common ground with his former master. Instead, he aggressively goes after Auld right from his opening salvo: "All will agree that a man guilty of theft, robbery, or murder, has forfeited the right to concealment and private life; that the community have a right to subject such a person to the most complete exposure." Of course the most complete exposure for most of Douglass's readers would have been the portrait of Auld in the *Narrative*, but when Douglass says that he will be "dragging you again before the public," the "you" is both the "Thomas Auld" of the *Narrative* and the flesh and blood person who continues to hold slaves after the chronological end point of his appearance in the *Narrative*.[23]

As in the *Narrative*, Douglass in "To My Old Master" writes about being under Auld's power and feeling like "a poor degraded chattel—trembling at the sound of your voice, lamenting that I was a man, and wishing myself a brute." But after describing his 1838 escape from slavery, Douglass quickly moves beyond the closing scenes of the *Narrative*, showing how over the past few years he has achieved personally and economically in ways that place him on an equal footing with Auld: "I can boast of as comfortable a dwelling as your own. I have an industrious and neat companion, and four dear children." Douglass's mention of his family in freedom prompts him to turn his attention to those of his family still in slavery. He pointedly asks Auld about his sisters and grandmother: "Sir, I desire to know how and where these dear sisters are. . . . And my dear old grandmother, who you turned out like an old horse to die in the woods—is she still alive?"[24] Having expressed his concerns (and anger) about his sisters and grandmother, he adopts the tactic of direct address that Harriet Beecher Stowe would use so effectively in *Uncle Tom's Cabin*, rhetorically demanding of Auld (as Stowe's George Harris would demand of his former employer Wilson), how he would like being in the position of a slave. Working with the interrelated issues he has been addressing all along—the separation of families and the violation of slave women (his missing sisters, his neglected grandmother, and implicitly his sexually violated mother)—Douglass raises the emotional and rhetorical stakes of his open letter by asking Auld what he would think and how he would respond if Douglass were to assume mastery over his daughter, Amanda, in the way that Anthony and then Auld had assumed mastery over the women of Douglass's family. By posing the question in this way, Douglass evinces a rhetorical violence that we simply do not see in his earlier antislavery writings but which would take on a new prominence in his writings of the 1850s. In the most shocking moment of the open letter, Douglass demands of Auld:

> How, let me ask, would you look upon me, were I some dark night in company with a band of hardened villains, to enter the precincts of your own elegant dwelling and seize the person of your own lovely daughter Amanda, and carry her off my slave— compel her to work, and I take her wages—place her name on my ledger as property—disregard her personal rights—fetter the powers of her immortal soul by denying her the right and privilege of learning to read and write—feed her coarsely— clothe her scantily, and whip her on the naked back occasionally; more, and still more horrible, leave her unprotected—a degraded victim to the brutal lust of fiendish overseers who would pollute, blight, and blast her fair soul—rob her of all dignity—destroy her virtue, and annihilate all in her person the graces that adorn the character of virtuous womanhood![25]

This imagined rape of Amanda is an extraordinary moment in Douglass's life histories, suggestive of his rage against Auld, a lack of "love" between the two, and Douglass's felt need (in 1848) to push readers as aggressively as possible to confront the evils of the slave system. David Walker's 1829 *Appeal* was republished in 1848, and in that militant text Walker similarly turns the tables on Jefferson and other proslavery writers by talking about the possibility of blacks asserting power over whites, though Walker scoffs at the notion that blacks would be interested in sexual relations with white women. The specters of Walker and Nat Turner inform the angry turn at the end of Douglass's open letter, which may been difficult for Douglass to write because in historical fact he had warm feelings about Lucretia (Auld's first wife) and, as we shall see in *Life and Times*, Amanda as well. McFeely finds Douglass's rhetorical violation here inexcusable, stating rather paternalistically that Amanda "had been a kind young friend to Frederick Bailey in St. Michaels," and then moving to a psycho-biographical reading that has no evidentiary support and (worse) factors in none of the risks Douglass took in underscoring the ubiquity of white rape by depicting himself, or his imagined black overseers, as possible rapists. "There is in this tormented letter," McFeely asserts, "a hint that the legacy of slavery that Douglass could not shake was a trace of hatred of himself."[26] But perhaps one of the legacies of slavery that Douglass could not shake was more than a trace of hatred for Thomas Auld.

Douglass concludes his open letter by promising Auld that he will continue "to make use of you as a weapon with which to as-sail the system of slavery." Somewhat disingenuously, I think, he says that "in doing this, I entertain no malice towards you per-sonally." And yet an effort to speak without personal malice does appear to motivate his last significant piece of writing on Auld prior to the publication of the 1855 *My Bondage and My Freedom:* a second open letter to Auld, which Douglass published in the September 3, 1849, *North Star*. By 1849 Douglass had learned that Auld had tried to help his grandmother, who it turns out had not died during the 1830s. As Douglass writes Auld, "a person inti-mately acquainted with your affairs" has recently told Douglass that Auld had freed his slaves, except for Douglass's grandmother, whom he is now "providing for . . . in a manner becoming a man and a Christian." Douglass allows that Auld's actions have "greatly increased my faith in man." Arguably, Auld's actions have also increased Douglass's faith in his own writing, for he could take pride in imagining that his grandmother (who died right around the time Douglass was writing this letter) was being provided for because of his earlier critique of Auld, and that Auld's freeing of his slaves had something to do with the moral-suasionist tactics of Douglass's antislavery writings. But even this conciliatory letter has an edge to it. Douglass says that for all Auld has recently done, he will hail Auld "as a friend" only under one condition, or what Douglass calls "one reasonable request": if Auld would write about his putatively newfound antislavery beliefs and join him at the lectern. "It would be truly an interesting and glorious spectacle to see *master and slave*, hand in hand, laboring together for the overthrow of slavery," Douglass writes.[27]

Given that Douglass could be absolutely certain that Auld would not take on this role, and that he may have known Auld still possessed at least six slaves, we ought to be suspicious of reading the letter as a moment of reconciliation. If anything, the letter reminds the reader of the antislavery work that still needs to be done, even as its ironies suggest the persistence of Douglass's anger against his former master. In that light, it should be noted that Douglass not only made no changes in his account of the grim fate of his grandmother for his 1855 *My Bondage and My Freedom*, choosing simply to reprint the set piece on her imminent death as it appeared in the *Narrative*, but he also chose to reprint his accusatory September 8, 1848, letter, now titled "To My Old Master, Thomas Auld," in *Bondage and Freedom*'s appendix.

THE DAUGHTER OF THE OWNER OF A SLAVE

Despite his partly conciliatory open letter to Thomas Auld of 1849, and despite his much later reunion with him in 1877, Douglass in his 1881 *Life and Times of Frederick Douglass* continues to characterize the antebellum Auld by his "meanness." As described in *Life and Times*, which draws on the 1845 *Narrative* and the 1855 *Bondage and Freedom* for its accounts of Douglass's experiences as a slave, when Douglass is sent back to Thomas Auld in St. Michaels after seven years with Hugh and Sophia Auld in Baltimore, he becomes the slave of a man whose "leading characteristic was intense selfishness" and who is newly married to a woman, Rowena Hambleton, who "was as cold and cruel as her husband was stingy." Douglass once again depicts Auld's torturing of the maimed slave Henny, whom Auld keeps "tied up by her wrists to a bolt in the joist, three, four, and five hours at a time." And he again underscores the hypocrisy of Auld's religious conversion by describing how the master and his friends attack Douglass's Sabbath school "armed with sticks and other missiles." At the moment of the attack, Douglass writes in 1881, Auld exhibits "all the cruelty and meanness *after* his conversion which he had exhibited before that time." Understandably, then, in the key scene with Covey, Douglass presents Auld as acting with the same cruelty and meanness that are on display in the earlier autobiographies. In all three autobiographies, Douglass describes himself fleeing from Covey's farm and walking five hours to Auld's house to display his bloodied body to what he hopes will be his sympathetic master. Douglass writes in 1881, as he had in 1855 (when he changed "iron" to "stone"), about how he "presented an appearance of wretchedness and woe calculated to move any but a heart of stone." Possessing the proverbial heart of stone, Auld orders Douglass to return the next day to Covey, while insisting that Douglass "no doubt . . . deserved the flogging."[28]

As in the *Narrative*, Thomas Auld's one shining moment occurs when he decides to send Douglass to Hugh and Sophia Auld in Baltimore following Douglass's arrest for attempting to lead a group of Freeland's hired slaves to freedom. According to Douglass, Auld initially plans to send Douglass to Alabama, with a promise to free him in eight years; but Douglass remains skeptical about whether he would be freed and of course fears what would happen to him in the Deep South. But then Auld changes his mind, and as Douglass reports in the 1845 *Narrative*, "from some cause or other, he did not send me to Alabama, but concluded to send me back to Baltimore, to live again with his brother Hugh, and to learn a trade." Douglass revised that account in the 1855 *Bondage and Freedom* in order to acknowledge that there was some generosity behind Auld's decision, allowing that Auld "had the power and the provocation to send me, without reserve, into the very everglades of Florida, beyond the remotest hope of emancipation; and his refusal to exercise that power, must be set down to his credit." Douglass retains nearly the same language in the 1881 *Life and Times* when he writes of Auld's change of mind: "He certainly did not exert his power over me as in the case he might have done, but acted, upon the whole, very generously, considering the nature of my offence." Douglass thus experiences "surprise and . . . relief" (and gratitude), as he puts it in both *Life and Times* and the earlier *Bondage and Freedom*, when Auld chooses to send him to Baltimore, but there are sound economic reasons behind his decision: Douglass produces income as a laborer in Baltimore and remains valuable property.[29] Still, this is a moment when Auld does seem uncharacteristically kind, though he quickly reverts to form, refusing Douglass's request to hire out his time in Baltimore. By contrast, Hugh in *Bondage and Freedom* and *Life and Times* continues to seem more appealing, showing his concern when Douglass is beaten by the white laborers at Fell's Point and initially allowing Douglass to do extra paid work in Baltimore. Though Hugh keeps a large portion of the additional earnings and soon ends the arrangement, in all of the autobiographies his generally relaxed oversight can be credited with helping Douglass to plan his escape.

We can now turn to scenes involving Thomas Auld and his family that are entirely new to the 1881 *Life and Times*, but not before noting a significant revision in *Bondage and Freedom*. In the *Narrative*, Douglass makes a single mention of Amanda, the daughter of Thomas Auld and his first wife, Lucretia, giving only her name in passing. In *Bondage and Freedom*, Douglass adds new details, saying that when he suffered from the cruelties of Auld's new wife, he thought of the more kindly, but now dead, Lucretia, "traces of whom I yet remembered, and the more especially, as I saw them shining in the face of little Amanda, her daughter, now living under a step-mother's government." In *Life and Times*, Douglass cuts that sentence, mentioning Amanda just once in the chapters on his slavery years, at the precise moment when he learns of Lucretia's death: "I had returned to Baltimore but a short time when the tidings reached me that my kind friend, Mrs. Lucretia, was dead. She left one child, a daughter, named Amanda, of whom I shall speak again."[30] By removing the comparison of Amanda to her mother early on, Douglass can make that comparison more resonantly later in the autobiography in his first reunion scene with an Auld.

In a key scene prior to the account of the 1877 reunion between Thomas Auld and Douglass, Douglass describes his 1859 reunion in Philadelphia with Auld's daughter Amanda—the very person whom Douglass tauntingly asked Auld in his 1848 open letter to imagine as a possible rape victim. Douglass places the scene artfully in the autobiography. Rather than follow chronology, which would have made the reunion a sidelight to John Brown's raid on Harpers Ferry, Douglass withholds the story of his 1859 meeting with Amanda until he describes a speech he delivers at the National Loyalist's Convention in Philadelphia in September 1866. Following the speech, Douglass joins a procession through Chestnut Street, where he notices Amanda, who has brought her two children to see the famous black abolitionist she knew from her childhood. Douglass remarks on her attendance: "Here was the daughter of the owner of a slave, following with enthusiasm that slave as a free man, and listening with joy to the plaudits he received as he marched along the crowded streets of the great city." His observation of Amanda at the 1866 parade leads him to insert into the narrative the account of their more dramatic 1859 reunion in Philadelphia, which Douglass says "should have found place earlier in this story."[31] But by withholding the story about Amanda until this later section, Douglass adds to its emotional force by linking it more closely to the reunion with Thomas Auld that comes just three chapters later in the autobiography.

As a storyteller, Douglass thus moves from his account of the 1866 procession on Chestnut Street to his 1859 speech at Philadelphia's National Hall, where he meets Amanda after a separation of over two decades. Amanda, who, we recall, is the daughter of Auld's first wife, Lucretia, and the granddaughter of Douglass's probable father, Aaron Anthony (and thus probably Douglass's half niece), has married coal merchant John Sears and is now opposed to slavery. Unbeknownst to Douglass, she attends his speech at National Hall, and he learns about this in Gothic fashion when a mysterious man, her servant William Needles, approaches him after the speech to ask if he knew "your once mistress has been listening to you tonight." (She was more his younger family member than mistress when he knew her.) Douglass is incredulous, but the next day he receives a note from Needles inviting him to meet with Sears at his office. When Douglass arrives, Sears is initially hesitant to talk with the former slave out of respect for the feelings of Thomas Auld, his father-in-law. But it turns out that his larger anxiety has to do with Douglass's position as an editor-journalist: he doesn't want their meeting written up in Douglass's newspaper. After Douglass promises that "no word shall go into its columns of our conversation," Sears opens up. "To make a long story short," Douglass writes, "we had then quite a long conversation, during which Mr. Sears said that in my 'Narrative' I had done his father-in-law injustice, for he was really a kind-hearted man, and a good master." Rather than making any concessions, Douglass defends his portrayal of Auld by asserting the right of the slave (or former slave) to his own perspective: "I replied that there must be two sides to the relation of master and slave, and what was deemed kind and just to the one was the opposite to the other." In effect, Douglass undermines the stereotype of the good master that remained central to white southerners' nostalgic memories of slavery by suggesting that the trope has nothing to do with the reality of the slave's experience. He claims that Sears accepts his explanation, and that "the longer we talked the nearer we came together." Douglass then asks for permission to see Amanda, "the little girl of seven or eight years when I left the eastern shore of Maryland."[32] Sears agrees to an afternoon visit at their home the very next day.

This first reunion scene with an Auld is unambiguously warm. Challenged to pick out Amanda from a group of young women, Douglass immediately recognizes her, whereupon she "bounded to me with joy in every feature, and expressed her great happiness at seeing me." Amanda, who seems unaware of the 1848 open letter to her father (or its reprinting in *Bondage and Freedom*), revels in Douglass's company while pressing him for more information about her beloved mother, Lucretia, whom she says she read about in Douglass's *Narrative*. Similarly, Douglass wants to learn more about members of his family still living on the Eastern Shore. They share in their disdain for Amanda's stepmother, Rowena; and after Amanda tells Douglass about how she had come to hate slavery and free her own slaves, she introduces Douglass to her two daughters. At a time that had seen an upsurge of lynchings on the pretext that blacks were sexually assaulting white women, Douglass is daringly physical in his 1881 account of this moment, describing how he takes Amanda's young daughters "in my arms" to embrace them. Throughout the scene he also conveys a brotherly affection for Amanda, so that one imagines there were warm embraces between the two of them as well. To some extent, then, Douglass rewrites or revises the most controversial part of the 1848 "To My Old Master," making clear that rape is the last thing he would wish on Amanda or her daughters. Douglass also uses the scene to convey his continued hope for the socially regenerative possibilities of a Reconstruction project that would move the nation beyond racial tensions—and even race itself. As he says about his 1859 reunion with Amanda: "All thought of slavery, color, or what might seem to belong to the dignity of her position vanished, and the meeting was as the meeting of friends long separated, yet still present in each other's memory and affection."[33]

Though depicted as a private, heartfelt reunion between Douglass and Amanda, there is much about the meeting that seems performed, as if on a stage, and not just for readers of the 1881 autobiography. Douglass notes, for instance, that Mr. Sears "had invited to his house a number of friends to witness the meeting between Mrs. Sears and myself." There is every sense that Douglass has those witnesses in mind as he delivers what is probably a heartfelt performance about his warm emotional response to Amanda. The performative quality of the reunion looks forward to the similarly theatrical reunion with Thomas Auld. The reunion also provided Douglass with a nice story for his lectures of the 1860s. In a speech delivered in Philadelphia on September 5, 1866, Douglass described his meeting with Amanda as "one of the most touching incidents of my life," and all the more moving because she was the daughter of Lucretia Auld, "from whom I received the first kindness that I ever experienced from one of a complexion different from my own."[34] On a public level, Douglass hoped that such kindness between whites and blacks, as exemplified by his relationships with Lucretia and her daughter, would become a model for post–Civil War America.

But there was clearly more than politics involved in his response to the reunion with Amanda. Buoyed by the happiness of the meeting, Douglass wrote Hugh Auld in October 1859 to report that "I have seen *Miss Amanda*," and to ask for more such meetings with the extended Auld family. In the letter, he expressed some of his warmest emotions for a former slaveholder: "I feel nothing but kindness for you all—I love you, but hate slavery. Now, my dear Sir, will you favor me by dropping me a line, telling me in what year I came to live with you."[35] The conflation of love with the request for information is telling, for Douglass had long been intent on trying to learn details about his early life. Still, even if the letter was written at an emotional pitch (right after his re-union with Amanda), and rhetorically conceived to break down Hugh's resistance to a meeting that he hoped would supply him with additional facts about his life history, he may well have gen-uinely loved this Baltimore-based family. Hugh Auld seemed to care about him; Sophia attempted to teach him to read and write and nursed him when he was beaten at the docks; and Tommy, the Aulds' son, who was Douglass's charge, was something of a little brother to him. In 1864, after Union victories made such a visit possible, Douglass traveled to Baltimore for the first time since his escape in 1838 and tried to visit Sophia, who was now a widow. (Hugh died in 1861.) Because of the interference of her younger son, Benjamin, a police officer to whom I will return later in the chapter, such a meeting never took place.[36]

In *Life and Times,* the reunion scene with Amanda doesn't stop with the 1866-inspired memory of the 1859 meeting. Douglass jumps chronologically forward to Amanda's death in 1877, which occurred shortly *after* Douglass visited her father but is presented earlier in the autobiography at the conclusion of a section focusing on his three meetings with Amanda. As in 1859, Amanda, who had summoned Douglass to her deathbed, remains eager to hear about her mother, whom she believes "she should meet in another and better world." In this sad scene, Douglass tells Amanda that of her two daughters, the older, Lucretia, looks very much like her mother. Hearing that the mother Lucretia lives on in her daughter Lucretia, Amanda says she is "ready to die." Douglass concludes the section on Amanda by moving back in time, re-marking that he had heard after his 1859 visit to Amanda and John Sears that Thomas Auld himself wanted to know how the meeting had gone. According to Douglass, "Mr. Sears then told him all about my visit, and had the satisfaction of hearing the old man say that he had done right in giving me welcome to his house."[37] Douglass claims to have heard about the exchange from the Reverend J. D. Long, a friend of the Sears family. In this way, Douglass introduces into his autobiography an image of Thomas Auld that is very different from what we have read in the earlier chapters. For the first time, Auld seems genuinely to care about Douglass.

A SORT OF FINAL SETTLEMENT
OF PAST DIFFERENCES

Near the end of the section on Amanda Auld Sears in *Life and Times*, Douglass allows that some might challenge him for being friendly with the daughter of his former master. Douglass remarks: "I have no heart to visit upon children the sins of their fathers." But what should be visited upon the sinning father? That became an issue when Douglass traveled to Auld's home on the Eastern Shore in 1877, and it remained an issue when he wrote up the meeting for his 1881 autobiography.[38]

In *Life and Times*, Douglass presents his June 18, 1877, visit to Thomas Auld in the larger context of his various political triumphs and honors, his other visits to Maryland between 1864 and 1880, and his continued hopes for Reconstruction (despite the Compromise of 1877). In the chapter immediately prior to the description of his meeting with Auld, he urges blacks to join him in laying claim to the South. It is at this point in the autobiography that he sets forth his controversial position on the Exoduster movement, which he opposed, as he somewhat overstates the issue, because he feared that it would "set in motion a wholesale exodus of colored people of the South to the Northern States." Convinced that African Americans should continue to insist on their rights in the South, he was criticized during the late 1870s for minimizing the dangers blacks were facing as a result of the Compromise of 1877, which greatly diminished the protective authority of federal troops in the southern states. Douglass conveys his frustrations to his readers by reporting on what he regarded as the outrageous charges that were brought against him: "It was said of me that I had deserted to the old master class, and that I was a traitor to my race."[39]

Concerned that he would have to fend off similar charges of desertion to the master class when he decided to visit the Eastern Shore, he enlisted a reporter from Baltimore's leading newspaper whom he hoped would present his meetings with whites as signs of the possibilities of racial reconciliation in the South, but not at the expense of black agency and not with racial hierarchies remaining unchallenged. Douglass tended to work collaboratively with photographers to make sure they produced the images that he wanted disseminated to the public.[40] Similarly, Douglass to some extent "posed" for his visit to Auld. The resulting article, "Frederick Douglass at His Old Home, A Visit to His Former Master—An Affectionate and Friendly Meeting—Sound Advice to the Colored People, &c.," appeared on the front page of the June 19, 1877, *Baltimore Sun*. But it was not what Douglass wanted or expected. Though there are some parallels between the reporter's account in 1877 and Douglass's own account in 1881, mostly the reporter got things wrong, or at least got things wrong from Douglass's perspective, thus prompting Douglass to provide his own narrative of the reunion in the autobiography he was soon to write. Before turning to Douglass's version in *Life and Times*, it would be useful to consider the article that he helped to produce and then sought to correct.

The *Baltimore Sun* article begins with a general description of the "colored people from Baltimore" on board a steamer to St. Michaels, and then focuses on the steamer's black celebrity: "Among the party was Frederick Douglass, United States marshal for the District of Columbia, who paid a visit for the first time since he left here forty-one years ago to the scenes of his youth. Mr. Douglass some time ago expressed a wish to visit his former master, Capt. Thomas Auld, a resident of St. Michael's, and an old man now on the verge of the grave, infirm in body, but with a clear and vigorous intellect." Throughout the article the reporter uses the phrase "colored people" to differentiate blacks from whites, at one point referring to "the colored part of his [Douglass's] audience." Still, he keeps Douglass's accomplishments and prestige front and center, and he clearly takes advantage of information that Douglass had provided him in order to shape the narrative as dramatically as possible. Thus the reporter can state the exact number of years that the "colored" Douglass had been away from "home," while reporting on the putative motivation for his return—his long-standing desire to visit his former master, presumably with the hope of reconciliation. (Douglass will correct an aspect of this story, emphasizing in *Life and Times* that it was Auld who had asked to see him.) The reporter describes Douglass's arrival at Auld's residence, "where he was received by Judge Wm. H. Bruff, Capt. Auld's son-in-law, who addressed him as 'Marshal Douglass.'" (President Rutherford Hayes had appointed Douglass U.S. marshal of the District of Columbia earlier that year.) According to the article, Douglass responds, "No, no, . . . I am Marshal Douglass in Washington; here let me be Fred Douglass again."[41] Was Douglass in some odd way asking to be a slave again or to be treated as a kind of boy, as some of his critics at the time suggested? In his 1881 autobiography, Douglass revised and corrected aspects of this exchange so that such questions would seem misguided.

In the one-paragraph account of the actual meeting between Douglass and Auld, the reporter tells of how Bruff led Douglass (and probably the reporter and some of Douglass's friends and Auld's other relatives) to Auld's sickbed, where the following scene ensued:

> The meeting between the former master and former servant was very affecting. Tenderly Douglass grasped the palsied hand of Captain Auld, addressed him as his old master, and manifested emotion creditable alike to his manhood and to his heart, as he saw how heavily time had laid his hands upon him. The interview was very pleasant throughout. Mr. Douglass stated that in his book written soon after his escape [the 1845 *Narrative*] he had made some statements that lapse of time and reflection had caused him to feel he had better have left unsaid, and for aught that he said that was unjust to his old master, or had wounded his feelings, he begged his forgiveness. Capt. Auld told him that he had never expected to keep him in slavery; that he knew forty-one years ago he was too smart to be a slave, and that when he sent him to Baltimore, after his difficulty at Freeland's, instead of selling him South, it was with the expectation that he would achieve his freedom. Douglass called upon Capt. Auld again in the afternoon, just before starting to the boat, to bid him good-bye, and when they parted both men wept.

Douglass in 1881 provided a somewhat different description of the meeting, though it is worth noting that in both accounts the scene that seems so intimate is being observed by several people. For the reporter, the scene is about the moving reconciliation between master and "former servant" (he leaves it to Auld to refer to Douglass as a former slave), and those identities remain pretty much intact. It is Douglass who offers apologies to his former master, and it is Auld who defends his earlier actions and fails to offer any apologies at all. The reporter initially identifies Douglass as the person who "manifested emotion creditable alike to his manhood and to his heart," but when Auld and Douglass briefly meet again later in the day, "both men wept."[42] Are the displays of emotion performances, real feeling, or the projections of the white reporter? It is impossible to say. In his own account in *Life and Times,* Douglass elides the afternoon meeting (with its tears) and presents himself as much more in control of his emotions. We sense that control even in the *Baltimore Sun* article when Douglass later in the day gives a speech in St. Michaels that touches on his meeting with Auld.

As described by the reporter, Douglass addressed "a large audience of both white and colored people," which included many "prominent [white] citizens of the town and adjacent country, many of whom were old men who knew well the boy 'Fred.'" The reporter's presentation of Marshal Frederick Douglass as "the boy 'Fred'" is obviously demeaning. But the reporter prints what he claims are Douglass's own words from the speech, and if he got those words reasonably close to the mark, Douglass supplies within the same article what already seems like a correction of the reporter's description of his meeting with Auld. Douglass remarks on the meeting: "I have had great joy in shaking that hand, in looking into that face, stricken with age and disease, but aglow with the light that comes from an honest heart, and reflecting the glory from the spirit world, upon whose border he is, and where we shall meet again."[43] As opposed to the reporter's initial description, in which Douglass seems apologetic and deferential, Douglass presents himself in the speech as an active agent, shaking the hand of his former master in a gesture that suggests he is forgiving him at what would appear to be the moment of his imminent death.

In the same speech, Douglass addresses the topic of black uplift, calling upon blacks, as he regularly did, to work at educating themselves "until we can do what white people can do." For the white reporter, this aspect of the speech offered "a eulogy of the white race and its achievements," while providing "the colored part of the audience some of the best advice and soundest instruction they have had for many a day." The reporter claims that the speech was "well received, especially by the white part of the audience," and that "among others who sought him out after his address was Mr. Wm. H. Bruff, who taught him reading, arithmetic, and geography fifty years ago." Here, the self-reliant Douglass, who had mostly taught himself to read and write, is presented as indebted to Bruff, whom Douglass does not even mention in his prior autobiographies. By the end of the article, Douglass has clearly lost control of his performance to the racially condescending reporter. The final sentence of the article is significant, though, for it reveals something else important about the visit: "Marshal Douglass learned his age from Capt. Auld, who has a record of his birth, wherein it appears 'Frederick Bailey was born in February, 1818.'"[44] All along, Douglass had said that one of his large motivations for visiting the Eastern Shore was to learn more about his personal history. On this trip, he learned something essential. Oddly, however, in the opening chapter of both the 1881 and 1892 *Life and Times* he neglects to revise the February 1817 birthdate he had used in *Bondage and Freedom*.

The *Baltimore Sun* article, or altered and embellished versions thereof, appeared in over twenty newspapers across the country, including the *New York Times* and Vicksburg, Mississippi's *Daily Commercial*. These articles did not do the political or cultural work Douglass had hoped for. In the North, Douglass was mocked in several newspaper articles for allegedly calling himself "Fred" and for appearing to subordinate himself to a former slave master. The title of the article about the reunion in the June 1877 Washington, DC, *Daily Critic* nicely captures the tone of these pieces: " 'Our Freddie': He Visits His Former Master and Speaks His Little Piece." From a different perspective, southern newspapers loved the way Douglass was depicted in the *Baltimore Sun* as in quest of forgiveness, as if he had at long last realized how misguided he had been in opposing slavery. As the reporter for the New Orleans *Picayune* wrote in his June 1877 article: "Douglass asked the old gentleman's forgiveness for whatever he had said that was unjust, and said that time and reflection had convinced him that much that he had written had better have been unuttered."[45] By the time Douglass wrote *Life and Times*, then, stories had already circulated about the reunion that the reporter claims was initiated by Douglass but that Douglass claims was initiated by Auld. In the 1881 *Life and Times*, Douglass responds directly to the 1877 *Baltimore Sun* article and the stories it spawned by asserting that the initial newspaper story itself was "in some respects defective," and that he now wants "to state exactly what was said and done at this interview."[46]

Douglass confesses in *Life and Times* that he was particularly upset about how the article had made him "the subject of mirth of heartless triflers" who thought he had been overly deferential to Auld. Offering a corrective of the *Baltimore Sun* account, Douglass writes that he was "formally invited by Captain Thomas Auld, then over eighty years old, to come to the side of his dying bed, evidently with a view to a friendly talk over our past relations." Rather than seeking out Auld on his own, Douglass asserts that he was kindly honoring the request of a dying man. Even the visit to the Eastern Shore, he declares, was suggested by someone else, his black friend Charles Cadwell, and the invitation to visit Auld came from Auld's friend or servant, a Mr. Green, after Douglass had already arrived in the area, perhaps because Auld was aware of the publicity surrounding Douglass's visit. Unlike the *Baltimore Sun*'s account, Douglass presents himself as a benefactor, the man who is willing to forgive and partially forget, and not the other way around. "The conditions were favorable for remembrance of all his good deeds," Douglass writes of Auld, "and generous extenuation of all his evil ones."[47]

The description of the actual meeting in *Life and Times* is prefaced by a long paragraph in which Douglass states his brief against Auld by remembering only his evil deeds. He writes (in part):

> To me Capt. Auld had sustained the relation of master—a relation which I had held in extremest abhorrence, and which for forty years I had denounced in all bitterness of spirit and fierceness of speech. He had struck down my personality, had subjected me to his will, made property of my body and soul, reduced me to a chattel, hired me out to a noted slave breaker to be worked like a beast and flogged into submission; he had taken my hard earnings, sent me to prison, offered me for sale, broken up my Sunday-school,

forbidden me to teach my fellow-slaves to read on pain of nine and thirty lashes on my bare back; he had, without any apparent disturbance of his conscience, sold my body to his brother Hugh and pocketed the price of my flesh and blood. I, on my part, had traveled through the length and breadth of this country and of England, holding up this conduct of his, in common with that of other slaveholders to the reprobation of all men who would listen to my words. I had by my writings made his name and his deeds familiar to the world in four different languages.

This hardly sounds loving. That Douglass is willing to rehearse these charges against Auld one more time, and in such sustained fashion, suggests that in 1881 Douglass continued to harbor at least some ill will toward his former master. The passage also makes clear just how wonderfully Auld has served Douglass's antislavery purposes. But with the end of slavery, both of their worlds have changed, and Douglass can't help marveling, in what he terms the "truth is stranger than fiction" mode of the overall chapter, that whereas during the time of slavery an invitation from Auld would have been regarded as "one to put fetters on my ankles and handcuffs on my wrists," now, with the end of slavery, and with Douglass's political ascent, "here we were, after four decades once more face to face—he on his bed, aged and tremulous, drawing near the sunset of life, and I, his former slave, United States Marshal of the district of the Columbia, holding his hand and in friendly conversation with him."[48]

Even with Douglass's proud reminder of his status as a U.S. marshal, there is something undeniably moving about the reunion scene itself, which Douglass presents as "a sort of final settlement of past differences" (and I take that "sort of" as a significant qualification). Douglass generously remarks about Auld that "I regarded him as I did myself, a victim of the circumstances of birth, education, law, and custom," though it's clear from the pre-1838 chapters of *Life and Times* that some slaveholders are worse than others. He says that he wants to remember all of his former master's "good deeds," while basically presenting only one such deed in *Life and Times* (Auld's decision not to send him to Alabama after his plot was discovered at Freeland's); and he says that he offers a "generous extenuation of all his evil ones," while failing to offer much extenuation at all. In the chapters focusing on his pre-1838 escape, Douglass tells the same stories about Auld in 1881 that he had been telling since the early 1840s. There are tears at the start of the visit, though Auld's tears, as Douglass explains, derive at least in part from Auld "having long been stricken with palsy," which makes him "shed tears as men thus afflicted will do when excited by any deep emotion." Douglass, too, experiences "deep emotion," for the sight of the stricken old man "choked my voice and made me speechless." Still, former slave and former master manage to recover rather quickly: "We both, however, got the better of our feelings, and conversed freely about the past."[49]

Douglass then reports on an actual conversation between himself and Auld, while noting that others, such as William Bruff, are listening in on the conversation *and* that the conversation had already been reported in the 1877 *Baltimore Sun* article, which implies the reporter's presence, too. As with the reunion scene with Amanda, Douglass knows that he is being watched, and he performs accordingly. Douglass addresses Auld (as opposed to Auld's son-in-law in the *Baltimore Sun*'s account) as "Captain

Auld," and when Auld calls him "Marshal Douglass," Douglass responds "not *Marshal,* but Frederick to you as formerly." That "Frederick" is a significant change from the diminutive "Fred" in the Baltimore *Sun* article. Notably, it's now Auld, and not Bruff, who is presented as the white man with whom Douglass had this exchange, which helps to keep the reunion in focus, even if Douglass is misremembering. Douglass can still seem just a bit deferential, and yet by forcefully reminding Auld of how he had been addressed as a slave ("Frederick to you as formerly"), Douglass highlights the gap between who he was then and who he is now at this moment of reunion. In crucial respects, then, there is an assertion of power over the man who is lying in bed virtually powerless.[50]

But that powerless man can speak. According to Douglass, Auld claims he would have acted like Douglass had he been in his situation, asserting that "you were too smart to be a slave." While Douglass fails to challenge the implication of Auld's contention—that most slaves were not very smart and thus belonged in their place—Douglass's inclusion of this comment works to keep Auld pretty much in character. Douglass returns Auld's "compliment" by saying something that is unsupported by *Life and Times,* to wit: "I did not run away from *you,* but from *slavery.*" (In the early chapters of *Life and Times,* and in the prior autobiographies, Auld is presented as the slave master anyone would want to run away from.) Their discussion then shifts to what Auld regards as Douglass's scurrilous presentation in the *Narrative,* in the 1848 open letter "To My Old Master," and in *Bondage and Freedom* of Auld as the person who had essentially sent Douglass's frail grandmother out to the woods to die.[51]

Biographers Preston and McFeely both criticize Douglass for his earlier misrepresentations of Auld's treatment of the grandmother. Preston characterizes Douglass's accounts in the autobiographies as "outright falsehood" and McFeely similarly describes them as rife with "peculiar distortions." In this reunion scene, Douglass now concedes that he may have got things wrong: "I told him that I had made a mistake in my narrative, a copy of which I had sent him, in attributing to him ungrateful and cruel treatment of my grandmother." Auld claims that the grandmother had not been his responsibility because she had become at the death of Aaron Anthony the property of his son and heir Andrew S. Anthony (Auld's brother-in-law), and after that, at the death of Andrew, the property of Andrew's son John P. Anthony (Auld's nephew). Even so, Auld declares that when he saw the grandmother was in need, "I brought her down here and took care of her as long as she lived." Douglass's response is to say that "this mistake of mine was corrected as soon as I discovered it, and that I had at no time any wish to do him injustice; that I regarded both of us as victims of a system."[52]

But several questions remain: Why does Douglass, who apparently knew of Auld's action by the late 1840s, choose *not* to correct this "mistake" in the 1848 open letter or the 1855 *Bondage and Freedom,* or in the republication of the 1848 open letter in *Bondage and Freedom*'s appendix? Why does he barely acknowledge the mistake in his 1849 open letter to Auld, and why does his phrasing in *Life and Times* about their mutual acts of "injustice" seem to do the opposite of exonerating Auld, suggesting instead that Auld remains implicated in his family's mistreatment of the grandmother? In his 1859 letter to Hugh Auld, Douglass acknowledges that Thomas might have been a better "Christian" than the man he had portrayed in his public writings and speeches. His more positive view of Thomas, enhanced by their 1877 meeting, was what probably motivated him to make a small but significant revision to the long sentimental passage about the grandmother's imminent death, first published in the *Narrative* and republished in *Bondage and Freedom,* by inserting into the *Life and Times* version a five-word mention of Aaron Anthony's grandson's legal ownership. But even with that addition, Douglass, as in the earlier versions, concludes the passage by juxtaposing the seemingly deadly exiling of the grandmother to the woods with the mention of Thomas Auld's second marriage, stressing what he continues to suggest is Auld's unconcern about the fate of the grandmother.[53] To be sure, Douglass *was* being unfair to Auld. But contra Preston and McFeely, I'm a bit suspicious, as I think Douglass was, too, of Auld's legalistic posturing, the idea that Auld was not responsible for the old woman who had been so central to his extended household. What are we to make of the fact that Auld's idea of responsibility remains consistent with the notion of the grandmother as property (as chattel that "belongs" to someone or other)? And what does it mean that Auld "cared for" her? Did he offer kind assistance or basic subsistence? Douglass's skepticism about the trope of the good master that Auld propounds during the reunion is conveyed through his unwillingness to provide any of the facts that would corroborate Auld's account. Too many questions remain unanswered; and the uncertainties about the grandmother are only underscored by Douglass's decision to retain the darker account of the treatment of the grandmother in the earlier chapter of *Life and Times,* when she (once again) is banished to the woods, seemingly to die.

Given Douglass's failure to significantly revise the account of the grandmother's imminent death, we have to consider the possibility that in 1877 (or 1881), Douglass remained uncertain about Auld's beneficence, which would only add to the sense that

the reunion isn't quite the moving achievement of mutual understanding and forgiveness (between men who love each other) that
some have taken it for. Even if Douglass's intention in 1877
and 1881 was to dramatize the possibility of interracial understanding and forgiveness during a period in which he still had
hopes for Reconstruction, it is crucial to note that the reunion
scene with Auld is basically a four-page account, in the much
longer chapter "Time Makes All Things Even," in a huge book,
of what Douglass describes as an "interview [that] did not last
more than twenty minutes."[54]

However we interpret the scene, its performative dimension—
famous former slave visiting his former master on what appears
to be his deathbed—has to be kept in mind, at the very least as a
caution against reading too much "love" into a reunion that in
some ways is presented as a form of vengeance (making things
even). As Douglass reports, those on hand for the reunion would
have observed a healthy man with an international reputation
standing over the frail Auld. Thus what comes across in the scene,
as much as anything else, is the profound reversal in social standing
between the two men, along with the sense that in making the
visit Douglass was doing Auld a favor. Douglass's final words on
the meeting seem more a self-celebration than an affirmation of
the emotional significance of the reunion: "His [Auld's] death was
soon after announced in the papers, and the fact that he had once
owned me as a slave was cited as rendering that event note-
worthy."[55] Douglass doesn't seem especially bereaved. Moreover, by suggesting that Auld died "soon after" the visit, when
he actually died three years later, Douglass creatively (and again
somewhat self-servingly, given the parallels with the Amanda
Auld Sears death scene just a few chapters earlier) makes the
reunion into a gratifying story about how Douglass's kind visit

allowed the old master to die in peace. In this way, the reunion scene serves to bolster Douglass's ethos as a former slave who ultimately transcends the oppression and oppressors of his early life. His humility and graciousness toward Auld demonstrate not so much love as moral superiority because his kindness is freely given, rather than coerced or otherwise forced. In *Life and Times*, Douglass emerges as more of a gentleman than the gentleman who had once owned him.[56]

Whatever he may have thought of Auld, Douglass insists that the tears he shed in his presence were prompted mainly by the uncanny collapse of past and present into a bizarre and unsettling new reality: "The sight of him, the changes which time had wrought in him . . . affected me deeply, and for a time choked my voice and made me speechless." Additionally making the chapter so memorable (and moving) is its presentation of the seemingly magical transformations brought about by the passage of time—transformations, as in Shakespearean romance, that suggest the possibility of reconciliation between formerly warring parties. In the overall chapter, Douglass highlights the "peculiar and poetic force" of returning decades later to key sites from his youth, such as the Lloyd plantation, where he and other slaves had suffered, and seeing new prospects for blacks in a world literally turned upside down. The return is not about deference; it is about transformation. That is no doubt why Douglass was so upset by the illustrations accompanying the first printing of *Life and Times*, which included an image showing him reverentially paying homage to Colonel Lloyd's gravestone (Figure 9). (Douglass dropped all the illustrations for the second printing.) Rather than worshiping the former masters, Douglass sought to emphasize the enormous historical and social changes that undid the power of the masters. Experiencing a profound sense of upheaval in which

REVISITS HIS OLD HOME.

FIGURE 9. *Life and Times of Frederick Douglass* (Hartford, CT: Park Publishing, 1882), p. 545. Courtesy of the Library Company of Philadelphia.

costumes and settings can so quickly be changed, Douglass says of his relatively short visit to Auld in particular that it "might well enough be dramatized for the stage"—which in some ways it was in *Life and Times*.[57]

A dramatic, staged reunion with the formerly loathed and once powerful slave master, a hope in 1877 (and then in 1881) for a social transformation in which masks fall by the wayside, blacks and whites discover their common humanity, and the process of national regeneration commences: this is Douglass's romance of reunion as depicted in *Life and Times*.[58] It is difficult not to note, however, that the Thomas Auld of *Life and Times*, with the exception of this single scene, remains as before, and that Douglass concludes the chapter, not by reporting on another visit to another white person or descendent from his days as a slave, but by describing his most famous post–Civil War speech on John Brown, which he delivered at Harpers Ferry (for more on the speech, see Chapter 4). Douglass presents the occasion of the speech as just as improbable as his Maryland reunions: "I was, after two decades, . . . allowed to deliver an address, not merely defending John Brown, but extolling him as a hero and martyr to the cause of liberty, and doing it with scarcely a murmur of disappropriation." Incredibly, Andrew J. Hunter, the Virginia state attorney who had prosecuted Brown, congratulates Douglass on his speech, and according to Douglass goes so far as to say that "if Robert E. Lee [who had captured Brown] were alive and present, he knew he would give me his hand also."[59] Kindness and human brotherhood truly seem to be dawning in the South. And yet despite Douglass's hopefulness at this moment of the autobiography, many of his speeches of the late 1870s and early 1880s angrily condemn the steady loss of blacks' civil rights. Thus it is not that surprising that a chapter that begins so hopefully with the

Auld-Douglass reunion should build to a scene invoking John Brown. With his celebration of Brown's attack on Harpers Ferry, Douglass concludes his seemingly hopeful chapter on white-black reunions in the post-slavery South with an implied warning: John Brown lives!

DEAR CAPTAIN AULD

Shortly after his reunion with Thomas Auld, Douglass wrote his friend and companion Ottilie Assing about what had transpired at Auld's home. Assing was the German woman who traveled to the United States to meet Douglass after the publication of *My Bondage and My Freedom*, translated it into German for an 1860 publication, and became Douglass's regular companion and perhaps lover from the late 1850s to the early 1880s. She committed suicide in 1884, the same year that Douglass married his white secretary, Helen Pitts. Douglass has virtually nothing to say about Assing in *Life and Times*, beyond two fleeting references. But as Maria Diedrich demonstrates in her masterly biography of Assing, Douglass and Assing had a long history of exchanging confidences. Though Douglass's letter to Assing does not survive, her July 12, 1877, response to Douglass suggests how he must have depicted the reunion to his close friend. She writes: "The meeting with your master naturally was one of the chief points of interest and under the circumstances you met him in, loaded with honor, one of the most prominent men in the country, it must have been quite gratifying to you and rather an act of condescention [*sic*] on your part than otherwise. If I only for once could see the Eastern shore in your company! Now as we see that you can venture to go there, I dare to hope that I may yet have that pleasure."[60] The letter points to what would come to characterize Douglass's account in 1881: Douglass as honored gentleman making a visit to his former master; Douglass in an act of literal condescension choosing to be generous toward the man who had once been so cruel to him; and, very importantly, Douglass laying claim to a part of the country that had historically been hostile to black people.[61]

In 1892, Douglass published an expanded version of *Life and Times*, adding to the text of the 1881 edition (which he lightly edited) a third part with thirteen new chapters covering the years 1881 to 1892. As with the 1881 edition of *Life and Times*, Douglass published his updated autobiography at a time of controversy, for just a year earlier he had resigned from his position as U.S. minister resident and consul general to Haiti. To many of his white critics, Douglass as a black man had chosen to side with a black country during the negotiations in which the United States was attempting to obtain Haiti's Môle St. Nicolas as a naval coaling station. In the third part of his updated autobiography, and in defenses published in the *North American Review*, Douglass insisted that his primary allegiance was to the United States. Still, he had a good relationship with Haiti's president, Louis Mondestin Florvil Hyppolite, and foreign minister, Anténor Firmin, and at the very least understood their point of view in wanting to maintain Haiti's independence from U.S. military and business interests. More than in the *North American Review* pieces, Douglass's remarks on the controversy in *Life and Times* reveal him as unapologetic about his divided loyalties, even as he maintains that he did his job: "I am charged with sympathy for Haïti. I am not ashamed of that charge, but no man can say with truth that my sympathy with Haïti stood between me and any honorable duty that I owed to the United States or to any citizen of the United States."[62]

And yet a man who in 1890–1891 could seem "black" in his political affiliations with Haiti had in January 1884, a year and a half after the death of his wife Anna, married his former secretary, the white Helen Pitts. If Douglass during the controversy over the Môle St. Nicolas could be accused of being more black than "American," during the mid-to-late 1880s he was criticized by a number of blacks for being more white than black, and he was criticized by a number of whites for presuming to marry a white woman. Douglass addresses this controversy as well in the 1892 *Life and Times,* remarking on how the marriage led whites and blacks alike to ask Douglass a version of this question: "Why did I marry a person of my father's complexion instead of marrying one of my mother's complexion?" Emphasizing "complexion" over "race," Douglass destabilizes the latter term while offering his own genealogy as evidence against binary conceptions of white and black. In an interview printed in the *Washington Post* shortly after his marriage to Helen, Douglass states: "I am not an African, as may be seen from my features and hair, and it is equally easy to discern that I am not a Caucasian." Thus he declares to the interviewer: "You may say that Frederick Douglass considers himself a member of the one race which exists."[63] But as the third part of *Life and Times* shows, it is not so easy to move beyond race in what Douglass portrays as a race-obsessed (and racist) nation.

Precisely because Douglass cannot escape race, tensions between a "white" and "black" Douglass inform the added third part of the 1892 autobiography, and not just in the sections on Helen Pitts and Haiti. Hopeful about social change at the end of the 1881 *Life and Times,* even as he invokes the specter of John Brown, Douglass in the 1892 *Life and Times* expresses his anger at the Supreme Court's dismantling of the 1875 Civil Rights Act in 1883, which he asserts is "the most flagrant example of . . . national deterioration," basically nullifying the Fourteenth Amendment and making all blacks, including himself, vulnerable to institutionalized forms of racism. He describes his 1886–1887 European and North African travels with Helen, noting that one of the main goals of this trip was to find evidence undermining the very idea of racial difference—evidence that he hoped would help him "in combating American prejudice against the darker colored races of mankind." When he travels to Rome and observes "an increase of black hair, black eyes, full lips, and dark complexions," he responds not only intellectually about detecting "proof of a common brotherhood" among dark and light peoples, but emotionally as a black man. As he says about the dark coloring of the famous statue of St. Peter: "I was glad to find him black. I have no prejudice against his color."[64] Overall the third part is a challenging addition to the 1881 *Life and Times* that puts Douglass's complex views about race at its very center.

With the pronounced focus on race in the 1892 *Life and Times'* third part, the reunion scene with Thomas Auld, though basically unchanged from the 1881 *Life and Times,* takes on new ramifications. While the 1881 version emphasizes Douglass's position as a black man and former slave who is meeting with a white man and former master at a time when Douglass is urging black Exodusters to remain in the South, the same meeting, described with mostly the same words, but read through the lens of the third part, seems much more about racial identity. The rhetorical question about why Douglass married someone of his father's instead of his mother's "complexion" forcefully reminds readers that Douglass is part white, and even more than in the 1881 edition, presses us to think about Douglass's reunion with Amanda Auld Sears, the granddaughter of the man who was probably Douglass's father, as a reunion with a half niece, and his reunion with Thomas Auld as a reunion with the man whose first marriage was to a woman who could be viewed as Douglass's half sister on his father's side. These are not just reunions between a slave and his former mistress and master, but between members of an extended biological family.

But by the time of the 1892 *Life and Times,* the reunions can seem almost quaint and nostalgic, exposing Douglass to the criticism that he had been naïve about the implications of the Compromise of 1877. Keeping faith with the ideals of Reconstruction, Douglass in the 1881 *Life and Times* presents himself as doing important cultural work in demonstrating the possibility of reconciliation in which blacks do not have to defer to white power. By contrast, in the 1892 *Life and Times,* published after the Supreme Court overturned the 1875 Civil Rights Act, Douglass can appear to have demeaned himself by participating in a ritual that could be read, as southern newspapers back in 1877 read it, as an affirmation of traditional racial hierarchies. In the added third part to *Life and Times,* Douglass is clear about the implications of the Supreme Court's decision on the hopes he had harbored for a multiracial nation based on social justice and equal rights for all: "The future historian will turn to the year 1883. . . . Here he will find the Supreme Court of the nation reversing the action of the Government, defeating the manifest purpose of the Constitution, nullifying the Fourteenth Amendment, and placing itself on the side of prejudice, proscription, and persecution."[65] Rereading the reunion scene while preparing the 1892 *Life and Times,* Douglass may have been troubled by his failure to anticipate the Supreme Court's decision, and thus by what he now could well have regarded as the failure of his trip to the Eastern Shore in 1877. Still, he lets the scene stand as published in 1881.

I conclude this chapter with a story that runs parallel to Douglass's work on the 1892 edition of *Life and Times* but does not make it into the volume itself. Had it done so, the story would have provided Douglass with a more hopeful vision of America's multiracial future based not only on black but also white agency. The story has its origins in Douglass's joyous reunion with Amanda in 1859. As mentioned above, after meeting with Amanda, Douglass wrote Hugh Auld with the hope of having a similarly happy reunion with Hugh and his wife, Sophia. Nothing came of that letter, but when Douglass visited Baltimore in 1864 he renewed his efforts to meet with the family, unaware that Hugh had died in 1861. Douglass called on Sophia and was met not by her son Tommy, who had been his charge when a slave in Baltimore, and who had died in 1848, but by her younger son, Benjamin, a Baltimore policeman, who angrily denied Douglass access to his mother because, as he later wrote Douglass, "I had been reading your Book and imagined that you had done Mother a great injustice in some of your remarks in regard to her."[66] It remains unclear whether Benjamin had been reading the *Narrative* or *My Bondage and My Freedom*, but in both books Sophia is presented in mostly positive terms as a person who genuinely cared about Douglass. Years pass, and shortly after Douglass was relieved of his Haitian consulship in 1891, he was invited to speak at the Centennial Methodist Episcopal Church in Baltimore, the very church he had attended as a slave during the early 1830s. After speaking on the social transformation of Baltimore brought about by the Civil War, he was approached by a white woman who introduced herself as the wife of Benjamin Auld. Benjamin, she informed Douglass, was now eager to make amends for his past intransigence.[67]

From this surprising encounter in a black church, Douglass began a correspondence with the Hugh and Sophia side of the

Auld family. In 1891, Benjamin was a far different person from the hotheaded young man who had denied Douglass access to Sophia in 1864. He writes Douglass on September 11, 1891: "What took place at mothers [*sic*] house on Ann St, during the War I have long Since regretted, and have felt that I did you a great wrong." Nearly three decades after that incident, he maintains that "I harbored not the least unkind feeling towards you, but on the contrary I have always felt a degree of pride when I have read, or heard of you being elevated to some important position, many of which you have filled with credit to yourself." Desirous of ending their "estrangement," he informs Douglass that he has "many friends both White & Colored in my district," and that he can "now thank God, that I have outlived all old animosities and have no ill will against any person in the world."[68]

This letter, and their subsequent exchanges, in which Douglass mainly asks Benjamin for information about his past, are among the most touching testimonials in the Douglass archive to the possibilities of black-white reconciliation, made all the more poignant by the fact that the worsening of conditions for African Americans did not stop this particular Auld from reaching out to Douglass. In the only extant letter from Douglass's side of the correspondence, he addresses Benjamin as "Dear Captain Auld," asks him about Hugh Auld's business partnerships and other matters related to 1830s Baltimore, and remarks on his improbable rise in the culture given his past as a slave: "I sometimes wonder that I ever amounted to any thing in this world."[69] Though the two men would never actually meet, Benjamin Auld's efforts to move beyond the color line, and his wife's bravery in actively seeking out Douglass in a black church, make this epistolary reconciliation all the more inspirational for the way it shows whites south of the Mason-Dixon Line actually doing the work of reaching out to a black man whose relationships with whites and blacks remained as complicated as ever.

After the publication of the 1892 edition of *Life and Times,* Douglass would proudly serve Haiti as its representative at the World's Columbian Exposition of Chicago and, along with Ida B. Wells, would help to produce the short book *The Reason Why the Colored American Is Not in the World's Columbian Exposition* (1893), a scathing attack on white racism. That same year Douglass delivered his great antilynching speech "The Lessons of the Hour." Angry and disillusioned about developments of the 1890s, he nevertheless remained a stalwart of the Republican Party and continued to cling to "the inspiration of hope," as he put it in one of his last extant speeches, that blacks and whites could work together to achieve "the promise of a brighter future."[70] When Douglass died in 1895, his remains were conveyed to the Metropolitan Methodist Episcopal Church in Washington, DC—the black church which he regularly attended—and the area around his casket was decorated with flowers from his many admirers. As reported in a commemorative volume published in 1903, the flowers themselves tell a story, without need of further commentary, about Douglass's complex racial, familial, and political identities: "A simple bunch of lilies decorated the casket but about the altar and the pulpit was banked a wonderful profusion of flowers in appropriate designs. Among the floral tributes besides the beautiful set pieces sent by the Haytien Government, was a cross by Capt. B. F. Auld, of Baltimore, a son of Mr. Douglass's former master."[71]

POSTHUMOUS DOUGLASS

He died in 1895.
He is not dead.

—Langston Hughes

O N FEBRUARY 20, 1895, Douglass gave a speech to the National Council of Women in Washington, DC. A long-standing supporter of women's rights ever since he had attended the epochal Seneca Falls women's rights convention in 1848, he was escorted to the speaker's platform by Susan B. Anthony. When he returned to his home in Anacostia later that day, he began to imitate some of the meeting's speeches for his wife, Helen, and then dropped to his knees in pain. According to the Unitarian minister and Douglass biographer Frederick May Holland, who published a tribute to Douglass two weeks after his death, "his wife thought it was only such mimicry as had always been his delight."[1] But Douglass was suffering from cardiac arrest, and he died, in effect, in the midst of giving a speech.

A memorial service was held several days later at the Metropolitan Methodist Episcopal Church in Washington, DC, where Douglass's body lay in state in an open casket and was viewed by thousands of mourners, including many of Washington's African American children. The black schools of the city's segregated school system canceled classes that day in honor of Douglass; the service itself was attended by Supreme Court Justice John Marshal Harlan, Senators George Hoar and John Sherman, the faculty of Howard University, family, friends, and hundreds of admirers. In his eulogy to Douglass, the pastor of the church, Reverend J. T. Jenifer, shared his vision of Douglass's arrival in heaven:

> On Wednesday, February 20, there was caused a great commotion in the Spirit World. There it was announced, "Frederick Douglass has come." There gathered about him others, Peter Landy, William Lloyd Garrison, William Wilberforce, Daniel O'Connell . . . John Brown, Lewis Hayden, Henry Highland Garnet, William Wells Brown, Charles Sumner, Abraham Lincoln . . . with many heroes prominent in the anti-slavery conflict.
>
> Garrison and Brown inquired, "Well, Frederick, how is it in the world from which you just came? What are the results of freedom for which we all struggled?" Douglass replied, "The victory has been achieved; slaves freed and enfranchised, and made citizens. They have schools, colleges, and great churches. Two millions of children in school, and sixty thousand teachers instructing them. They have their own press, paper and periodicals. They have accumulated

since freedom $200,000,000, and my people are advancing along every line and are rising generally.

The angels heard the tidings, took down their harps, and sang, "Alleluia, Alleluia, the Lord God omnipotent reigneth."[2]

Jenifer's eulogy was followed by a tribute from Susan B. Anthony, who included in her remarks the praise sent by Elizabeth Cady Stanton: "As an orator, writer and editor, Douglass holds an honored place among the gifted men of his day." In 1869, Anthony and Stanton had turned on Douglass during the debates on the Fifteenth Amendment for refusing to withhold his support for a bill that granted black men, but not white women, the franchise. In their anger, they betrayed their racism at a meeting of the American Equal Rights Association, which Douglass attended. According to the proceedings, Stanton remarked that "she did not believe in allowing ignorant negroes and foreigners to make laws for her to obey," and Anthony similarly stated that "if intelligence, justice, and morality are to have precedence in the Government, let the question of woman be brought up first and that of the negro last." From Douglass's point of view, by supporting the Fifteenth Amendment he was defending the idea that black men were men, and thus should have the legal rights accorded "men" in the nation's legal documents. As Angela Y. Davis observes, at a time that saw an upsurge of antiblack violence in the South, Douglass believed that "Black people's need for electoral power was more urgent than that of middle-class white women." The late 1860s conflict between Douglass and women reformers, with whom he had been aligned since the 1840s, was significant, but Douglass remained true to his convictions that women should have the same rights as men, and by the 1880s he had restored his friendships with Anthony and Stanton and was once again an invited speaker at the major women's rights meetings in New York, Boston, and Washington, DC. "I am a radical woman suffrage man," he declared in 1888 before the New England Woman Suffrage Association; and he died hours after speaking to women's rights advocates at the invitation of Anthony.[3]

A number of other religious and cultural leaders offered eulogies to Douglass at Washington's Metropolitan Methodist Episcopal Church. His body was then taken by train to Rochester for a second memorial service, where the Reverend W. C. Gannett of Rochester's First Unitarian Church proposed building a monument to Douglass to stand with the city's monument to Lincoln. The monument would be unveiled just a few years later. Tribute followed tribute, and at the end of the service, Douglass was buried in Rochester's Mount Hope Cemetery beside his first wife, Anna, and daughter Annie.

Douglass had been writing and speaking about his life for over fifty years, often in response to how others had represented him. Beginning with his death, the lives of Douglass would be imagined by those who could not be challenged, refuted, or supplemented by the man himself. That process began with the memorial services. Would he have appreciated Jenifer's heavenly vision of Douglass reporting simultaneously to John Brown and William Lloyd Garrison? We'll never know. But Douglass surely would have been pleased that many of the memorial tributes of 1895 (which were collected by Helen Pitts Douglass for her 1897 *In Memoriam: Frederick Douglass*) drew on the 1881/1892 *Life and Times of Frederick Douglass*. At the memorial gathering at Metropolitan Methodist Episcopal Church, for example, the Reverend J. E. Rankin, president of Howard University, referred to Douglass's account of his 1877 visit to Thomas Auld: "And if we turn from his public life to his private career, what more striking and unusual scene, save perhaps Joseph's forgiveness of his brethren, ever was introduced into the lot of man than his visit to his old and dying master, so many years after his escape from bondage? Was there ever an experience more pathetic? Was there ever forgiveness more generous?" Two weeks later, at a memorial service held at the Fifteenth Street Presbyterian Church in Washington, DC, the Reverend Francis J. Grimké commented extensively on his recent rereading of *Life and Times:* "In looking back over this life, in studying it carefully, as he himself has written it out, the first thing that impresses us, and that gives promise that something may yet come out of it, is his rebellion against the system under which he was born." By learning to read and write, Grimké says, Douglass "wrote his own emancipation proclamation" and then impelled Lincoln to produce one for the nation. Grimké asserts that "it was due largely to the influence of Mr. Douglass, that the colored man was allowed to shoulder his musket and strike a blow for his own freedom and for the preservation of the Union." For those who might be skeptical about Douglass's impact on Lincoln and the Civil War, Grimké refers them to "chapter eleventh of his Life, entitled 'Secession and War.'" In the course of his tribute, Grimké allows that Douglass has some detractors who regard him as "selfish," but he defends Douglass from this "base insinuation" by stating that he has "read his life carefully" and sees nothing that would "justify such an accusation." If anything, he insists, "we get a true insight into the spirit which animated him during his long and eventful life, as well as the motives which prompted him to make a record of that life." The Reverend Alexander Crummell also reflected on *Life and Times* in a eulogy delivered right after Grimké's. "In reading his biography," Crummell observes, "you will see this rich strata of poetic gold cropping out all along through his pages." Like Garrison in 1845, he is particularly taken by Douglass's "fine apostrophe to the gallant ships floating down the Chesapeake," which Douglass included in all versions of his autobiography. Crummell paused in his eulogy to read that passage aloud to the assembly.[4]

"When God finishes a life, it is as though he had written a book," Rankin remarked at the second memorial service in Washington. Just a few years before his death, Douglass finished a book, the expanded second edition of *Life and Times*. By the time of his death, that book for many of his admirers had become the definitive life of Douglass, which was exactly what Douglass had hoped for. Published during his lifetime, it was to some extent a posthumous life, too, a vision of his "several lives as one" shaped by a man who for good reason, given his age, increasingly imagined himself as dead.[5]

In a hostile review of the poorly produced first printing of the 1881 *Life and Times,* an anonymous writer for the *Critic* pronounced: "Here is reason enough why a man should wait till there is five feet of good solid earth over him before he provokes the world to talk about him by taking it into his confidence."[6] Given that Douglass would not be able to write his autobiography from the grave, it made sense that he would want to revise and update *Life and Times* when he thought he would be in the grave relatively soon. During the 1880s, Douglass had the vigor to remarry and travel to Europe and Africa, but he became increasingly convinced that he was not long for the world, especially as he contemplated the deaths of his antislavery friends and associates from the pre–Civil War era. Speaking at the memorial service for Wendell Phillips on February 22, 1884, Douglass remarks on his vanishing generation of abolitionists: "Death has been very busy during the last years, in thinning out the ranks of such men." Douglass has the dead on his mind a year later, during a celebration of West Indies emancipation and the Emancipation Proclamation, when he intones in the midst of his speech: "We are walking amid sacred graves. Garrison, Phillips, Sumner, Wilson, Stevens, Wade, and Lincoln, with other friends of liberty, have passed on to the silent continent of the dead and to-day we stand in the valley and shadow of the death of Ulysses S. Grant, the most illustrious warrior and statesman of modern times." Several years later, on the occasion of a memorial service for the former U.S. senator Roscoe Conkling of New York, Douglass laments that "only two of the original signers of the Constitution of the American Anti-Slavery Society still survive, and these are Robert Purvis of Pennsylvania and John G. Whittier of Massachusetts, both far beyond their three score and ten. The leaves are falling all around us, and soon all that remain must fade and fall." Douglass gave this speech the year he turned seventy. In 1890, at the age of seventy-two, he attended a reunion of abolitionists at Boston's Tremont Temple, and as nostalgia gripped him, he was moved to honor the dead Garrison above all other abolitionists: "How well I knew Mr. Garrison! How much I loved him!" Then he makes a claim that conflicts with his condemnation of Garrison in *My Bondage and Freedom* and his celebration of Lincoln in *Life and Times:* "We would never have heard of Abraham Lincoln but for the men I have mentioned [Garrison and his associates at the Massachusetts Anti-Slavery Society]. It was they who made Abraham Lincoln, Charles Sumner, William H. Seward, possible."[7]

Douglass continued to speak publicly about his old age. During an interview with the *Baltimore American,* at a time when he was working on the second edition of *Life and Times,* he remarks that "I am seventy-four years of age, and I can say, as to my future, that I think I have arrived at an age when I have a right to retire from all official duties." As he explains to the interviewer, he needs to quickly complete the final version of his life history, "for being past seventy years I have not in the course of nature long to stay here." He comments on his goals for this final version of his autobiography: "My life has been a remarkable one, coming, as I have, from the slave cabin and the cornfield to the prominent position which I hold, especially as a representative of my race. Thus, I can tell my descendants a little something of what I have seen and experienced and how I have acted in the world."[8] Adopting a similar tone in a letter to his friend Marshall Pierce about his work on the second edition of *Life and Times*, Douglass confesses: "When I laid down my pen a dozen years ago I thought I had reached the end, not of life, but of autobiographic writing, and was glad to have done with it. I have always found it easier to speak than to write." And yet he chooses to write, "though my eyes are failing and my hand is not as nimble as it once was."[9]

More than any of his other autobiographies, *Life and Times* is haunted by Douglass's vision of impending death and driven by his desire to create the figure of "Douglass" that he wants to bequeath to posterity. An awareness of death and a desire to address future generations inform both editions of *Life and Times*. Near the end of the 1881 edition, for instance, and reprinted in the 1892 edition, Douglass marvels at what he has constructed over the first 500 pages of his autobiography: "The most of my story is now before the reader. . . . As I review the last decade up to the present writing, I am impressed with a sense of completeness; a sort of rounding up of the arch to the point where the keystone may be inserted, the scaffolding removed, and the work, with all its perfections of faults, left to speak for itself." He underscores that sense of completeness at the 1881 edition's "Conclusion" (also reprinted in 1892): "As far as this volume can reach that point I have now brought my readers to the end of my story. What may remain of life to me, through what experiences I may pass, what heights I may attain, into what depths I may fall, . . . all this, if thought worthy and useful, will probably be told by others when I have passed from the busy stage of life." Is there happiness or anxiety at the thought of his life (or lives) being left to others to use and interpret as they see fit? There would appear to be anxiety more than anything else, for eleven years after making this statement he decided to expand *Life and Times* by adding a new third part that would chronicle his life from 1881 to the present. At this point he is understandably even more convinced that his life will soon be over. In this new section Douglass expresses his surprise that he's still alive to tell his story: "When the first part of this book was written, I was, as before intimated, already looking toward the sunset of human life and thinking that my children would probably finish the recital of my life, or that possibly some other persons outside of family ties to whom I am known might think it worth while to tell what he or she might know of the remainder of my story." He praises "the scrupulous justice done me in the biography of myself lately written by Mr. Frederick May Holland of Concord, Massachusetts," but he's even happier that he still has the vigor to complete "the recital of my life." He candidly remarks: "Like most men who give the world their autobiographies I wish my story to be told as favorably towards myself as it can be with a due regard to truth."[10]

The final edition of *Life and Times* does have a sense of completeness. But there are contradictory and mysterious components of the autobiography, too. Readers continue to debate about the extent of Douglass's closeness to the Auld family. Was he unfair to Garrison? And what about the role of women in his life? Douglass says virtually nothing about his first wife, Anna, or the loyal managing editor of his newspapers, Julia Griffiths, and there are just two quick mentions of Ottilie Assing, who is described in the autobiography as "a German lady, deeply interested in the John Brown scheme," but who we now know was Douglass's close friend and probable paramour for a twenty-year period.[11] Sophia Auld and Douglass's grandmother have an important place in all of the autobiographies, and Amanda Auld Sears is crucial to *Life and Times*. Seeking to lay claim to the manhood that white racist culture denied him, Douglass in much of his autobiographical writings emphasizes his performance of black manhood in the public arena, whether fighting back against the Eastern Shore's most notorious slave breaker, Covey, debating Garrison, defending Brown, working with and sometimes against Lincoln, or making sure that his visit to Thomas Auld was front-page news. But where is the private Douglass? Did he have close friends? What did he like to read? What kind of relationship did he have with his children? Though Douglass's images of a keystone and scaffolding suggest that he built a monument to himself in his final autobiography, one of the most compelling aspects of *Life and Times* is that no single or transparent Douglass emerges from this very long text. As Douglass himself seemed to realize, the monument that he constructed (in the revised and expanded autobiography) consists of multiple, successive selves—and enigma.

But there are controversies that Douglass sees fit to describe on his own terms. He spends considerable space in the new third part defending his marriage to the white Helen Pitts and his service as minister resident and consul general to the Republic of

Haiti. Rejecting the notion that he is "more a Haïtian than an American," as he was "so characterized in American journals" when he argued for Haiti's right to reject the development of a U.S. naval site on the island, he nonetheless gives Haiti a central place in the remarkable closing sentence of the 1892 edition of his autobiography: "I have been the recipient of many honors, among which my unsought appointment by President Benjamin Harrison to the office of Minister Resident and Consul-General to represent the United States at the capital of Haïti, and my equally unsought appointment by President Florvil Hyppolite to represent Haïti among all the civilized nations of the globe at the World's Columbian Exposition, are crowning honors to my long career and a fitting and happy close to my whole public life."[12] Here, Douglass puts his U.S. and Haitian honors in an equivalent balance, and thus, as in *My Bondage and My Freedom*, to some extent works against his representative identity as a leader of African Americans. Or, perhaps more accurately, he enlarges that identity by locating himself in a transnational context. That broader identity is anticipated in chapters just prior to his account of his diplomatic work in Haiti, when he describes the tour of England, France, Italy, Greece, and Egypt that he undertook from October 1886 to May 1887 with his wife Helen. The tour, he says, had "an ethnological purpose," insofar as he sought to find evidence of racial hybridity in Europe that would counter what he terms "the steady march of the slave power toward national supremacy since the agonies of the war." But in his account of his travels, he does something more than simply offer lessons about race. In Egypt, at age seventy, he climbs "to the top of the highest Pyramid," where he achieves a sublime vision of the "millions on millions that lived, wrought, and died there"; and then upon returning to Rome, he contemplates the limits of human ambition and power in a manner consistent with what he intimated in Egypt: "The lesson of the vanity of all things is taught in deeply buried palaces, in fallen columns, in defaced monuments, in decaying arches, and in crumbling walls; all perishing under the silent and destructive force of time and the steady action of the elements, in utter mockery of the pride and power of the great people by whom they were called into existence."[13]

In the final chapters of the 1892 *Life and Times,* and thus at the conclusion of his series of autobiographies, Douglass directly addresses the vanity and futility of human actions, the tenuousness of nations and institutions, and the mocking reality of death. On the level of sheer politics, Douglass also seems dumbfounded in 1892 by the persistence of white supremacy and racial hierarchies over the nearly fifty years from his first to last autobiography. Whether he is gazing at the Chesapeake or imagining himself looking down on the world from a pyramid, there are complexities of desire and anxiety that inform all of Douglass's autobiographical writings and suggest the possibility of the imminent collapse of any particular construction of identity at any particular moment. In that light, perhaps the most heroic aspect of Douglass's efforts to write himself into being is his faith in writing itself. Beginning with his death in 1895, to circle back to the introduction of this study, Douglass has had a continued impact on American culture in large part because of his autobiographical writing, which for well over one hundred years has made the posthumous Douglass a significant presence even beyond the United States. *"He is not dead,"* Langston Hughes asserts. Douglass's lives produced afterlives—conflicting, elusive, and inspirational—which are among his greatest legacies.[14]

NOTES

ACKNOWLEDGMENTS

INDEX

⚘ NOTES ⚘

Correspondence   *The Frederick Douglass Papers: Series Three: Correspondence: Volume 1: 1842–1852*, ed. John R. McKivigan et al. (New Haven: Yale University Press, 2009)

FDP   *The Frederick Douglass Papers, Series One: Speeches, Debates, and Interviews*, 5 vols., ed. John W. Blassingame et al. (New Haven: Yale University Press, 1979–1992)

INTRODUCTION

1. Douglass, *Life and Times of Frederick Douglass, Written by Himself* (1881; Hartford, CT: Park Publishing, 1882), 581–82. Douglass preferred this printing, which corrected many of the errors in the 1881 first edition.

2. See, for instance, the discussion in Chapter 4 of the different stories Douglass told about Lincoln in the late 1880s and early 1890s.

3. For an example of this sort of comparative work, see James Matlack, "The Autobiographies of Frederick Douglass," *Phylon* 40.1 (1979): 15–28.

4. Douglass, "The Freedmen's Monument to Abraham Lincoln: An Address Delivered in Washington, D.C., on 14 April 1876," *FDP*, vol. 4, 431; Douglass, "Good Men Are God in the Flesh: An Address Delivered in Boston, Massachusetts, on 22 September 1890," *FDP*, vol. 5, 435.

5. The sculpture was later moved to Rochester's Highland Park.

6. James Monroe Gregory, *Frederick Douglass the Orator* (Springfield, MA: Willey, 1893), 21; Waldo E. Martin, Jr., "Foreword: The Enduring Douglass," Frederick S. Voss, *Majestic in His Wrath: A Pictorial Life of Frederick Douglass* (Washington, DC: Smithsonian Institution Press, 1995), xiv.

7. Booker T. Washington, *Frederick Douglass* (1906; Honolulu: University Press of the Pacific, 2003), 15, 339; W. E. B. Du Bois, *John Brown* (1909; New York: Modern Library, 2001), 205–6. For an excellent discussion of Washington and Douglass, see James Olney, "The Founding Fathers—Frederick Douglass and Booker T. Washington," *Slavery and the Literary Imagination: Selected Papers from the English Institute, 1987,* ed. Deborah E. McDowell and Arnold Rampersad (Baltimore: Johns Hopkins University Press, 1989), 1–24.

In *Race Adjustments* (New York: Neale Publishing, 1908), Kelly Miller was the first to raise pointed questions about Washington's appropriation of Douglass: "Douglass was like a lion, bold and fearless; Washington is lamblike, meek and submissive" (reprinted in *Critical Essays on Frederick Douglass,* ed. William L. Andrews [Boston: G. K. Hall, 1991], 36). Miller saw Du Bois as more in the tradition of Douglass. Debate continues about Douglass's political legacy. Peter C. Myers makes a good case for a tradition that runs from Douglass to Washington (and beyond) unified around the natural rights arguments central to political liberalism (*Frederick Douglass and the Rebirth of American Liberalism* [Lawrence: University of Kansas Press, 2008]). In direct response to Myers, Nicholas Buccola argues that Douglass was a more radical progressive reformer (*The Political Thought of Frederick Douglass* [New York: New York University Press, 2012]).

8. For this information I am indebted to Waldo E. Martin, Jr., "Images of Frederick Douglass in the Afro-African Mind: The Recent Black Freedom Struggle," *Frederick Douglass: New Literary and Historical Essays,* ed. Eric J. Sundquist (Cambridge: Cambridge University Press. 1990), 271–85.

9. Douglass also shaped his image through his love of posing for photographers; see Celeste-Marie Bernier, John Stauffer, and Zoe Trodd, eds., *Picturing Frederick Douglass: An Illustrated Biography of the Nineteenth-Century's Most Photographed American* (New York: W. W. Norton, 2015).

10. William Lloyd Garrison, "Preface," *Narrative of the Life of Frederick Douglass, An American Slave, Written by Himself* (Boston: Anti-Slavery Office, 1845), iv; David W. Bartlett, *Modern Agitators; or, Pen Portraits of Living American Reformers* (New York: Miller, Orton and Mulligan, 1856), 63; quoted in James A. Colaiaco, *Frederick Douglass and the Fourth of July* (New York: Palgrave Macmillan, 2006), 5; Pauline Hopkins,

"Hon. Frederick Douglass," *Colored American* 2.2 (1900): 125; George L. Ruffin, "Introduction," *Life and Times*, 20; Charles Chesnutt, *Frederick Douglass* (1899; New York: Dover, 2002), 46; W. S. Scarborough, "Introduction," Gregory, *Frederick Douglass the Orator*, 9. In her important anthology, *Masterpieces of Negro Eloquence: The Best Speeches Delivered by the Negro from the Days of Slavery to the Present Time* (New York: Bookery Publishing, 1914), Alice Moore Dunbar emphatically calls Douglass *"the greatest of Negro orators"* (41). For information on the various editions of *Life and Times*, see *The Frederick Douglass Papers: Series Two: Autobiographical Writings: Volume 3: Life and Times and Frederick Douglass: Book 1: The Text and Editorial Apparatus*, ed. John R. McKivigan et al. (New Haven: Yale University Press, 2012).

11. Douglass, *My Bondage and My Freedom* (New York: Miller, Orton and Mulligan, 1855), 223; Douglass, *Life and Times*, 121.

12. For information on the various editions of the *Narrative*, see *The Frederick Douglass Papers: Series Two: Autobiographical Writings: Volume 1: Narrative*, ed. John Blassingame et al. (New Haven: Yale University Press, 1999).

13. William Wells Brown, *The Black Man: His Antecedents, His Genius, and His Achievements* (Boston: James Redpath, 1863), 180–81; Hopkins, "Hon. Frederick Douglass," 125.

14. Benjamin Griffith Brawley, *The Negro in Literature and Art* (Atlanta: n.p., 1910), 37; Brawley, *The Negro in Literature and Art* (1918; New York: Duffield, 1930), 3, 4, 48. See also Brawley, *A Short History of the American Negro* (New York: Macmillan, 1929).

15. Brawley, *The Negro Genius: A New Appraisal of the Achievement of the American Negro in Literature and the Fine Arts* (New York: Dodd, Mead, 1937), 58, 54, 55; John Sekora, "Black Message/White Envelope: Genre, Authenticity, and Authority in the Antebellum Slave Narrative," *Callaloo* 32 (2007): 497; Brawley, *Negro Genius*, 55. See also Brawley, *Early American Negro Writers: Selections with Biographical and Critical Introductions* (Chapel Hill: University of North Carolina Press, 1935).

16. Vernon Loggins, *The Negro Author: His Development in America to 1900* (New York: Columbia University Press, 1931), 141, 144; Benjamin Quarles, *Frederick Douglass* (Washington, DC: Associated Publishers, 1948), 35. In his eloquent *To Make a Poet Black* (1939; Ithaca: Cornell

University Press, 1988), J. Saunders Redding writes that *Bondage and Freedom* is Douglass's best book, in part because it enlarges upon "the simple plan of the *Narrative*" (35). Still, Redding has an appreciative paragraph on the *Narrative*'s "stringent simplicity of style" (32).

17. Philip S. Foner, *The Life and Writings of Frederick Douglass: Early Years, 1817–1849* (New York: International Publishers, 1950), 13, 12.

18. Benjamin Quarles, "Introduction," *Narrative of the Life of Frederick Douglass, an American Slave* (Cambridge, MA: Harvard University Press, 1960), xvi–xvii, xviii, xix.

19. Ephraim Peabody, "Narratives of Fugitive Slaves" (1849), reprinted in *Critical Essays on Frederick Douglass*, ed. William L. Andrews (Boston: G. K. Hall, 1991), 19; James Miller, "Frederick Douglass," *The Heath Anthology of American Literature: Volume B: Early Nineteenth-Century: 1800–1865*, ed. Paul Lauter (Boston: Houghton Mifflin, 2006), 1881; Quarles, "Introduction," xix.

20. Quarles, "Introduction," xxiv, xix. Douglass's *Narrative* continues to have an important place on the Harvard University Press list. When the John Harvard Library Series was recently revived, Robert B. Stepto was commissioned to do a new edition of the *Narrative*, which was published in 2009 with other of the series' inaugural volumes.

21. Harold Cruse, *The Crisis of the Negro Intellectual* (New York: William Morrow, 1967), 563; Lerone Bennett, Jr., "Frederick Douglass: Father of the Protest Movement," *Ebony* 18.11 (1963): 51; Stokely Carmichael and Charles V. Hamilton, *Black Power: The Politics of Liberation in America* (New York: Vintage, 1967), x; Malcolm X, *By Any Means Necessary* (1970; New York: Pathfinder, 1992), 124; Eric J. Sundquist, "1855/1955: From Antislavery to Civil Rights," *Frederick Douglass and Herman Melville: Essays in Relation*, ed. Robert S. Levine and Samuel Otter (Chapel Hill: University of North Carolina Press, 2008), 419; and Martin Luther King, Jr., "The Ethical Demands of Integration" (1962), *A Testament of Hope: The Essential Writings of Martin Luther King, Jr.*, ed. James Melvin Washington (San Francisco: Harper and Row, 1986), 119. For a good overview of debate on Douglass during the 1960s, see Martin, "Images of Frederick Douglass."

22. John Hope Franklin, "Rebels, Runaways, and Heroes: The Bitter Years of Slavery," *Life* 65.21 (1968): 102.

23. See Courtland Milloy, "Douglass Still Battling the Old South," *Washington Post*, 15 February 2006, B3.

24. Charles T. Davis and Henry Louis Gates, Jr., eds., *The Slave's Narrative* (New York: Oxford University Press, 1985), x; James Olney, "'I Was Born': Slave Narratives, Their Status as Autobiography and Literature," Davis and Gates, *Slave's Narrative*, 153; Houston A. Baker, Jr., "Introduction," *Narrative of the Life of Frederick Douglass, an American Slave* (New York: Penguin, 1982), 24. On the reevaluation of the slave narrative, see Charles H. Nichols's *Many Thousands Gone: The Ex-Slaves' Account of Their Bondage and Freedom* (1963; Bloomington: Indiana University Press, 1969); Stephen Butterfield's *Black Autobiography in America* (Amherst: University of Massachusetts Press, 1974); and Sidonie Smith's *Where I'm Bound: Patterns of Slavery and Freedom in Black American Autobiography* (Westport, CT: Greenwood Press, 1974).

25. In an influential essay, Deborah E. McDowell argued that the emphasis on the *Narrative* as the representative nineteenth-century African American autobiography contributed to the omission of African American women from the canon; see "In the First Place: Frederick Douglass and the Afro-American Narrative Tradition," *Critical Essays on Frederick Douglass*, ed. William L. Andrews (Boston: G. K. Hall, 1991), 192–214. For a discussion of Douglass and racial representativeness in the nineteenth century, see Gene Andrew Jarrett, *Representing the Race: A New Political History of African American Literature* (New York: New York University Press, 2011), ch. 2.

26. William L. Andrews, "Towards a Poetics of Afro-American Autobiography," *Afro-American Literary Study in the 1990s*, ed. Houston A Baker, Jr., and Patricia Remond (Chicago: University of Chicago Press, 1989), 87; Celeste-Marie Bernier, "A 'Typical Negro' or a 'Work of Art': The 'Inner' via the 'Outer Man' in Frederick Douglass's Manuscripts and Daguerreotypes," *Slavery & Abolition* 33.2 (2012): 292. On the seriality of Douglass's writings, see Fionnghuala Sweeney, *Frederick Douglass and the Atlantic World* (Liverpool: Liverpool University Press, 2007), esp. 68–70.

27. Paul John Eakin, *Fictions in Autobiography: Studies in the Art of Self-Invention* (Princeton: Princeton University Press, 1985), 36; Waldo E. Martin, Jr., *The Mind of Frederick Douglass* (Chapel Hill: University of

North Carolina Press, 1984), 273. On Douglass's belief that identity was constantly changing, see John Stauffer, "Frederick Douglass's Self-Fashioning and the Making of a Representative American Man," *The Cambridge Companion to the African American Slave Narrative*, ed. Audrey Fisch (Cambridge: Cambridge University Press, 2007), 201–17.

1. THE MASSACHUSETTS ANTI-SLAVERY
SOCIETY *NARRATIVE*

1. See the discussion of Douglass during the summer and fall of 1845 in Chapter 2.

2. John Sekora, "Black Message/White Envelope: Genre, Authenticity, and Authority in the Antebellum Slave Narrative," *Callaloo* 32 (1987): 509, 502. In somewhat the same vein, Celeste-Marie Bernier asserts about the *Narrative:* "There can be little doubt that Douglass's first autobiography was written upon command to prove his fugitive slave status and dispel the doubts of white sceptics" ("From Fugitive Slave to Fugitive Abolitionist: The Oratory of Frederick Douglass and the Emerging Heroic Slave Tradition," *Atlantic Studies* 3.2 [2006]: 206).

3. William Lloyd Garrison, "To the Abolitionists of the United States," 28 February 1840, *The Letters of William Lloyd Garrison: Volume 2: A House Dividing against Itself,* ed. Louis Ruchames (Cambridge, MA: Harvard University Press, 1971), 564; hereafter *Letters*; Garrison, "To the Abolitionists of the United States," 24 April 1840, *Letters,* 580; Garrison, "Address to the Friends of Freedom and Emancipation in the United States," *Liberator,* 31 May 1844, 86.

4. This paragraph draws on William S. McFeely, *Frederick Douglass* (New York: W. W. Norton, 1991), chs. 7–8. On Douglass's importance to the Massachusetts Anti-Slavery Society, see also John Stauffer, "Douglass's Self-Making and the Culture of Abolitionism," *The Cambridge Companion to Frederick Douglass,* ed. Maurice S. Lee (Cambridge: Cambridge University Press, 2009), 13–30.

5. Douglass, *My Bondage and My Freedom* (New York: Miller, Orton and Mulligan, 1855), 358, 359, 360, 361, 362.

6. Douglass to William Lloyd Garrison, letter of 27 October 1844, *Correspondence,* 33. For examples of Douglass's lectures of the period on a

wide range of topics, see "The Union, Slavery, and Abolitionist Petitions: Addresses Delivered in Hingham, Massachusetts, on 4 November 1841," *FDP*, vol. 1, 5–8; "American Prejudice and Southern Religion: An Address Delivered in Hingham, Massachusetts, on 4 November 1841," *FDP*, vol. 1, 9–13; and "Southern Slavery and Northern Religion: Two Addresses Delivered in Concord, New Hampshire, on 11 February 1844," *FDP*, vol. 1, 23–27. On Douglass's early career as a lecturer, see Gregory P. Lampe, *Frederick Douglass: Freedom's Voice, 1818–1845* (East Lansing: Michigan State University Press, 1998).

7. McFeely, *Frederick Douglass*, 108; Sekora, "Black Message/White Envelope," 498.

8. On this point see also Sekora, "Black Message/White Envelope," 501.

9. Douglass, *My Bondage and My Freedom*, 358; Nathaniel Peabody Rogers, "Rhode Island Meeting" (1841), *A Collection from the Miscellaneous Writings of Nathaniel Peabody Rogers* (Manchester, NH: William H. Fisk, 1849), 201, 203, 204.

10. Douglass, "I Have Come to Tell You Something about Slavery: An Address Delivered in Lynn, Massachusetts, in October 1841," *FDP*, vol. 1, 3, 5. On Auld, see also "American Prejudice and Southern Religion: An Address Delivered in Hingham, Massachusetts, on 4 November 1841," *FDP*, vol. 1, 13, along with the many speeches and essays I discuss in Chapter 5.

11. Douglass, "Southern Slavery and Northern Religion: Two Addresses Delivered in Concord, New Hampshire, on 11 February 1844" (as reported by Nathaniel P. Rogers in the 16 February 1844 *Concord Herald of Freedom*), *FDP*, vol. 1, 25, 26.

12. See Douglass, "My Slave Experience in Maryland: An Address Delivered in New York, New York, on 6 May 1845," *FDP*, vol. 1, 27–34.

13. Benjamin Quarles, *Frederick Douglass* (1948; New York: Atheneum, 1968), 34–35.

14. Douglass to Garrison, letter of 8 November 1842, *Correspondence*, 5; Douglass to Maria Weston Chapman, letter of 10 September 1843, *Correspondence*, 12; Douglass to Chapman, letter of 27 October 1844, *Correspondence*, 43; Henry Mayer, *All on Fire: William Lloyd Garrison and the Abolition of Slavery* (New York: St. Martin's Press, 1998), 350.

15. Gérard Genette, *Paratexts: Thresholds of Interpretation* (Cambridge: Cambridge University Press, 1997), 197.

16. From a completely different perspective, the editors of the Yale University Press "Frederick Douglass Papers" edition of the *Narrative* present Douglass as actively engaged with all aspects of the composition and publication of his canonical work, including the "envelope," which they claim is essentially Douglass's. They assert the following: "Douglass knew well that perhaps the central problem he faced was to establish his credibility. To do so, he adopted several strategies. First, he placed a daguerreotype of himself on the book's frontispiece and signed his name below it. . . . Next he preceded his text with letters from William Lloyd Garrison and Wendell Phillips, who served as witnesses to his veracity." See *The Frederick Douglass Papers: Series Two: Autobiographical Writings: Volume 1: Narrative*, ed. John W. Blassingame et al. (New Haven: Yale University Press, 1999), xxx–xxxi. It is much more likely that the publisher placed the daguerreotype of Douglass on the frontispiece (though probably with Douglass's approval), and that the publisher (Garrison) made the decision to preface Douglass's first-person narrative with white authentication because that's how slave narratives were typically presented to white readers. That Douglass textual scholars would insist on Douglass's control over all aspects of a publication coming out of the Massachusetts Anti-Slavery Society suggests that many continue to remain uncomfortable about the *Narrative*'s connection to the white abolitionist organization that Douglass eventually turned on. So the editors (incorrectly) make the 1845 Boston *Narrative* into a Douglass production.

17. Douglass, *Narrative of the Life of Frederick Douglass, an American Slave. Written by Himself* (Boston: Anti-Slavery Office, 1845), iv, iii–iv, v, vi, xii.

18. On this point see also Robert P. Stepto, *From behind the Veil: A Study of Afro-American Narrative* (1979; Urbana: University of Illinois Press, 1991), 18–19.

19. Douglass, *Narrative*, 85–86, xv.

20. Ibid., iv, 117, 125, 31, iv, vii, viii, 63, ix.

21. Ibid., viii, xiv, xv.

22. Ibid., 1, 8. Douglass was a great admirer of Dickens; he serialized *Bleak House* in 1852–1853 issues of *Frederick Douglass' Paper*.

23. In an influential essay, Deborah E. McDowell argues that Douglass's "sexualized scene of whipping projects him into a voyeuristic relation to the violence against slave women, which he watches, and thus he enters into a symbolic complicity with the sexual crime he witnesses" ("In the First Place: Making Frederick Douglass and the Afro-American Narrative Tradition," *Critical Essays on Frederick Douglass,* ed. William L. Andrews [Boston: G. K. Hall, 1991], 203). See also Jenny Franchot, "The Punishment of Esther: Frederick Douglass and the Construction of the Feminine," *Frederick Douglass: New Literary and Historical Essays,* ed. Eric J. Sundquist (Cambridge: Cambridge University Press, 1990), 141–65; Jeannine DeLombard, " 'Eye-Witness to the Cruelty': Southern Violence and Northern Testimony in Frederick Douglass's 1845 *Narrative,*" *American Literature* 73.2 (2001): 245–75, esp. 258–60; and (for a somewhat different perspective), David Van Leer, "A View from the Closet: Reconcilable Differences in Douglass and Melville," *Frederick Douglass and Herman Melville: Essays in Relation,* ed. Robert S. Levine and Samuel Otter (Chapel Hill: University of North Carolina Press, 2008), 279–99. On Douglass and gender, see also Cynthia Hamilton, "Frederick Douglass and the Gender Politics of Reform," *Liberating Sojourn: Frederick Douglass and Transatlantic Reform,* ed. Alan J. Rice and Martin Crawford (Athens: University of Georgia Press, 1999), 73–92; and Hester Blum, "Douglass's and Melville's 'Alphabets of the Blind,' " Levine and Otter, *Frederick Douglass and Herman Melville,* 233–56.

It is worth noting that the two best known women reviewers of Douglass's *Narrative*—the American Margaret Fuller and the Briton Mary Howitt—both commented positively on this opening scene, with Howitt in particular praising Douglass for having the honesty to depict the white male slave owners as having children with their slave women in order to add to their property. She specifically recommends to her readers Douglass's "forcible words" on how Anthony "tied up a poor female slave to a joist, and whipped her upon the naked back till she was literally covered with blood." See Mary Howitt, "Memoir of Frederick Douglass," *People's Journal* 2 (1847), reprinted in Blassingame et al., *Frederick Douglass Papers: Series Two: Autobiographical Writings: Volume 1: Narrative,* 193. Fuller's review appeared in the *New York Tribune,* 10 June 1845, 2.

24. Douglass, *Narrative*, 6, x, 5.

25. Aliyyah I. Abdur-Rahman, " 'This Horrible Exhibition': Sexuality in Slave Narratives," *The Oxford Handbook of the African American Slave Narrative*, ed. John Ernest (New York: Oxford University Press, 2014), 237.

26. Douglass, *Narrative*, 21, 22, 23, 24, 15; Abdur-Rahman, " 'This Horrible Exhibition,' " 237; Douglass, *Narrative*, 17, 46, 67.

27. Douglass, *Narrative*, 12. Arthur Riss argues that the *Narrative*, which is generally taken as a paradigmatic liberal text, also develops a counternarrative on the limits of personal action; see *Race, Slavery, and Liberalism in Nineteenth-Century American Literature* (Cambridge: Cambridge University Press, 2006), esp. 164–69.

28. Douglass, *Narrative*, 31. On the influence of Franklin on Douglass's autobiographical writings, see Rafia Zafar, "Franklinian Douglass: The Afro-American as Representative Man," Sundquist, *Frederick Douglass: New Literary and History Essays*, 99–117.

29. On the importance of Scottish commonsense philosophy to Douglass as a philosopher of race, see Maurice S. Lee, *Slavery, Philosophy, and American Literature, 1830–1860* (Cambridge: Cambridge University Press, 2005), ch. 3.

30. Douglass, *Narrative*, 33, 117, 38, 40.

31. Ibid., 41–42.

32. Ibid., 72.

33. It should be noted that though Garrison regularly preached nonviolence, he was prepared to support violence that could be understood as self-defensive, divinely inspired, or in the American revolutionary tradition. Garrison had come to the defense of one of the most violent rebels in American history, Nat Turner, whose violence Garrison linked to "the vengeance of Heaven," and had published celebratory pieces about the slave rebels Cinqué, who led the rebellion at sea on the *Amistad* in 1839, and Madison Washington, who led the rebellion at sea on the *Creole* in 1841 (the subject of Douglass's only work of fiction, *The Heroic Slave*). On Nat Turner, see [William Lloyd Garrison], "The Insurrection," *Liberator*, 3 September 1831, 143. For Garrison's response to the *Creole* rebellion, see Chapter 3.

34. Douglass, *Narrative*, 64–65, 57, 63, 68.

35. See the discussion in Chapter 3.

36. Douglass, *Narrative*, 71, 72, 73.

37. Ibid., 82, 14, 82, 81, 83.

38. See the discussion in Chapter 3.

39. Douglass, *Narrative*, 86, 98.

40. Ibid., 111, 116.

41. Ibid., 117.

42. Should we be suspicious of such affirmation in a Garrisonian publication? Perhaps. But the sentiments are consistent with Douglass's letters and speeches of the 1841–1845 period; and in the Dublin editions, where he had the freedom to revise, he kept these passages as is.

43. Douglass, *Narrative*, 117. I have been influenced by Stepto's reading of the symmetry of the *Narrative*'s conclusion, though my emphasis is more on the coming together of Garrison's and Douglass's perspectives. Stepto argues that Douglass at the conclusion "supplant[s] Garrison as the definitive historian of his past" (*From behind the Veil*, 25). I'm not sure that Garrison ever regarded himself as Douglass's definitive historian. For a reading that raises questions about tensions between Garrison and Douglass in this final scene, see Maurice O. Wallace, "'I Rose a Freeman': Power, Property, and the Performance of Manhood in Slave Narratives," Ernest, *Oxford Handbook*, esp. 262. On the way that the *Narrative* comes full circle in this final scene, see also Albert E. Stone's seminal "Identity and Art in Frederick Douglass's *Narrative*," *CLA Journal* 17.2 (1973): 192–213.

44. For a provocative argument that Douglass's autobiographical narrative itself is ultimately an attack on Christianity, see Zachary McLeod Hutchins, "Rejecting the Root: The Liberating Anti-Christ Theology of Douglass's *Narrative*," *Nineteenth-Century Literature* 68.3 (2013): 292–322.

45. Douglass, *Narrative*, 118, 119, 120, 122.

46. "Narrative of the Life of Frederick Douglass," *Liberator*, 9 May 1845, 75.

47. "Selections. Narrative of Frederick Douglass," *Liberator*, 30 May 1845, 85; "Narrative of Frederick Douglass," *Liberator*, 23 May 1845, 82.

48. "Narrative of Frederick Douglass," *Liberator*, 23 May 1845, 82; "Frederick Douglass," *Liberator*, 30 May 1845, 86; "Narrative of Frederick Douglass," *Liberator*, 20 June 1845, 99; [untitled advertisement], *Liberator*,

29 August 1845, 139; "Cheap Edition—Douglass," *Liberator,* 29 August 1845, 139.

2. TAKING BACK THE *NARRATIVE*

1. See, for example, Patricia J. Ferreira, "Frederick Douglass in Ireland: The Dublin Edition of His *Narrative,*" *New Hibernia Review* 5.1 (2001): 53–67; and Fionnghuala Sweeney, *Frederick Douglass and the Atlantic World* (Liverpool: Liverpool University Press, 2007), 13–53. On Douglass and Great Britain, see also Alan J. Rice and Martin Crawford, eds., *Liberating Sojourn: Frederick Douglass and Transatlantic Reform* (Athens: University of Georgia Press, 1999); Paul Giles, *Virtual Americas: Transnational Fictions and the Transatlantic Imaginary* (Durham, NC: Duke University Press, 2002), 22–46; Giles, "Douglass's Black Atlantic: Britain, Europe, Egypt," *The Cambridge Companion to Frederick Douglass,* ed. Maurice S. Lee (Cambridge: Cambridge University Press, 2009), 132–45; Audrey A. Fisch, *American Slaves in Victorian England: Abolitionist Politics in Popular Literature and Culture* (Cambridge: Cambridge University Press, 2000); and R. J. M. Blackett, *Building an Antislavery Wall: Black Americans in the Atlantic Abolitionist Movement, 1830–1860* (Baton Rouge: Louisiana State University Press, 1983), 67–117.

2. Gerald Fulkerson, "Textual Introduction," *The Frederick Douglass Papers: Series Two: Autobiographical Writings: Volume 1: Narrative,* ed. John W. Blassingame et al. (New Haven: Yale University Press, 1999), 97, 104.

3. On this point, see Rice and Crawford, *Liberating Sojourn,* 2–4.

4. Douglass, *My Bondage and My Freedom* (New York: Miller, Orton and Mulligan, 1855), 366. James N. Buffum's very positive recollections about Douglass, included in *Commemoration of the Fiftieth Anniversary of the Organization of the American Anti-Slavery Society in Philadelphia* (1884), can be found in John Ernest, ed., *Douglass in His Own Time: A Biographical Chronicle of His Life, Drawn from Recollections, Interviews, and Memoirs by Family, Friends, and Associates* (Iowa City: University of Iowa Press, 2014), 12–16.

5. Douglass, *My Bondage and My Freedom,* 367. For a good overview of the *Cambria* incident, see Tom Chaffin, *Giant's Causeway: Frederick*

Douglass's Irish Odyssey and the Making of an American Visionary (Charlottesville: University of Virginia Press, 2014), ch. 3.

6. Douglass to Garrison, letter of 1 September 1845, *Correspondence*, 48, 49, 50, 48.

7. Douglass, "American Prejudice against Color: An Address Delivered in Cork, Ireland, 23 October 1845," *FDP*, vol. 1, 63, 64, 65–66.

8. Douglass, "Slavery and America's Bastard Republicanism: An Address Delivered in Limerick, Ireland, on 10 November 1845," *FDP*, vol. 1, 83; Douglass, "The *Cambria* Riot, My Slave Experience, and My Irish Mission: An Address Delivered in Belfast, Ireland, on 5 December 1845," *FDP*, vol. 1, 91; Douglass, "America's Compromise with Slavery and the Abolitionists' Work: An Address Delivered in Paisley, Scotland, on 6 April 1846," *FDP*, vol. 1, 215.

9. Douglass, "The *Cambria* Riot," 90.

10. Isabel Jennings to Maria Weston Chapman, letter of 26 November 1845, Boston Public Library. Webb admired Garrison and helped to found the Garrisonian Hibernian Anti-Slavery Society in 1837; see Douglass C. Riach, "Richard Davis Webb and Antislavery in Ireland," *Antislavery Reconsidered: New Perspectives on the Abolitionists,* ed. Lewis Perry and Michael Fellman (Baton Rouge: Louisiana State University Press, 1979), 149–67. For a good overview of Webb's career, see Richard S. Harrison, *Richard Davis Webb: Dublin Quaker Printer (1805–72)* (Dublin: R. S. Harrison, 1993).

11. See Meredith L. McGill, *American Literature and the Culture of Reprinting, 1834–1853* (Philadelphia: University of Pennsylvania Press, 2003), 1–44.

12. Douglass to Garrison, letter of 16 September 1845, *Correspondence*, 52.

13. Quoted in Laurence Fenton, *Frederick Douglass in Ireland: 'The Black O'Connell'* (Cork, Ireland: Collins Press, 2014), 73; see also 60–73.

14. R. D. Webb to Maria Weston Chapman, letter of 16 May 1846, *British and American Abolitionists: An Episode in Transatlantic Understanding*, ed. Clare Taylor (Edinburgh: Edinburgh University Press, 1974), 260, 259. Webb's wife, Hannah, referred to Douglass as "a child—a savage," which suggests that Douglass had to deal with racist condescension and paternalism from both Webbs (see Fenton, *Frederick Douglass in Ireland*, 72). William S. McFeely, however, argues that the conflict

between Webb and Douglass was less about race than Douglass's bad manners (*Frederick Douglass* [New York: W. W. Norton, 1991], 122). Tom Chaffin more sympathetically sees reasons why each person was angry at the other (*Giant's Causeway*, ch. 5). According to Ezra Greenspan, Webb got along much better with William Wells Brown (*William Wells Brown: An African American Life* [New York: W. W. Norton, 2014], 208–14).

15. On tensions between Douglass and the Garrisonians, see William H. Pease and Jane H. Pease, "Boston Garrisonians and the Problem of Frederick Douglass," *Canadian Journal of History* 2.2 (1967): 29–48.

16. Gérard Genette's *Paratexts: Thresholds of Interpretation* (Cambridge: Cambridge University Press, 1997) is discussed in Chapter 1.

17. On Douglass's dissatisfaction with the Adler engraving, see Julia Sun-Joo Lee, *The American Slave Narrative and the Victorian Novel* (New York: Oxford University Press, 2010), 2–5.

18. See Douglass, *Narrative of the Life of Frederick Douglass, an American Slave, Written by Himself* (Dublin: Webb and Chapman, 1845). For a useful discussion of various editions of the *Narrative*, see Fulkerson, "Textual Introduction," 87–97; and on the Dublin editions, see Ferreira, "Frederick Douglass in Ireland," and Sweeney, *Frederick Douglass*, 13–36.

19. See Chapter 1 for a discussion of John Sekora's "Black Message/ White Envelope: Genre, Authenticity, and Authority in the Antebellum Slave Narrative," *Callalo* 32 (1987): 482–515.

20. Douglass, "Preface," *Narrative* (Webb and Chapman, 1845), iii.

21. Ibid., iv, ii.

22. Douglass to Garrison, letter of 29 September 1845, *Correspondence*, 58; Douglass, "Slavery and America's Bastard Republicanism," 82, 76; Douglass to Webb, letter of 6 December 1845, *Correspondence*, 69–70; *Narrative of the Life of Frederick Douglass, an American Slave. Written by Himself*, Second Dublin Edition (Webb and Chapman, 1846), cxxxii; Douglass to Webb, letter of 24 December 1845, *Correspondence*, 72n.2, 71.

23. Fenton, *Frederick Douglass in Ireland*, 97; Douglass to Garrison, letter of 16 September 1845, *Correspondence*, 54. On Douglass and Ireland, see esp. Sweeney, *Frederick Douglass*. Also useful is Lee Jenkins, "The Black O'Connell: Frederick Douglass and Ireland," *Nineteenth-Century Studies* 13 (1999): 22–46; Nina Rogers, *Ireland, Slavery, and Anti-Slavery:*

1612–1865 (New York: Palgrave, 2007), 278–89; Lee M. Jenkins, "Beyond the Pale: Green and Black and Cork," *The Black and Green Atlantic: Cross-Currents of the African and Irish Diasporas*, ed. Peter D. O'Neill and David Lloyd (New York: Palgrave Macmillan, 2009), 165–77; George Bornstein, *The Colors of Zion: Blacks, Jews, and Irish from 1845 to 1945* (Cambridge, MA: Harvard University Press, 2011), 2–9; Ferreira, "Frederick Douglass in Ireland"; and Fenton, *Frederick Douglass in Ireland*. For a provocative fictional reimagining of Douglass's visit to Ireland, see Colum McGann's *Transatlantic: A Novel* (New York: Random House, 2013).

24. Douglass to Garrison, letter of 26 February 1846, *Correspondence*, 96, 95, 96, 97; Douglass to Thomas Van Rensselaer, letter of 18 May 1847, *Correspondence*, 212; Douglass, *My Bondage and My Freedom*, 98. For an excellent discussion of problematic aspects of Douglass's tendency to "fall into the trap of stubbornly accentuating the difference between chattel slavery and Irish poverty, thereby diminishing the extent and significance of the latter" (103), see Bruce Nelson, *Irish Nationalists and the Making of the Irish Race* (Princeton: Princeton University Press, 2012), ch. 4.

25. See Elisa Tamarkin, *Anglophilia: Deference, Devotion, and Antebellum America* (Chicago: University of Chicago Press, 2008), 213–31.

26. Douglass to Webb, letter of mid-January 1846, *Correspondence*, 79; Douglass to Webb, letter of 20 January 1848, *Correspondence*, 81.

27. R. D. Webb to Maria Weston Chapman, letter of 26 February 1846, Taylor, *British and American Abolitionists*, 254; Webb to Chapman, letter of 16 May 1846, Taylor, *British and American Abolitionists*, 260; Buffum to Chapman, letter of 26 June 1846, Taylor, *British and American Abolitionists*, 271.

28. Webb to Chapman, letter of 26 February 1846, Taylor, *British and American Abolitionists*, 254; Douglass to Chapman, letter of 29 March 1846, *Correspondence*, 99.

29. Ferreira, "Frederick Douglass in Ireland," 63. Ferreira claims that Douglass "revered" (63) the second Dublin edition of the *Narrative*.

30. Douglass, *Narrative* (Webb and Chapman, 1846), iv, v–vi.

31. Ibid., vi.

32. Ibid., cxxiii.

33. Ibid.

34. Ibid., cxxiv, cxxiv–cxxv, cxxiv, cxxiii, cxxv.

35. Douglass to Garrison, letter of 27 January 1846, *Correspondence*, 81.

36. Douglass, *Narrative* (Webb and Chapman, 1846), cxxiv, cxxvii.

37. Ibid., cxxvi, cxxvii.

38. Ibid., cxxvii.

39. Ibid., cxxviii, cxxxii.

40. Webb to Edmund Quincy, letter of 2 February 1846, quoted in Sweeney, *Frederick Douglass*, 38; Douglass, "American Slavery, American Religion, and the Free Church of Scotland: An Address Delivered in London, England on 22 May 1846," *FDP*, vol. 1, 291.

41. Webb to Chapman, letter of 31 October 1846, Taylor, *British and American Abolitionists*, 294.

42. Garrison to Edmund Quincy, letter of 18 August 1846, *The Letters of William Lloyd Garrison, Volume 3, No Union with Slave-Holders, 1841–1849*, ed. Walter M. Merrill (Cambridge, MA: Harvard University Press, 1973), 379; hereafter *Letters*; Garrison to Webb, letter of 19 August 1846, *Letters*, 384; Garrison to Helen E. Garrison, letter of 17 September 1846, *Letters*, 415; Garrison to John B. Estlin, letter of 8 September 1846, *Letters*, 400; Garrison to Webb, letter of 8 September 1846, *Letters*, 409. On Douglass and the "Send Back the Money" campaign in Scotland, see Alasdair Pettinger, "Send Back the Money: Douglass and the Free Church of Scotland," Rice and Crawford, *Liberating Sojourn*, 31–55.

43. J. B. Estlin to Samuel May, letter of 12 January 1847, Taylor, *British and American Abolitionists*, 305; Douglass to Anna Richardson, letter of 29 April 1847, *Correspondence*, 208. Though Douglass and his wife Anna may not have been all that close by the 1850s, Douglass did miss his wife and children while abroad. In a letter of 17 September 1846, Garrison reported to his wife, Helen E. Garrison, that Douglass is "sighing to see his wife and children, but he is satisfied that it will enhance his personal safety, and be the better for them in the end, to remain here until spring" (*Letters*, 415). In another letter of 29 April 1847, Douglass wrote the British Quakers William and Robert Smeal: "I am at home—in the warm bosom of my family, caressed and administered to, by the beloved ones of my heart. It is good to be here" (*Correspondence*, 205).

44. *Report of Proceedings at the Soirée Given to Frederick Douglass, London Tavern, March 30, 1847* (London: R. Yorke Clarke, 1847), 3. Julia Griffiths's "The Farewell Song of Frederick Douglass" was published by Duff and Hodgson and reviewed in the *New Monthly Belle Assemblée; A Magazine of Literature and Fashion* 27 (July–December 1847), which called it "far better than amateur compositions in general," and particularly worthy because "Frederick Douglass well deserves to be celebrated in song" (125).

45. Ibid., 6, 7.

46. Ibid., 22, 26, 29.

47. Ibid., 31.

48. Garrison to Helen E. Garrison, letter of 20 October 1847, *Letters*, 532–33. On Douglass's founding of the *North Star* and his initial coediting with Delany, see Robert S. Levine, *Martin Delany, Frederick Douglass, and the Politics of Representative Identity* (Chapel Hill: University of North Carolina Press, 1997), ch. 1.

49. Douglass, *My Bondage and My Freedom*, 361.

50. Douglass, "Our Paper and Its Prospects," *North Star*, 3 December 1847, 1. For William C. Nell's accounts of the black patriots and freedom fighters of the Americas, see his *Services of Colored Americans, in the Wars of 1776 and 1812* (Boston: Robert F. Wallcut, 1851), and *The Colored Patriots of the American Revolution, with Sketches of Several Distinguished Colored Persons: To Which Is Added a Brief Survey of the Condition and Prospects of Colored Americans* (Boston: Robert F. Wallcut, 1855). On Douglass and women's rights, see the pioneering volume edited by Philip S. Foner, *Frederick Douglass on Women's Rights* (1976; New York: Da Capo Press, 1992).

51. Douglass, "A Few Facts and Personal Observations of Slavery: An Address Delivered in Ayr, Scotland, on 24 March 1846," *FDP*, vol. 1, 199. On Garrison's tacit support for the *Creole* rebels, see Chapter 3.

3. HEROIC SLAVES

1. Douglass, "A Tribute for the Negro," *North Star*, 7 April 1849, 2. The biographical portrait and image can be found in Wilson Armistead, *A Tribute for the Negro: Being a Vindication of the Moral, Intellectual, and*

Religious Capabilities of the Colored Portion of Mankind (Manchester: William Irwin, 1848), 454–58. On Douglass's displeasure with the image in Armistead's book, see Julia Sun-Joo Lee, *The American Slave Narrative and the Victorian Novel* (New York: Oxford University Press, 2010), 4–6. For a discussion of Douglass's concerns about how he was imaged during the 1840s and 1850s, see John Stauffer, "Creating an Image in Black: The Power of Abolition Pictures," *Beyond Blackface: African Americans and the Creation of American Popular Culture, 1890–1930*, ed. W. Fitzhugh Brundage (Chapel Hill: University of North Carolina Press, 2011), 66–94; Celeste-Marie Bernier, " 'The Face of a Fugitive Slave': Representing and Reimagining Frederick Douglass in Popular Illustrations, Fine Art Portraiture and Daguerreotypes," *Life Writing and Political Memoir*, ed. Magnus Brechtken (Göttingen: Vandenboeck and Ruprecht, 2012), 11–33; and Sean Ross Meehan, *Mediating American Autobiography: Photography in Emerson, Thoreau, Douglass, and Whitman* (Columbia: University of Missouri Press, 2008), 130–80.

2. Ephraim Peabody, "Narratives of Fugitive Slaves," *Christian Examiner* 47.1 (1849), reprinted in *The Slave's Narrative*, ed. Charles T. Davis and Henry Louis Gates, Jr. (New York: Oxford University Press, 1985), 23, 25; Douglass, "Narratives of Fugitive Slaves. By the Rev. Ephraim Peabody," *North Star*, 3 August 1849, 2.

3. Douglass, *My Bondage and My Freedom* (New York: Miller, Orton and Mulligan, 1855), vii, xxv, xxx.

4. Robert B. Stepto, "Storytelling in Early Afro-American Fiction: Frederick Douglass' 'The Heroic Slave,' " *Georgia Review* 36.2 (1982): 359; Eric J. Sundquist, *To Wake the Nations: Race in the Making of American Literature* (Cambridge, MA: Harvard University Press, 1993), 115. See also Celeste-Marie Bernier, "A 'Typical Negro' or a 'Work of Art'? The 'Inner' via the 'Outer Man' in Frederick Douglass's Manuscripts and Daguerreotypes," *Slavery & Abolition* 33.2 (2012): 287–303.

5. I am thus going against the grain of William L. Andrews's argument that "the fundamental importance of *The Heroic Slave* to the evolution of African American narrative from 'natural' to 'fictive' discourse" is that "priority in *The Heroic Slave* is given to the empowering of a mode of fictive discourse whose authority does not depend on the authentication of what is asserted in that discourse" ("The Novelization of Voice in Early

African American Narrative," *PMLA* 105.1 [1990]: 30). In my reading of *The Heroic Slave* in this chapter, I argue that Douglass was highly attentive to the historical facts of the rebellion as he understood them.

6. Douglass, *The Heroic Slave*, in *Autographs for Freedom*, ed. Julia Griffiths (Boston: John P. Jewett, 1853), 176; Douglass, *Narrative of the Life of Frederick Douglass, an American Slave. Written by Himself* (Boston: Anti-Slavery Office, 1845), 1.

7. Sundquist, *To Wake the Nations*, 120; William S. McFeely, *Frederick Douglass* (New York: W. W. Norton, 1991), 174.

8. On Douglass and Smith, see John R. McKivigan, "The Frederick Douglass–Gerrit Smith Friendship and Political Abolitionism in the 1850s," *Frederick Douglass: New Literary and Historical Essays*, ed. Eric J. Sundquist (Cambridge: Cambridge University Press, 1990), 205–35; and John Stauffer, *The Black Hearts of Men: Radical Abolitionists and the Transformation of Race* (Cambridge, MA: Harvard University Press, 2002), 61–64, 82–88, 174–81. For a discussion of how Douglass's turn to political abolitionism led to changes in his literary self-representations, see Hoang Gia Phan, *Bonds of Citizenship: Law and the Labors of Emancipation* (New York: New York University Press, 2013), ch. 4. Douglass changed the name of his newspaper from the *North Star* to *Frederick Douglass' Paper* in 1851.

9. Douglass, *Narrative*, 117. In this and the prior paragraphs, I have focused on the facts most relevant to Douglass's speeches and novella. For fuller historical discussions of the *Creole* rebellion, see Howard Jones, "The Peculiar Institution and National Honor: The Case of the *Creole* Slave Revolt," *Civil War History* 21.1 (1975): 28–50; Edward D. Jervey and C. Harold Huber, "The *Creole* Affair," *Journal of Negro History* 65.3 (1980): 196–211; Stanley Harrold, "Romanticizing Slave Revolt: Madison Washington, the *Creole* Mutiny, and Abolitionist Celebration of Violent Means," *Antislavery Violence: Sectional, Racial, and Cultural Conflict in Antebellum America*, ed. John R. McKivigan and Stanley Harrold (Knoxville: University of Tennessee Press, 1999), 89–107; Roy E. Finkenbine, "The Symbolism of Slave Mutiny: Black Abolitionist Responses to the *Amistad* and *Creole* Incidents," *Rebellion, Repression, Reinvention: Mutiny in Comparative Perspective*, ed. Jane Hathaway (Westport, CT: Praeger, 2001), 233–52; and George Hendrick and Willene Hendrick, *The Creole Mutiny: A Tale of Revolt aboard a Slave Ship* (Chicago: Ivan R. Dee, 2003). The best

recent study is Walter Johnson, "White Lies: Human Property and Domestic Slavery aboard the Slave Ship *Creole*," *Atlantic Studies* 5.2 (2008): 237–63. On connections between the *Amistad* and *Creole* rebellions, see Marcus Rediker, *The Amistad Rebellion: An Atlantic Odyssey of Slavery and Freedom* (New York: Viking, 2012), 224–27. And on the importance of the diplomatic and legal context to *The Heroic Slave*, see Maggie Montesinos Sale, *The Slumbering Volcano: American Slave Ship Revolts and the Production of Rebellious Masculinity* (Durham, NC: Duke University Press, 1997); and Jeffrey Hole, "Enforcement on a Grand Scale: Fugitive Intelligence and the Literary Tactics of Douglass and Melville," *American Literature* 85.2 (2013): 217–46.

10. "Protest," *Liberator*, 31 December 1841, 210. For a comprehensive discussion of a wider range of writings about the *Creole* beyond what appeared in the *Liberator*, see Cynthia S. Hamilton, "Models of Agency: Frederick Douglass and 'The Heroic Slave,'" *Proceedings of the American Antiquarian Society* 114 (2005): 87–136. For selections from the "Protest" and a number of other texts discussed in this section, see Frederick Douglass, *The Heroic Slave: A Cultural and Critical Edition*, ed. Robert S. Levine, John Stauffer, and John R. McKivigan (New Haven: Yale University Press, 2015).

11. "The Hero Mutineers," *Liberator*, 7 January 1842, 1. See also "The *Creole* Mutiny," in the 25 December 1841 *Colored American*, and "The Case of the *Creole*," in the 6 January 1842 *National Anti-Slavery Standard*.

12. "Madison Washington: Another Chapter in His History," *Liberator*, 10 June 1842, 89.

13. Andrews, "The Novelization of Voice," 28; and see also Ellen Weinauer, "Writing Revolt in the Wake of Nat Turner: Frederick Douglass and the Construction of Black Domesticity in 'The Heroic Slave,'" *Studies in American Fiction* 33.2 (2005): 193–202.

14. See "Madison Washington," *National Anti-Slavery Standard*, 28 April 1842, 187; Douglass, "Slavery, The Slumbering Volcano: An Address Delivered in New York, New York, on 23 April 1849," *FDP*, vol. 2, 155; and "A Priceless Picture: History of Sinque, the Hero of the Amistad," *Philadelphia Inquirer*, 26 December 1889, 3. To be sure, Purvis could have been fabricating aspects of the story, but there are consistencies

between this 1889 newspaper article and the information in the essay in the 28 April 1842 *National Anti-Slavery Standard* and Douglass's 1849 "Slavery, the Slumbering Volcano." On Washington, Purvis, and the Jocelyn painting, see also Rediker, *The Amistad Rebellion,* 172–74, 224–26; and Celeste-Marie Bernier, *Characters of Blood: Black Heroism in the Transatlantic Imagination* (Athens: University of Georgia Press, 2012), 169–70.

15. See Henry Highland Garnet's "Address" in *Walker's Appeal, with a Brief Sketch of His Life. By Henry Highland Garnet. And also Garnet's Address to the Slaves of the United States* (New York: J. H. Tobitt, 1848), 93, 92, 95, 96. On Madison Washington in Garnet's speech, see Sale, *Slumbering Volcano,* 176–77.

16. *Minutes of the National Convention of Colored Persons: Held at Buffalo, on the 15th, 16th, 17th, 18th of August, 1843. For the Purposes of Considering Their Moral and Political Condition as American Citizens* (New York: Piercy and Reed, 1843), 13; Douglass, *Narrative,* 84–85.

17. Douglass, "The Union, Slavery, and Abolitionist Petitions: Address Delivered in Hingham, Massachusetts, on 4 November 1841," *FDP,* vol. 1, 8; Douglass, "My Slave Experience in Maryland: An Address Delivered in New York, New York, on 6 May 1845," *FDP,* vol. 1, 33. Waldo E. Martin, Jr., observes that Douglass, even before his public break with Garrison in 1851, implicitly conveyed in his speeches of the 1840s that he regarded Garrisonian nonresistance to be "lofty and impractical" (*The Mind of Frederick Douglass* [Chapel Hill: University of North Carolina Press, 1984], 24).

18. Douglass, "American Prejudice against Color: An Address Delivered in Cork, Ireland, 23 October 1845," *FDP,* vol. 1, 68. Reporters sometimes spelled "Madison" as "Maddison."

19. Douglass, "America's Compromise with Slavery and the Abolitionists' Work: An Address Delivered in Paisley, Scotland, on 6 April 1846," *FDP,* vol. 1, 211–12; Douglass, "American and Scottish Prejudice against the Slave: An Address Delivered in Edinburgh, Scotland, on 1 May 1846," *FDP,* vol. 1, 244, 245. For a complementary reading of the autobiographical dimensions of Douglass's speech of 1 May 1846, see Celeste-Marie Bernier, "From Fugitive Slave to Fugitive Abolitionist: The Oratory of Frederick Douglass and the Emerging Heroic Slave Tradition," *Atlantic Studies* 3.2 (2006): 212–14.

20. Douglass, "Farewell to the British People: An Address Delivered in London, England, on 30 March 1847," *FDP*, vol. 2, 47, 50.

21. Gerrit Smith to Frederick Douglass, letter of 8 December 1847, *Correspondence*, 277.

22. On Douglass and Smith, see McKivigan, "Frederick Douglass—Gerrit Smith Friendship"; and on Smith's racial egalitarianism, see Stauffer, *Black Hearts of Men*, 1–7, 14–20, 60–65.

23. Douglass, "The Slave's Right to Revolt: An Address Delivered in Boston, Massachusetts, on 30 May 1848," *FDP*, vol. 2, 131; Douglass, "Slavery, the Slumbering Volcano," 153.

24. Ibid., 154, 155.

25. Ibid., 155, 156. On Douglass's personal investment in Washington in this speech, see also Bernier, "From Fugitive Slave to Fugitive Abolitionist," 216–19.

26. Douglass, "What to the Slave Is the Fourth of July? An Address Delivered in Rochester, New York, on 5 July 1852," *FDP*, vol. 2, 364; "Letter from Wm. C. Nell," *Frederick Douglass' Paper*, 18 March 1852, 1; Douglass to Henry Wadsworth Longfellow, letter of 16 June 1852, *Correspondence*, 542. Douglass had written Longfellow with the hope he would contribute a poem or essay to *Autographs for Freedom;* for unspecified reasons, Longfellow did not contribute. On ship of state imagery during this time, see Robert S. Levine, *Conspiracy and Romance: Studies in Brockden Brown, Cooper, Hawthorne, and Melville* (Cambridge: Cambridge University Press, 1989), ch. 4.

27. *The Heroic Slave* first appeared in *Autographs for Freedom*, ed. Julia Griffiths (Boston: John P. Jewett, 1853), 174–239. *Autographs* was advertised in the 7 January 1853 *Frederick Douglass' Paper* as available for purchase at that time, so it was probably published in late 1852. A British edition appeared shortly thereafter with the title *Autographs for Freedom. By Mrs. Harriet Beecher Stowe, and Thirty-five Other Eminent Writers* (London: Sampson Low and Son, 1853). The novella was serialized in 1853 in the 4, 11, 18, and 25 March issues of *Frederick Douglass' Paper*. There was even a pirated edition published in 1853 or 1863, *The Heroic Slave; A Thrilling Narrative of the Adventures of Madison Washington in Pursuit of Liberty,* with a considerably altered text; see Celeste-Marie Bernier, "A Comparative Exploration of Narrative Ambiguities in Frederick Douglass's Two Versions

of *The Heroic Slave* (1853, 1863?)," *Slavery & Abolition* 22.2 (2001): 69–86. After the March 1853 newspaper serialization, *The Heroic Slave* was not republished in Douglass's lifetime; it was neglected until the 1970s, when Abraham Chapman reprinted it in his *Steal Away: Stories of the Runaway Slaves* (New York: Praeger, 1971), and Philip Foner included it in his *The Life and Writings of Frederick Douglass: Supplementary Volume 5: 1844–1860* (New York: International Publishers, 1975). On Douglass and Stowe, see Robert B. Stepto, "Sharing the Thunder: The Literary Exchanges of Harriet Beecher Stowe, Henry Bibb, and Frederick Douglass," *New Essays on Uncle Tom's Cabin* (New York: Cambridge University Press, 1986), 135–53; and on Douglass, Delany, and Stowe, see Robert S. Levine, *Martin Delany, Frederick Douglass, and the Politics of Representative Identity* (Chapel Hill: University of North Carolina Press, 1997), ch. 2; and Levine, *Martin R. Delany: A Documentary Reader* (Chapel Hill: University of North Carolina Press, 2003), 224–37.

28. Douglass to Gerrit Smith, letter of 6 November 1852, *Correspondence*, 552; Douglass to Smith, letter of 21 January 1851, *Correspondence*, 443.

29. McFeely, *Frederick Douglass*, 175.

30. Douglass, *The Heroic Slave*, 174, 175, 176. As Jeannine Marie DeLombard points out, blacks generally made their way into the archives when they were criminalized (*In the Shadow of the Gallows: Race, Crime, and American Civic Identity* [Philadelphia: University of Pennsylvania Press, 2012]). For that reason there are records about Washington once he led a slave revolt.

31. Douglass, *The Heroic Slave*, 177, 179, 182; Carrie Hyde, "The Climates of Liberty: Natural Rights in the *Creole* Case and 'The Heroic Slave,'" *American Literature* 85.3 (2013): 487. On the importance of the visual in the novella, see also Fionnghuala Sweeney, "Visual Culture and Fictive Technique in Frederick Douglass's *The Heroic Slave*," *Slavery & Abolition* 33.2 (2012): 305–20. Celeste-Marie Bernier, in "A 'Typical Negro' or a 'Work of Art'?," describes Washington as Douglass's "imaginative surrogate" (293); see also Bernier's *Characters of Blood*, 277. For an excellent reading of the sublime setting of the forest "conversation," see John Stauffer, "Interracial Friendship and the Aesthetics of Freedom," *Frederick Douglass and Herman Melville: Essays in Relation*, ed. Robert S. Levine

and Samuel Otter (Chapel Hill: University of North Carolina Press, 2008), 134–58.

32. On this point, see Hyde, "Climates of Liberty," 476–504.

33. Raymond Hedin notes in his influential narratological study of the novella that though "everything Washington does and says in the story is either heard or seen by one of two white participants/observers," the storytelling framework nonetheless "conveys not only Washington's dependence on his white observers but his considerable power over them" ("Probable Readers, Possible Stories: The Limits of Nineteenth-Century Black Narrative," *Readers in History: Nineteenth-Century American Literature and the Contexts of Response*, ed. James L. Machor [Baltimore: Johns Hopkins University Press, 1993], 187, 188). On the interplay in the novella between artful talk and sympathetic listening, see Marianne Noble, "Sympathetic Listening in Frederick Douglass's 'The Heroic Slave' and *My Bondage and My Freedom*," *Studies in American Fiction* 34.1 (2006): 53–69.

34. Douglass, *The Heroic Slave*, 182, 185.

35. Ibid., 195, 203, 205.

36. Ibid., 211, 215, 216. On Douglass's use of Listwell as an informant, see Stepto, "Storytelling in Early Afro-American Fiction," 367–69.

37. Douglass, *The Heroic Slave*, 217, 220, 221. Decades after Douglass published his novella, Pauline Hopkins retold the *Creole* rebellion in the short story "Dash for Liberty" (1901). Hopkins imagines Washington's wife as still alive and places her at the center of the rebellion. Douglass's decision to excise her at this point in the novella is consistent with the white officers' "Protest," which says little about the black women aboard the ship, and is consistent as well with Douglass's tendency to valorize black manhood and black representative leadership. For important critiques of Douglass's gender politics, see Richard Yarborough, "Race, Violence, and Manhood: The Masculine Ideal in Frederick Douglass's 'The Heroic Slave,'" Sundquist, *Frederick Douglass: New Literary and Historical Essays*, 166–88; and P. Gabrielle Foreman, "Sentimental Abolition in Douglass's Decade: Revision, Erotic Conversion, and the Politics of Witnessing in *The Heroic Slave* and *My Bondage and My Freedom*," *Sentimental Men: Masculinity and the Politics of Affect in American Culture*, ed. Mary Chapman and Glenn Hendler (Berkeley: University of California

Press, 1999), 149–62. On Douglass and black manhood, see Maurice O. Wallace, *Constructing the Black Masculine: Identity and Ideality in African American Men's Literature and Culture, 1775–1995* (Durham, NC: Duke University Press, 2002), ch. 3.

At this point in the novella it is tempting to view Listwell as a kind of paternalistic Garrisonian (or as surrogate for Garrison himself), given his unwillingness to risk any sort of direct action to help his black friend. For example, Bernier refers to Listwell as a "pseudo-William Lloyd Garrison figure ironically so named to leave his inadequacies in plain sight" (*Characters of Blood*, 276). But as Listwell's subsequent actions reveal, he is no moral suasionist, for his proffering of the files leads directly to the violent revolt on the *Creole*.

38. Douglass, *The Heroic Slave*, 223.

39. Other traces of Douglass's life history can be discerned in Part III. For instance, Douglass mentions that the ship taking the slaves to New Orleans is a "Baltimore built American Slaver" (*The Heroic Slave*, 223). Douglass escaped from slavery in 1838, but prior to that he had been working in the shipyards at Baltimore's Fell's Point. When reading about the *Creole*, he likely would have considered the possibility that he had helped caulk the slave ship. Douglass's 1852 lecture "What to the Slave Is the Fourth of July" also points to connections between Douglass and the story he tells in *The Heroic Slave*. In that Fifth of July speech, Douglass relates how he had observed chained slaves led through Baltimore to ships heading for New Orleans. In the most autobiographical moment of the speech, Douglass describes his viewing of a slave coffle in ways that suggest his own perceptions informed Listwell's first viewing: "The flesh-mongers gather up their victims by dozens, and drive them, chained, to the general depot at Baltimore. When a sufficient number have been collected here, a ship is chartered, for the purpose of conveying the forlorn crew to Mobile, or to New Orleans" ("What to the Slave Is the Fourth of July?," 374).

40. Douglass, *The Heroic Slave*, 226, 230, 225. The other epigraph to Part IV is from the Irish poet George Moore's "Where Is the Slave?"

41. Douglass, *The Heroic Slave*, 230.

42. Ibid., 233, 234, 234–235, 236. On Madison Washington's saving intervention aboard the historical *Creole*, see especially Senate Document

51, 27th Congress, 2nd session, 1842, 20–21. In the actual rebellion, one white was killed; Douglass describes two deaths in the novella. Though he doubles the number of killings, one of Douglass's aims in his characterization of Washington and the other black rebels in the novella, as Larry J. Reynolds suggests, is to show that "love of liberty, not hatred of whites, motivates the killings on the fictional *Creole*" (*Righteous Violence: Revolution, Slavery, and the American Renaissance* [Athens: University of Georgia Press, 2011], 104). For a different perspective, see Hamilton, who argues that Douglass "pointedly made the revolt more violent that it actually was" ("Models of Agency," 112), in part because he was moving toward a more violent politics of resistance.

43. Douglass, *The Heroic Slave*, 238, 239. Sundquist comments on how Douglass during the 1840s and 1850s linked himself "alternately with the white founding fathers and those black men—Toussaint L'Ouverture, Gabriel Prosser, Denmark Vesey, Nat Turner, and Madison Washington, among others—who also belong to the era of revolutionary greatness and its aftermath" (*To Wake the Nations*, 85). On nationalism in the novella, see also Krista Walter, "Trappings of Nationalism in Frederick Douglass's *The Heroic Slave*," *African American Review* 34.2 (2000): 233–47.

44. Ivy G. Wilson, "On Native Ground: Transnationalism, Frederick Douglass, and 'The Heroic Slave,'" *PMLA* 121.2 (2006): 463.

45. Douglass, *Narrative*, 40; Douglass, *The Heroic Slave*, 190, 197, 217.

46. Douglass to Gerrit Smith, letter of 14 January 1853, Gerrit Smith Papers, Syracuse University; Douglass, "The Claims of the Negro Ethnologically Considered: An Address Delivered in Hudson, Ohio, on 12 July 1854," *FDP*, vol. 2, 510; Douglass, *My Bondage and My Freedom*, xxxi, xxii. For a good discussion of Douglass's paratexts in his second autobiography, see John Sekora, "'Mr. Editor, If You Please': Frederick Douglass, *My Bondage and My Freedom*, and the End of the Abolitionist Imprint," *Callaloo* 17.2 (1994): 608–626. On theological debates about race, see Jared Hickman, "Douglass Unbound," *Nineteenth-Century Literature* 68.3 (2013): 323–62.

47. For a different, but complementary, perspective on Douglass and revolutionism, see Cody Marrs's fine discussion of Douglass's engagement with the European revolutions of the period, "Frederick Douglass in 1848," *American Literature* 85.3 (2013): 447–73.

48. Sundquist, *To Wake the Nations*, 90.

49. Douglass, *My Bondage and My Freedom*, 34, 35, 59, 60. For a provocative discussion of Douglass's presentation of his mother in his second autobiography, see Michael A. Chaney, "Picturing the Mother, Claiming Egypt: *My Bondage and My Freedom* as Auto(bio)ethnography," *African American Review* 35.3 (2001): 391–408. Chaney calls attention to Douglass's at times contradictory deracialization of his mother. My own sense is that Douglass seeks to destabilize race by unsettling connections between color and intelligence, and by the end of his essay Chaney makes a similar point (405–6). On Douglass's presentation of his mother and grandmother in *Bondage and Freedom*, see also Cynthia Hamilton, "Frederick Douglass and the Gender Politics of Reform," *Liberating Sojourn: Frederick Douglass and Transatlantic Reform*, ed. Alan J. Rice and Martin Crawford (Athens: University of Georgia Press, 1999), 73–92; and Arthur Riss, "Sentimental Douglass," *The Cambridge Companion to Frederick Douglass*, ed. Maurice S. Lee (Cambridge: Cambridge University Press, 2009), 103–17. For an intriguing discussion of the importance of mothers to Barack Obama's and Douglass's autobiographies, see Robert B. Stepto, *A Home Elsewhere: Reading African American Classics in the Age of Obama* (Cambridge, MA: Harvard University Press, 2010), 7–26.

50. Douglass, *My Bondage and My Freedom*, 91, 122, 115, 187.

51. Ibid., 189, 190–91, 205.

52. Douglass, *Narrative*, 65–66, 73; Douglass, *My Bondage and My Freedom*, 247.

53. Douglass, *My Bondage and My Freedom*, 227, 245, 249. On the importance of the Byron passage to *Bondage and Freedom*, see Phan, *Bonds of Citizenship*, 162–64; and on Douglass's more communal rendering of the rebellion against Covey, see Sekora, " 'Mr. Editor, If You Please,' " 623–625.

54. Douglass, *My Bondage and My Freedom*, 269, 275, 269, 280, 284, 288.

55. Ibid., 296, 319.

56. John Stauffer, "Foreword," Douglass, *My Bondage and My Freedom* (New York: Modern Library, 2003), xxv; David W. Blight, "Introduction," Douglass, *My Bondage and My Freedom* (New Haven: Yale University Press, 2014), xi.

57. Douglass, "The Liberator," *Frederick Douglass' Paper*, 9 December 1853, 2; *Liberator*, 16 December 1853, 196; William Lloyd Garrison, "The Mask Entirely Removed," *Liberator*, 16 December 1853, 196. Shocked by the venom of Garrison's attack, Harriet Beecher Stowe wrote him privately to ask: "Why is he [Douglass] any more to be called an apostate for having spoken ill-tempered things of former friends than they for having spoken severely and cruelly as they have of him? Where is this work of excommunication to end? Is there but one true anti-slavery church and all others infidels?" (Stowe to Garrison, letter of 19 December 1853, in *Life and Letters of Harriet Beecher Stowe*, ed. Annie Fields [Boston: Houghton, Mifflin, 1898], 214–15). Julia Griffiths returned to England early in 1855. For a helpful collection of letters and other primary documents about the conflict between Douglass and Garrison, see John Ernest, ed., *Douglass in His Own Time: A Biographical Chronicle of His Life, Drawn from Recollections, Interviews, and Memoirs by Family, Friends, and Associates* (Iowa City: University of Iowa Press, 2014), 63–101. See also William H. Pease and Jane H. Pease, "Boston Garrisonians and the Problem of Frederick Douglass," *Canadian Journal of History* 2.2 (1967): 29–48.

58. Douglass, "The Anti-Slavery Movement: An Address Delivered in Rochester, New York, on 19 March 1855," *FDP*, vol. 3, 19–20.

59. Douglass, *My Bondage and My Freedom*, 354–55, 359, 361. Douglass also chose not to obey the edict of Garrison's associate George Foster, who, for the sake of authenticity, tells him to retain "a *little* of the plantation manner of speech" in his lectures (362).

60. Ibid., 394, 395, 396, 398.

61. Ibid., 405, 406.

62. Garrison's review of *My Bondage and My Freedom* appeared in the 15 December 1855 London *Empire* and is reprinted in *The Frederick Douglass Papers: Series Two: Autobiographical Writings: Volume 2: My Bondage and My Freedom*, ed. John W. Blassingame et al. (New Haven: Yale University Press, 2003), 417; Douglass to William Lloyd Garrison, letter of 13 January 1856, reprinted in ibid., 431.

63. *Frederick Douglass' Paper*, 24 August 1855, 3; *Frederick Douglass' Paper*, 7 September 1855, 4; "New Publications," *Frederick Douglass' Paper*, 21 September 1855, 1; Douglass to Gerrit Smith, letter of 13 Jan-

uary 1856, quoted in Blassingame et al., *The Frederick Douglass Papers: Series Two: Autobiographical Writings: Volume 2: My Bondage and My Freedom*, 431. On Douglass's exploitation of the "scandal" of his relationship with Garrison to sell copies of *My Bondage and My Freedom*, see Susan M. Ryan, "Douglass, Melville, and the Moral Economies of American Authorship," Levine and Otter, *Frederick Douglass and Herman Melville*, 88–109.

64. See Stauffer, *Black Hearts of Men*, 42.

65. Douglass, "The Significance of Emancipation in the West Indies: An Address Delivered in Canandaigua, New York, on 3 August 1857," *FDP*, vol. 3, 207, 187, 206. Garnet was in attendance for the speech.

66. Douglass, "A Black Hero," *Douglass' Monthly* 4.3 (August 1861), 499. Green and Copeland participated in John Brown's raid on Harpers Ferry. Douglass began *Douglass' Monthly* in January 1859; it superseded *Frederick Douglass' Paper*.

4. TALES OF ABRAHAM LINCOLN
(AND JOHN BROWN)

1. *Reminiscences of Abraham Lincoln by Distinguished Men of His Time*, ed. Allen Thorndike Rice (1881; New York: North American Review, 1888), 195; Douglass, "The Spirit of Colonization," *Douglass' Monthly* 5 (September 1862), 706.

2. Douglass, *Life and Times of Frederick Douglass, Written by Himself* (Hartford, CT: Park Publishing, 1882), 400, 397, 410, 398. An error-ridden first printing of *Life and Times* was published in November 1881; Douglass was happiest with the Hartford 1882 printing. For the textual history of *Life and Times*, see Joseph R. McElrath, Jr., and Jesse S. Crisler, "Textual Afterword: A Critical Edition of *Life and Times of Frederick Douglass*," *The Frederick Douglass Papers: Series Two; Autobiographical Writings: Volume 3: Life and Times of Frederick Douglass: Book 1: The Text and Editorial Apparatus*, ed. John R. McKivigan et al. (New Haven: Yale University Press, 2012), 485–507.

3. Walt Whitman, "The Death of Abraham Lincoln" (1879), in Whitman, *Memoranda during the War: Written on the Spot in 1863–'65*, ed. Peter Coviello (New York: Oxford University Press, 2004), 157.

4. See James Oakes, *The Radical and the Republican: Frederick Douglass, Abraham Lincoln, and the Triumph of Antislavery Politics* (New York: W. W. Norton, 2007), esp. xiii–xxii.

5. The best recent accounts are Oakes, *Radical and the Republican;* David W. Blight, "Abraham Lincoln and Frederick Douglass: A Relationship in Language, Politics, and Memory," Blight, *Beyond the Battlefield: Race, Memory, and the Civil War* (Amherst: University of Massachusetts Press, 2002), 76–90; and Paul Kendrick and Stephen Kendrick, *Douglass and Lincoln: How a Revolutionary Black Leader and a Reluctant Liberator Struggled to End Slavery and Save the Union* (New York: Walker, 2008). John Stauffer's parallel biography also discusses the friendship or relationship in helpful ways; see Stauffer, *Giants: The Parallel Lives of Frederick Douglass and Abraham Lincoln* (New York: Twelve, 2008).

6. Douglass, "The Proclamation and a Negro Army: An Address Delivered in New York, New York, on 6 February 1863," *FDP*, vol. 3, 562; Douglass, "John Brown's Contributions to the Abolition Movement: An Address Delivered in Boston, Massachusetts, on 3 December 1860," *FDP*, vol. 3, 413.

7. Oakes, *Radical and the Republican*, 98, 101.

8. Douglass's letter on Brown to an anonymous recipient appeared in the *New York Times*, 30 April 1881, 2.

9. See Nathaniel Hawthorne to Richard Milnes, letter of 18 November 1854, in Hawthorne, *The Letters, 1853–1856*, ed. Thomas Woodson et al. (Columbus: Ohio State University Press, 1988), 279–80.

10. Robin L. Condon and Peter P. Hinks, "Introduction to Volume Three," McKivigan et al., *Frederick Douglass Papers*, xxxii. The negative assessments of *Life and Times* come from James Olney, "The Founding Fathers—Frederick Douglass and Booker T. Washington," *Slavery and the Literary Imagination: Selected Papers from the English Institute, 1987*, ed. Deborah E. McDowell and Arnold Rampersad (Baltimore: Johns Hopkins University Press, 1989), 19; William S. McFeely, *Frederick Douglass* (New York: W. W. Norton, 1991), 311; Eric J. Sundquist, *To Wake the Nations: Race in the Making of American Literature* (Cambridge, MA: Harvard University Press, 1993), 89; Blight, *Beyond the Battlefield*, 23; and Zoe Trodd, "A Hid Event, Twice-Lived: The Post-War Narrative Sub-Versions

of Douglass and Melville," *Leviathan* 10.2 (2008): 52. Blight in his chapter on *Life and Times* in *Beyond the Battlefield* concedes that "some of the writing in *Life and Times* is revealing, despite its function more as reminiscence than as a personal story" (23–24). In this and the next chapter, I work against the distinction that Blight makes between reminiscence and personal story; in Douglass, reminiscence often *is* personal story, and vice versa.

11. Condon and Hinks, "Introduction to Volume Three," xxxiii; J. Saunders Redding, *To Make a Poet Black* (1939; Ithaca: Cornell University Press, 1988), 37; Alain Locke, "Foreword," *Life and Times of Frederick Douglass, Written by Himself* (New York: Pathway Press, 1941), xv. For recent reconsiderations of *Life and Times*, see "Rediscovering the *Life and Times of Frederick Douglass*," a special issue of the *Journal of African American History* 99.1–2 (2014).

12. Celeste-Marie Bernier, " 'His Complete History'? Revisioning, Recreating and Reimagining Multiple Lives in Frederick Douglass's *Life and Times* (1881, 1892)," *Slavery & Abolition* 33.4 (2012), 597.

13. Douglass, *Life and Times*, 363, 371.

14. Douglass, "Editorial Correspondence," *North Star*, 11 February 1848, 2.

15. The critical work on Brown is voluminous. Particularly useful recent books include David S. Reynolds, *John Brown, Abolitionist: The Man Who Killed Slavery, Sparked the Civil War, and Seeded Civil Rights* (New York: Alfred A. Knopf, 2005); Evan Carton, *Patriotic Treason: John Brown and the Soul of America* (New York: Free Press, 2006); Bruce A. Ronda, *Reading the Old Man: John Brown in American Culture* (Knoxville: University of Tennessee Press, 2008); R. Blakeslee Gilpin, *John Brown Still Lives! America's Long Reckoning with Violence, Equality, and Change* (Chapel Hill: University of North Carolina Press, 2011); and John Stauffer and Zoe Trodd, eds., *The Tribunal: Responses to John Brown and the Harpers Ferry Raid* (Cambridge, MA: Harvard University Press, 2012), esp. xix–lix. On Brown and Douglass, see (in addition to the works mentioned in Note 6 and immediately above), Benjamin Quarles, *Allies for Freedom: Blacks and John Brown* (New York: Oxford University Press, 1974), esp. 19–21, 32–33, 38–39, 60–61, 114–16, 164–65;

McFeely, *Frederick Douglass*, esp. 188–200; and John Stauffer, *The Black Hearts of Men: Radical Abolitionism and the Transformation of Race* (Cambridge, MA: Harvard University Press, 2001), 58–60, 171–73, 197–200, 246–51.

16. Douglass, "The Present Condition of Slavery: An Address Delivered in Bradford, England, on 6 January 1860," *FDP*, vol. 3, 303, 304; Douglass, "John Brown and the Slaveholders' Insurrection: An Address Delivered in Edinburgh, Scotland, on 30 January 1860," *FDP*, vol. 3, 315, 314, 315, 316, 317, 318. Douglass published letters declaring that he had decided against participating in the raid. In a letter to the editor of the Rochester *Democrat and American*, which he wrote in Canada West on 31 October 1859 and then published in the November *Douglass' Monthly*, Douglass stated that he absolutely did not promise "to be present in person at the Harper's Ferry Insurrection," and that rumors that he planned to be there were "a very grave impeachment" (*Douglass' Monthly* 2 [November 1859], 163). Douglass never denied knowledge of the plot, and of course his decision not to betray Brown by revealing the plot implicated him in it.

17. Douglass, "Slavery and the Irrepressible Conflict: An Address Delivered in Geneva, New York, on 1 August 1860," *FDP*, vol. 3, 386, 387; Douglass, "John Brown's Contributions to the Abolition Movement: An Address Delivered in Boston, Massachusetts, on 3 December 1860," *FDP*, vol. 3, 416, 418. On Douglass and Haiti, see Robert S. Levine, *Dislocating Race and Nation: Episodes in Nineteenth-Century American Literary Nationalism* (Chapel Hill: University of North Carolina Press, 2008), ch. 4.

18. Douglass to James Redpath, letter of 29 June 1860, *Liberator*, 27 July 1860.

19. Douglass, *Life and Times*, 371, 372, 374.

20. Ibid., 381, 387, 389, 390–91.

21. Ibid., 389, 395, 361.

22. Abraham Lincoln, "'House Divided' Speech at Springfield, Illinois, June 16, 1858," *The Portable Abraham Lincoln*, ed. Andrew Delbanco (New York: Penguin Books, 1993), 89; Douglass, "Freedom in the West Indies: An Address Delivered in Poughkeepsie, New York, on 2 August 1858," *FDP*, vol. 3, 237; Douglass, *Life and Times*, 363–64.

23. See *The Lincoln-Douglas Debates: The First Complete, Unexpurgated Text,* ed. Harold Holzer (New York: HarperCollins Publishers, 1993), 51, 55, 111, 143, 218.

24. As Douglass almost certainly knew, Smith was one of the six wealthy benefactors who were secretly offering financial support to Brown; see Jeffrey S. Rossbach, *Ambivalent Conspirators: John Brown, the Secret Six, and a Theory of Slave Violence* (Philadelphia: University of Pennsylvania Press, 1982); and Stauffer, *Black Hearts of Men,* 240–48, 267–75.

25. Douglass, "The Inaugural Address," *Douglass' Monthly* 3 (April 1861), 433; Douglass, "The Progress of the War," *Douglass' Monthly* 4 (September 1861), 513; Douglass, "General Fremont's Proclamation to the Rebels of Missouri," *Douglass' Monthly* 4 (October 1861), 530; Douglass, "The State of the War," *Douglass' Monthly* 4 (February 1862), 593; Douglass, "The President and His Speeches," *Douglass' Monthly* 5 (September 1862), 707; "Speech of Frederick Douglass on the War," *Douglass' Monthly* 4 (February 1862), 595.

26. "Address on Colonization to a Deputation of Negroes," *New-York Tribune,* 15 August 1862, reprinted in *The Collected Works of Abraham Lincoln,* ed. Roy Basler (New Brunswick: Rutgers University Press, 1953), vol. 5, 371.

27. Douglass, "The President and His Speeches," 707, 708. Among the historians who believe that Lincoln staged the meeting with black leaders in order to appease the border states and tactfully set the stage for the Emancipation Proclamation are Oakes, Holzer, and Burt; see Oakes, *Radical and the Republican,* 193–95; Harold Holzer, *Emancipating Lincoln: The Proclamation in Text, Context, and Memory* (Cambridge, MA: Harvard University Press, 2012), 40–42; and John Burt, *Lincoln's Tragic Pragmatism: Lincoln, Douglas, and Moral Conflict* (Cambridge, MA: Harvard University Press, 2013), 360–66. On Lincoln's interest in black colonization, see George Fredrickson, *Big Enough to Be Inconsistent* (Cambridge, MA: Harvard University Press, 2008), 104–14; and Eric Foner, *The Fiery Trial: Abraham Lincoln and American Slavery* (New York: W. W. Norton, 2010), 127–29, 184–86, 221–40.

28. Douglass, "Emancipation Proclaimed," *Douglass' Monthly* 5 (October 1862), 721; Douglass, "January First 1863," *Douglass' Monthly* 5 (January 1863), 721.

29. Douglass, "The Proclamation and a Negro Army," 551, 553, 566. See the discussion of Garnet's use of Byron in Chapter 3.

30. Douglass, *Life and Times*, 422, 423, 444.

31. Ibid., 422; Douglass, "The Commander-in-Chief and His Black Soldiers," *Douglass' Monthly* 5 (August 1863), 849, 850. On 12 August 1863, two days after meeting with Lincoln, Douglass wrote George L. Stearns to express his admiration for Lincoln's Order of Retaliation, which would have allowed for retaliation against southern prisoners, but there is no evidence that Lincoln or his generals used that order to exact retaliation for the deaths of black soldiers.

32. Douglass, "Emancipation, Racism, and the Work before Us: An Address Delivered in Philadelphia, Pennsylvania, on 4 December 1863," *FDP*, vol. 3, 606–7.

33. Ibid., 607, 608, 609.

34. Douglass, "The Mission of the War: An Address Delivered in New York, New York, on 13 January 1864," *FDP*, vol. 4, 24.

35. Douglass, *Life and Times*, 436, 438–39.

36. Oakes, *Radical and the Republican*, 233.

37. Douglass, *Life and Times*, 436, 437.

38. Ibid., 435.

39. As George Kateb demonstrates, Lincoln's "deepest commitment was to human equality, to the equal humanity of all persons and races" (*Lincoln's Political Thought* [Cambridge, MA: Harvard University Press, 2015], 55). Douglass's concern was that at least to the time of the Thirteenth Amendment, Lincoln, the man who had supported colonizing blacks to Central America, seemed unable to imagine African Americans as U.S. citizens with equal social and political rights. Douglass may have also picked up on what Kateb suggests was Lincoln's generalized "dislike of black people" (98).

40. "Frederick Douglass on President Lincoln," *Liberator*, 16 September 1864, 3. In a letter to Garrison of 17 September 1864, Douglass expressed his anger at Garrison for printing the letter, saying that it "was flung off in haste; and was not written for publication." Still, he says that he would have preferred a Republican presidential candidate "of more decided and anti-slavery convictions" (*Liberator*, 23 September 1864, 3).

41. "Frederick Douglass on Northern Politics," *Nonconformist* 24 (12 October 1864), 829. The editors of this London weekly paper of reformist Protestantism date the letter 1 September 1864 and note that they reprinted it from another British paper, the *Inquirer*. My thanks to Kevin Dier-Zimmel for calling this letter to my attention.

42. Douglass to Theodore Tilton, letter of 15 October 1864, *The Life and Writings of Frederick Douglass: Volume 3: The Civil War, 1861–1865*, ed. Philip S. Foner (New York: International Publishers, 1952), 424.

43. Douglass, *Life and Times*, 444–45.

44. Ibid., 442, 443; Douglass, "Our Martyred President: An Address Delivered in Rochester, New York, on 15 April 1865," *FDP*, vol. 4, 76, 77. In a letter of 17 August 1865 to Mrs. Abraham Lincoln, Douglass writes of the "cane which was formerly the property and the favorite walking stick of your lamented husband": "I assure you that this inestimable memento of his excellency will be retained in my possession while I live, an object of sacred interest" (*The Life and Writings of Frederick Douglass: Volume 4: Reconstruction and After*, ed. Philip S. Foner [New York: International Publishers, 1955], 175).

45. Douglass, *Life and Times*, 425; Douglass to Abraham Lincoln, letter of 29 August 1864, Foner, *Life and Writings of Frederick Douglass: Volume 3*, 405; Douglass, *Life and Times*, 425.

46. As Douglass writes in *Life and Times*: "I called again on Mrs. Stowe, and was much disappointed to learn from her that she had reconsidered her plan for the industrial school" (358). On Lincoln's commissioning of up to a hundred African American officers, see Benjamin Quarles, *The Negro in the Civil War* (Boston: Little Brown, 1953), 208.

47. On Douglass, Delany, Stowe, *Uncle Tom's Cabin*, and the debate on black emigration, see Robert S. Levine, *Martin Delany, Frederick Douglass, and the Politics of Representative Identity* (Chapel Hill: University of North Carolina Press, 1997), ch. 2; and *Martin R. Delany: A Documentary Reader*, ed. Robert S. Levine (Chapel Hill: University of North Carolina Press, 2003), 224–37.

48. Frank A. Rollin [Frances A. Rollin], *Life and Public Services of Martin R. Delany* (Boston: Lee and Shepard, 1868), 168, 169, 170, 171. On Lincoln's meetings with a wide range of African Americans during the

Civil War, see Benjamin Quarles, *Lincoln and the Negro* (New York: Oxford University Press, 1962), 194–210; and Manisha Sinha, "Allies for Emancipation? Lincoln and Black Abolitionists," *Our Lincoln: New Perspectives on Lincoln and His World*, ed. Eric Foner (New York: W. W. Norton, 2008), 167–96.

49. For a discussion of Delany's important role at the Chatham Convention, see Benjamin Quarles, *Allies for Freedom*, 37–41. One wonders if Brown discussed with the group his provisional plans for Harpers Ferry.

50. On Delany's insurrectionary novel, *Blake; or, The Huts of America* (1859; 1861–1862), see Levine, *Martin Delany, Frederick Douglass*, ch. 5.

51. Historians continue to debate Lincoln's attitude toward colonization. Some see him as deeply committed; others are more skeptical. John Burt, for example, argues that "perhaps the fairest thing to say about Lincoln's embrace of colonization is that it usually served a rhetorical rather than a policy purpose" (*Lincoln's Tragic Pragmatism*, 362). Eric Foner, on the other hand, sees a more serious commitment through most of 1862, as does David W. Blight. See Foner's *Fiery Trial*, 127–29, 184–86, 221–26, 231–40; and Blight, *Frederick Douglass' Civil War*, ch. 6. My own view is that Lincoln remained committed to colonization up to the time of the Emancipation Proclamation, and that he never completely turned against it (there is no moment of renunciation), though his admiration for the work of black troops beginning in mid-1863 clearly had an impact on his thinking about the matter. But for an argument that Lincoln through most of 1863 attempted to develop a plan for black colonization to the Caribbean, and may have been interested in reviving a plan for black colonization in the months before his assassination, see Philip W. Magness and Sebastian N. Page, *Colonization after Emancipation: Lincoln and the Movement for Black Resettlement* (Columbia: University of Missouri Press, 2014).

52. "The Eulogy of Albion W. Tougée," *A Memorial of Frederick Douglass from the City of Boston* (Boston: Rockwell and Churchill, 1896), 56, 57.

53. For a complementary discussion of how Walt Whitman made use of Lincoln to develop his status as a celebrity, see David Haven Blake,

Walt Whitman and the Culture of Celebrity (New Haven: Yale University Press, 2006), 183–90.

54. Douglass, "The Assassination and Its Lessons: An Address Delivered in Washington, D.C., on 13 February 1866," *FDP*, vol. 4, 109, 110.

55. Douglass, "We Are Not Quite Free: An Address Delivered at Medina, New York, on 3 August 1869," *FDP*, vol. 4, 230–31.

56. Douglass, "The Assassination and Its Lessons," 111; Douglass, "We Are Here and Want the Ballot-Box: An Address Delivered in Philadelphia, Pennsylvania, on 4 September 1866," *FDP*, vol. 4, 138.

57. I am not alone in admiring this speech. Oakes calls it Douglass's "most complex and compelling evaluation of Abraham Lincoln" (*Radical and the Republican*, 266). See also Blight, "Abraham Lincoln and Frederick Douglass," 83–85.

58. Douglass, *Life and Times*, 511. In 1865, Douglass objected to plans by black abolitionist William J. Wilson to develop a monument to Lincoln on the grounds that he wanted the funding to come exclusively from African Americans; see Douglass to W. J. Wilson, letter of 8 August 1865, in *Life and Writings of Frederick Douglass: Volume 4*, 171–73. Ball's statue may have reminded Douglass of the frontispiece to the 1853 *Autographs for Freedom*, which depicted a black man kneeling before a white Christ while they grasp hands. Perhaps to Douglass's chagrin, Ball's statue makes Lincoln into a Christ figure who, instead of taking hold of the hand of a black man in an act of brotherhood, more distantly offers a benediction.

59. Douglass, "The Freedmen's Monument to Abraham Lincoln: An Address Delivered in Washington, D.C., on 14 April 1876," *FDP*, vol. 4, 431, 433, 432.

60. Ibid., 433–34, 436–37, 440.

61. Douglass, *Life and Times*, 548.

62. Douglass, "Did John Brown Fail? An Address Delivered in Harpers Ferry, West Virginia, on 30 May 1881," *FDP*, vol. 5, 8, 11, 10, 11, 22. The title of the talk was created by the editors of the Frederick Douglass Papers; Douglass published the lecture in 1881 under the title *John Brown* (Dover, NH: Morning Star Job Printing House, 1881).

63. Douglass, "Did John Brown Fail?," 11, 25, 34, 35.

64. Douglass, "Wendell Phillips Cast His Lot with the Slave: An Address Delivered in Washington, D.C., on 22 February 1884," *FDP*, vol. 5, 159; Douglass, "Our Destiny Is Largely in Our Own Hands: An Address Delivered in Washington, D.C., on 16 April 1883," *FDP*, vol. 5, 68; Douglass, "The Negro Problem: An Address Delivered in Washington, D.C., on 21 October 1890," *FDP*, vol. 5, 439.

65. Douglass, "The Black Man's Debt to Abraham Lincoln: An Address Delivered in Washington, D.C., on 12 February 1888," *FDP*, vol. 5, 340, 339, 341, 344. The dressmaker was the African American Elizabeth Keckley, who told her own stories about Abraham Lincoln and especially Mary Todd Lincoln in her *Behind the Scenes; or, Thirty Years a Slave, and Four Years in the White House* (New York: G. W. Carleton, 1868).

66. Douglass, "Abraham Lincoln, the Great Man of Our Century: An Address Delivered in Brooklyn, New York, on 13 February 1893," *FDP*, vol. 5, 533, 535, 536, 538.

67. Ibid., 540, 541, 542, 544, 545.

68. Douglass, "The Blessings of Liberty and Education: An Address Delivered in Manassas, Virginia, on 3 September 1894," *FDP*, vol. 5, 626. On Lincoln's draft of the 1865 speech he never gave on Lincoln, see Oakes, *Radical and the Republican*, 256.

5. THOMAS AULD AND THE REUNION NARRATIVE

1. Douglass, *Life and Times of Frederick Douglass: Written by Himself. His Early Life as a Slave, His Escape from Bondage, and His Complete History to the Present Time* (Hartford, CT: Park Publishing, 1882), 533.

2. Dickson J. Preston, *Young Frederick Douglass: The Maryland Years* (Baltimore: Johns Hopkins University Press, 1980), 186; William S. McFeely, *Frederick Douglass* (New York: W. W. Norton, 1991), 41, 294.

3. On Douglass's disillusionment with reunion rituals involving northern and southern whites, see David Blight, *Race and Reunion: The Civil War in American Memory* (Cambridge, MA: Harvard University Press, 2001), 92–93.

4. Quoted in Marcia Muelder Eaton, "Laughing at the Death of Little Nell: Sentimental Art and Sentimental People," *American Philosophical Quarterly* 26.4 (1989): 269.

5. Peter F. Walker, *Moral Choices: Memory, Desire, and Imagination in Nineteenth-Century American Abolition* (Baton Rouge: Louisiana State University Press, 1978), 247. On Douglass's interest in Haiti, see Robert S. Levine, *Dislocating Race and Nation: Episodes in Nineteenth-Century American Literary Nationalism* (Chapel Hill: University of North Carolina Press, 2008), ch. 4.

6. Preston, *Young Frederick Douglass*, 182. On Douglass's nostalgia for the Eastern Shore, see also Wayne Mixon, "The Shadow of Slavery: Frederick Douglass, the Savage South, and the Next Generation," *Frederick Douglass: New Literary and Historical Essays*, ed. Eric J. Sundquist (Cambridge: Cambridge University Press, 1990), 233–52.

7. Douglass, "The Final Test of Self-Government: An Address Delivered in Rochester, New York, on 13 November 1864," *FDP*, vol. 4, 32.

8. Douglass to James Hall, letter of 10 June 1859, Maryland Colonization Society Papers, Maryland Historical Society; Douglass to Lydia M. Child, letter of 30 July 1865, *The Life and Writings of Frederick Douglass: Volume 4: Reconstruction and After*, ed. Philip S. Foner (New York: International Publishers, 1955), 170. At the time, Child was working on a biographical sketch of Douglass, which appeared in her *The Freedmen's Book* (1865).

9. Blight, *Race and Reunion*, 92, 43.

10. See Nell Irvin Painter, *Exodusters: Black Migration to Kansas after Reconstruction* (New York: Alfred A. Knopf, 1977), 249–50.

11. Douglass, "American Slavery, American Religion, and the Free Church of Scotland: An Address Delivered in London, England, on 22 May 1846," *FDP*, vol. 1, 292.

12. The evidence suggests that Auld read the *Narrative* before May 1846, but it's not clear if Douglass actually sent him a copy. See McFeely, *Frederick Douglass*, 159–60; and John W. Blassingame, "Introduction to Volume One," *The Frederick Douglass Papers: Series Two: Autobiographical Writings: Volume 1: Narrative*, ed. John W. Blassingame et al. (New Haven: Yale University Press, 1999), xxxi.

13. Douglass, *Narrative of the Life of Frederick Douglass, an American Slave. Written by Himself* (Boston: Anti-Slavery Office, 1845), 47, 48, 49.

14. Ibid., 52, 51, 57.

15. Ibid., 68, 69.

16. Ibid., 93.

17. Ibid., 97, 103.

18. Douglass, "I Am Here to Spread Light on American Slavery: An Address Delivered in Cork, Ireland, on 14 October 1845," *FDP*, vol. 1, 43; Douglass, "Slavery and America's Bastard Republicanism: An Address Delivered in Limerick, Ireland, on 10 November 1845," *FDP*, vol. 1, 86; Douglass, "A Few Facts and Personal Observations of Slavery: An Address Delivered in Ayr, Scotland, on 24 March 1846," *FDP*, vol. 1, 196–97; Douglass, "Emancipation Is an Individual, a National, and an International Responsibility: An Address Delivered in London, England, on 18 May 1846," *FDP*, vol. 1, 252.

19. A. C. C. Thompson, "Narrative of Frederick Douglass," *Liberator*, 20 February 1846, 1; Douglass, "Emancipation," 252; Douglass to Garrison, letter of 16 April 1846, *Correspondence*, 109.

20. Douglass to Henry C. Wright, letter of 22 December 1846, *Correspondence*, 189, 184, 189.

21. Douglass, "Farewell to the British People: An Address Delivered in London, England, on 30 March 1847," *FDP*, vol. 2, 42, 43. For a different published version of the same speech, see *Report of Proceedings at the Soirée Given to Frederick Douglass, London Tavern, March 30, 1847* (London: R. Yorke Clarke, 1847), esp. 24–26.

22. Douglass, "Farewell to the British People," 43.

23. Douglass to Thomas Auld, letter of 8 September 1848, *Correspondence*, 309–10, 309.

24. Ibid., 310, 313, 314.

25. Ibid., 315.

26. McFeely, *Frederick Douglass*, 159, 160. On Douglass's use of rape imagery in the letter to Auld, see William M. Ramsey, "Frederick Douglass, Southerner," *Southern Literary Journal* 11.1 (2007): 19–38, esp. 22–23.

27. Douglass to Thomas Auld, letter of 8 September 1848, 315; Douglass to Thomas Auld, letter of 3 September 1849, *Correspondence*, 391, 392.

28. Douglass, *Life and Times*, 128, 130, 128, 137, 136, 137, 160, 161.

29. McFeely celebrates Auld's decision not to send Douglass to Alabama as the great beneficent action that eventually enabled Douglass's escape. As he remarks in his biography: "Frederick Bailey owed his

chance to seek freedom . . . to the largesse of . . . Thomas Auld. For his freedom—for his life—he would for the rest of his life be beholden to a white man whom he had loved and whom he now had to remember to loathe" (*Frederick Douglass*, 57). Leaving aside the question of how McFeely knows that Douglass loved Auld, the fact is that Douglass emphasizes the immediate economic benefits to Auld of not selling his young male slave.

30. Douglass, *My Bondage and My Freedom* (New York and Auburn: Miller, Orton and Mulligan, 1855), 187; Douglass, *Life and Times*, 187.

31. Douglass, *Life and Times*, 477.

32. Ibid., 477, 478, 479.

33. Ibid., 480.

34. Ibid., 479; Douglass, "The Altered State of the Negro: An Address Delivered in Philadelphia, Pennsylvania, on 5 September 1866," *FDP*, vol. 4, 136.

35. Douglass to Hugh Auld, letter of 4 October 1859, Mrs. Howard V. Hall Collection, box 1, folder 4, Maryland State Archive Hall of Records Building.

36. See Preston, *Young Frederick Douglass*, 165–66.

37. Douglass, *Life and Times*, 480, 481.

38. Ibid., 481.

39. Ibid., 523; and see Painter, *Exodusters*.

40. On Douglass and photography, see John Stauffer, *The Black Hearts of Men: Radical Abolitionists and the Transformation of Race* (Cambridge, MA: Harvard University Press, 2001), ch. 2.

41. [Anon.], "Frederick Douglass at His Old Home, A Visit to His Former Master—An Affectionate and Friendly Meeting—Sound Advice to the Colored People, &c.," *Baltimore Sun*, 19 June 1877, 1.

42. Ibid.

43. Ibid.

44. Ibid.

45. "'Our Freddie': He Visits His Former Master and Speaks His Little Piece," *Daily Critic* (Washington, DC), 19 June 1877, 4; "Capt. Thomas Auld," *Daily Picayune* (New Orleans), 27 June 1877, 4. In an article in the 26 June 1877 *Daily Commercial* (Vicksburg, Mississippi), Douglass is

described as similarly telling Auld that "lapse of time and reflection had convinced him that much he had written had better have been unsaid—he begged his forgiveness" (2).

46. Douglass, *Life and Times*, 535.

47. Ibid., 535, 534, 535.

48. Ibid., 534, 533, 535, 534.

49. Ibid., 534, 535, 536.

50. Ibid., 536. Despite Douglass's efforts to present himself as more forceful than the figure represented in the *Baltimore Sun* article, some critics remain unpersuaded. William Andrews, for example, describes Douglass, even with the "Frederick" instead of "Fred," as "reactionary" in seeming to reinstate the hierarchies of slave culture ("Reunion in the Postbellum Slave Narrative: Frederick Douglass and Elizabeth Keckley," *Black American Literature Forum* 33.1 [1989]: 7). For a good discussion of these issues, see Robin L. Condon and Peter P. Hinks's "Introduction to Volume Three," *The Frederick Douglass Papers: Series Two: Autobiographical Writings: Volume 3: Life and Times of Frederick Douglass: Book 1: The Text and Editorial Apparatus*, ed. John R. McKivigan et al. (New Haven: Yale University Press, 2012), esp. xlii–xliii.

51. Douglass, *Life and Times*, 536.

52. Preston, *Young Frederick Douglass*, 188; McFeely, *Frederick Douglass*, 158; Douglass, *Life and Times*, 537.

53. See Douglass, *Life and Times*, 121–23. For an argument that Douglass's mention of the legal responsibility of Aaron Anthony's grandson was a more substantial act of reconciliation, see Condon and Hinks, "Introduction to Volume Three," xliv–xlvi.

54. Douglass, *Life and Times*, 538.

55. Ibid.

56. Much of this paragraph is indebted to my conversations with rhetorician par excellence Glenn McClish.

57. Douglass, *Life and Times*, 536, 533.

58. On the importance of romance conventions to reunions of the period (mainly between white northerners and southerners), see Nina Silber, *The Romance of Reunion: Northerners and the South, 1865–1900* (Chapel Hill: University of North Carolina Press, 1993).

59. Douglass, *Life and Times*, 548–49, 550. Douglass's speech, "Did John Brown Fail? An Address Delivered in Harpers Ferry, West Virginia, on 30 May 1881," can be found in *FDP*, vol. 5, 7–35.

60. Ottilie Assing to Douglass, letter of 12 July 1877, *Radical Passion: Ottilie Assing's Reports from America and Letters to Frederick Douglass*, ed. and trans. Christoph Lohmann (New York: Peter Lang, 1999), 337. See also Maria Diedrich, *Love across the Color Lines: Ottilie Assing and Frederick Douglass* (New York: Hill and Wang, 1999).

61. On this point see Andrews, "Reunion in the Postbellum Slave Narrative," 5–16.

62. Douglass, *Life and Times of Frederick Douglass, Written by Himself: His Early Life as a Slave, His Escape from Bondage, and His Complete History to the Present Time* (Boston: De Wolfe and Fiske, 1892), 731; hereafter *Life and Times* (1892).

63. Douglass, *Life and Times* (1892), 622; "God Almighty Made but One Race: An Interview Given in Washington, D.C. on 25 January 1884," *FDP*, vol. 5, 146, 147.

64. Douglass, *Life and Times* (1892), 653, 703, 682, 700. On the racial implications of Douglass's trip to Rome, see Robert S. Levine, "Road to Africa: Frederick Douglass's Rome," *African American Review* 34.2 (2000): 217–31; and McFeely, *Frederick Douglass*, 329–33.

65. Douglass, *Life and Times* (1892), 653.

66. Benjamin Auld to Douglass, letter of 11 September 1891, Frederick Douglass Papers, Library of Congress.

67. See the editors' headnote to Douglass's "Boyhood in Baltimore: An Address Delivered in Baltimore, Maryland, on 6 September 1891," *FDP*, vol. 5, 479–80.

68. Benjamin Auld to Douglass, letter of 11 September 1891.

69. Douglass to Benjamin Auld, letter of 16 September 1891, Frederick Douglass Papers, Library of Congress.

70. Douglass, "The Blessings of Liberty and Education: An Address Delivered in Manassas, Virginia, on 3 September 1894," *FDP*, vol. 5, 629, 628.

71. J. W. Thompson, *An Authentic History of the Douglass Monument: Biographical Facts and Incidents in the Life of Frederick Douglass* (Rochester:

Rochester Herald Press, 1903), 17. John Thompson, the African American who spearheaded the initiative for a memorial statue of Douglass in Rochester, worked as a waiter at Rochester's Powers Hotel.

EPILOGUE

Epigraph: From Langston Hughes, "Frederick Douglass: 1817–1895" (1966), *The Collected Works of Langston Hughes: The Poems, 1951–1967* (Columbia: University of Missouri Press, 2001), 153. Hughes had a long-standing interest in Douglass; see his chapters on Douglass in *Famous American Negroes* (New York: Dodd, Mead, 1954) and *Famous Negro Heroes of America* (New York: Dodd, Mead, 1958). Both chapters draw on the 1892 *Life and Times,* which perhaps helps to explain Hughes's use of the 1817 birthdate in his 1966 poem. Hughes addresses Douglass in a number of other poems as well.

1. F. M. Holland, "Frederick Douglass," *Open Court: A Weekly Journal Devoted to the Religion of Science,* 7 March 1895, 1.

2. *In Memoriam: Frederick Douglass* (Philadelphia: John C. Yorston, Publishers, 1897), 28.

3. Ibid., 44; "Proceedings of the American Equal Rights Association Convention, Steinway Hall, New York City, May 12, 1869," *Frederick Douglass on Women's Rights,* ed. Philip S. Foner (1976; New York: Da Capo Press, 1992), 90, 87; Angela Y. Davis, *Women, Race and Class* (New York: Random House, 1981), 79; Douglass, "Emancipation of Women: Speech at the Twentieth Annual Meeting of the New England Woman Suffrage Association, Tremont Temple, Boston, May 28, 1888," Foner, *Frederick Douglass on Women's Rights,* 119. On Douglass and women's rights over the course of his career, see (in addition to Foner's excellent volume) John Stauffer, *The Black Hearts of Men: Radical Abolitionists and the Transformation of Race* (Cambridge, MA: Harvard University Press, 2001), 224–32; and Gary L. Lemons, *Womanist Forefathers: Frederick Douglass and W. E. B. Du Bois* (Albany: State University of New York Press, 2009).

4. *In Memoriam,* 35, 182–83, 188, 187, 217.

5. Ibid., 195; Douglass, *Life and Times of Frederick Douglass, Written by Himself* (Boston: De Wolfe and Fiske, 1892), 581. My thinking about

Douglass as imagining his autobiography from the perspective of the grave has been influenced by Stanley Plumly's *Posthumous Keats: A Personal Biography* (New York: W. W. Norton, 2008).

6. *Critic*, 28 January 1892, reprinted in *Critical Essays on Frederick Douglass*, ed. William L. Andrews (Boston: G. K. Hall, 1991), 30.

7. Douglass, "Wendell Phillips Cast His Lot with the Slave: An Address Delivered in Washington, D.C., on 22 February 1884," *FDP*, vol. 5, 148–49; Douglass, "Great Britain's Example Is High, Noble, and Grand: An Address Delivered in Rochester, New York, on 6 August 1885," *FDP*, vol. 5, 201; Douglass, "The Black People Have Lost a Firm Friend: An Address Delivered in Washington, D.C., on 24 April 1888," *FDP*, vol. 5, 375; Douglass, "Good Men Are God in the Flesh: An Address Delivered in Boston, Massachusetts, on 22 September 1890," *FDP*, vol. 5, 435.

8. "I Am Unwilling to Be an Idler: An Interview Given in Baltimore, Maryland, on 6 September 1891," *FDP*, vol. 5, 478.

9. Douglass to Marshall Pierce, letter of 18 February 1892, Moorland-Spingarn Research Center, Howard University.

10. Douglass, *Life and Times*, 494, 680–81, 622, 625, 622–23.

11. See Maria Diedrich, *Love across the Color Lines: Ottilie Assing and Frederick Douglass* (New York: Hill and Wang, 1999).

12. Douglass, *Life and Times*, 748, 752. On Douglass, Haiti, and *Life and Times*, see Kenneth W. Warren, "Frederick Douglass's *Life and Times*: Progressive Rhetoric and the Problem of Constituency," *Frederick Douglass: New Literary and Historical Essays*, ed. Eric J. Sundquist (Cambridge: Cambridge University Press, 1990), 253–70; and Robert S. Levine, *Dislocating Race and Nation: Episodes in Nineteenth-Century American Literary Nationalism* (Chapel Hill: University of North Carolina Press, 2008), ch. 4.

13. Douglass, *Life and Times*, 703, 670, 711, 714.

14. There are numerous ways that one might explore Douglass's afterlives from 1895 to the present. As I discuss in the Introduction, one might consider Douglass's impact on the Civil Rights Movement and on political thought more generally. See, for example, the discussion of Douglass in Nick Bromell, *The Time Is Always Now: Black Thought and the Transformation of US Democracy* (New York: Oxford University Press, 2013). One might also consider Douglass's influence on autobiographies ranging from Booker T. Washington's to Barack Obama's, on poetry and

fiction (see, for example, the poetry of Paul Laurence Dunbar, Ralph Ellison's *Invisible Man*, and John Updike's *Rabbit Redux*), and on painting, music, and theater. For an excellent discussion of Douglass's broad influence on the arts, see Celeste-Marie Bernier, *Characters of Blood: Black Heroism in the Transatlantic Imagination* (Charlottesville: University of Virginia Press, 2012), ch. 5.

♪ ACKNOWLEDGMENTS ❧

I am pleased to acknowledge the assistance I have received from a number of individuals and institutions. Fellowships from the National Endowment for the Humanities and the John Simon Guggenheim Memorial Foundation provided much appreciated time for research and writing. I thank John R. McKivigan and the staff at the Frederick Douglass Papers at Indiana University-Purdue University, Indianapolis, for sharing their archival collections and answering my many questions. My thanks as well to the librarians at the Library of Congress and the University of Maryland. As I was completing the book, I was fortunate to be named a Visiting Faculty Fellow at the Texas A&M University Institute for Advanced Study. During my visits, I tried out much of the manuscript in talks and workshops. For their invitation, hospitality, and helpful responses, I thank Alfred Bendixen, José Luis Bermúdez, Dennis Berthold, Ira Dworkin, Clifford Fry, Lucia Hodgson, John L. Junkins, Jerome Loving, Nancy Warren, the Americanist graduate students, and especially my host, Larry Reynolds, superb scholar, good friend, and resistant-reader par excellence.

I have had the opportunity to present sections of the book in progress at other universities as well, and the questions and comments from various audiences have helped me to hone the manuscript. For their invitations and helpful suggestions, I am especially grateful to Caroline Levander at Rice University,

Cristobal Silva and Rachel Adams at Columbia University, John R. McKivigan and Robin Condon at Indiana University-Purdue University, Joel Pfister and Ashraf Rushdy at Wesleyan University, Tess Chakkalakal at Bowdoin University, Rodrigo Lazo at the University of California-Irvine, Coleman Hutchison and Evan Carton at the University of Texas, Jennifer James at George Washington University, and Judith Madera at Wake Forest University. I have also tried out early discussions of some themes presented here in several publications: *American Cultural Icons: The Production of Representative Lives* (2010), *Journal of African American History* (2014), and *The Cambridge History of American Civil War Literature* (2015). My thanks to Günter Leypoldt, V. P. Franklin, and Coleman Hutchison for the invitations and useful forums. For their help along the way, I also thank June Can, Ann Coughlin, Kevin Dier-Zimmel, Patricia Herron, Glen McClish, Katie Nash, and Karen Nelson.

My colleagues and friends at the University of Maryland and elsewhere have offered encouragement and advice that have contributed in various ways to the project. My warm thanks to Jonathan Auerbach, Ralph Bauer, Nina Baym, Celeste-Marie Bernier, Lenny Cassuto, Chris Castiglia, Russ Castronovo, Tita Chico, Jeannine DeLombard, Betsy Duquette, John Ernest, Neil Fraistat, Susan Gillman, Ezra Greenspan, Maurice Lee, Ted Leinwand, Caroline Levander, Marilee Lindemann, Peter Mallios, Sam Otter, Carla Peterson, Jean Pfaelzer, Elizabeth Renker, Xiomara Santamarina, Martha Nell Smith, John Stauffer, Julia Stern, Priscilla Wald, Mary Helen Washington, and Edlie Wong. To my two Chairs over the duration of the project, Kent Cartwright and William Cohen: thank you for your generous support and thoughtfulness.

This book began as a study of Frederick Douglass as a cultural presence in the twentieth and twenty-first centuries, but I soon found myself pulled back into the nineteenth century by the brilliance of Douglass's writings. My editor at Harvard University Press, John Kulka, who thought I was going to write one sort of book, has remained strongly encouraging of this end result. I am grateful for his support over the past five years, and I am especially indebted to him for his meticulous commentary on the first draft of the manuscript, which helped me to sharpen and clarify my arguments. My thanks to the Press's two anonymous readers; and to Maria Louise Ascher, Susan Wallace Boehmer, Joy Deng, Hope Stockton, and Anne Zarrella—all of Harvard University Press—who have assisted me in various ways over the past few years. My thanks as well to Angela Piliouras and Paul Vincent for their work in the copyediting and production process, and to Helene Ferranti for her work on the index.

My wife, Ivy Goodman, read the manuscript multiple times and remains my very best reader. I am grateful for her sustaining love and editorial skills. I am also grateful to our son, Aaron, whose interest in particle physics has helped to enlarge my world.

George Dekker, my mentor and friend, was a magnificent transatlantic scholar and the kindest person I've met in the profession. I continue to be inspired by his example.

↗ INDEX ↖

Page references in italics indicate illustrations.